ABANDONED TRACKS

ABANDONED TRACKS

The Underground Railroad
in Washington County, Pennsylvania

W. THOMAS MAINWARING

University of Notre Dame Press
Notre Dame, Indiana

University of Notre Dame Press
Notre Dame, Indiana 46556
undpress.nd.edu

Library of Congress Cataloging-in-Publication Data

Names: Mainwaring, W. Thomas, 1952- author.
Title: Abandoned tracks : the Underground Railroad in Washington County,
Pennsylvania / W. Thomas Mainwaring.
Description: Notre Dame, Indiana : University of Notre Dame Press, [2018] |
Includes bibliographical references and index. |
Identifiers: LCCN 2018011944 (print) | LCCN 2018012417 (ebook) | ISBN
9780268103590 (pdf) | ISBN 9780268103606 (epub) | ISBN 9780268103576
(hardcover : alk. paper) | ISBN 0268103577 (hardcover : alk. paper)
Subjects: LCSH: Underground railroad—Pennsylvania—Washington County. |
Antislavery movements—Pennsylvania—Washington County—History. |
Fugitive slaves—Pennsylvania—Washington County—History. |
Abolitionists—Pennsylvania—Washington County—Biography. | Washington
County (Pa.)—History—19th century.
Classification: LCC E450 (ebook) | LCC E450 .M25 2018 (print) | DDC
326/.80974882—dc23
LC record available at https://lccn.loc.gov/2018011944

∞ *This paper meets the requirements of*
ANSI/NISO Z39.48-1992 (Permanence of Paper).

CONTENTS

LIST OF TABLES AND FIGURES

TABLES

PHOTOGRAPHS

LIST OF MAPS

All maps prepared by Mark D. Swift, except map 12, prepared by Tim Brown.

ACKNOWLEDGMENTS

Many people have provided advice, assistance, and encouragement during the long time that it has taken to write this book. Thanks first of all to Joan Ruzika, who believed in this project when it was just a germ of an idea when we were board members at the Washington County Historical Society. Her support has been crucial during the fruition of the book.

I owe a huge debt to Mark Swift, a colleague in the Department of Music at Washington & Jefferson College, who volunteered to produce the maps for *Abandoned Tracks*. Mark spent countless hours discussing the concepts for maps, producing sample copies, and then going through numerous iterations to achieve high-quality maps. Mark's expertise in geographical information systems has been invaluable, and his patience has been extraordinary. I can't thank him enough.

Several other colleagues at Washington & Jefferson College played crucial roles in seeing this book through to publication. Robert Dodge, emeritus professor of history, offered encouraging words of advice from the inception of this project. He read numerous drafts of *Abandoned Tracks* and greatly improved its readability. Jennifer Harding in the Department of English also read the manuscript and raised penetrating questions. Her enthusiasm for the project was infectious and timely.

I owe a special thanks to Patrick Trimble, who spent many hours with me traipsing around the eastern part of the county in search of Underground Railroad sites. I knew I was in for an adventure any time he called or dropped by my office. His familiarity with the network of Underground Railroad agents in eastern Washington County saved me untold amounts of time. He also pointed me to a number of important documents in the Washington County Courthouse. Patricia Stavovy, who was then working in the Law Library at the courthouse, was unfailingly helpful in locating materials for me.

Jim Craig was an excellent companion in exploring Underground Railroad sites in the West Alexander area. He also alerted me to the existence of the *Claysville Recorder*, which offered valuable information about the Liberty Line that was otherwise unknown. He also helped me to nail down the locations of several people who had proven previously elusive.

The staff of the Washington County Historical Society was very helpful in locating materials and in assisting me in general. Thanks especially to Executive Director Clay Kilgore and Chuck Edgar, who were always willing to lend a hand. The Washington County Historical Society graciously allowed me to use the Doran Map of Washington Borough as it existed in 1855.

Anna Mae Moore did a splendid job of finding archival materials in the Washington & Jefferson library. I am happy to be able to tell her that this book will finally appear. Thanks also to Amy Welch for her assistance in locating and digitizing maps. Ronalee Ciocco, the college's head librarian, helped track down some elusive references, and for that I am very thankful.

A number of former students also helped this project along. Natalie Rocchio at the Library of Congress spared me many trips to Washington, DC. Her willingness to track down and scan antislavery petitions from Washington County added substantially to my understanding of local abolitionism and opened avenues of understanding that I had not anticipated. Joe Smydo shared his work on the relationship between local colonizationists and abolitionists in several graduate seminar papers and in his excellent master's thesis. His perspective raised important questions and helped me think through this relationship. Jason Haley did some very good work on the involvement of Presbyterian churches in the Underground Railroad. His honors thesis, "Washington County Presbyterians: Abolitionism in a Divided Denomination" (2002), proved very helpful.

My students in the Underground Railroad course I taught during the January 2005 Intersession unearthed some valuable information about local sites. Thanks especially to Megan McGee and Michael Batalo.

Several of my friends provided very helpful advice and encouragement during the preparation of this book. John Mark Scott Jr., my longtime colleague at Washington & Jefferson, went on several expeditions to help find sites along the backcountry roads of the county. Tom Hatley provided perspective and cheer when we talked about this project. Tim Brown read several versions of this manuscript and provided levity when the occasion demanded. His skill with Photoshop is much in evidence here. My brother Scott Mainwaring was also unfailingly helpful and provided crucial support for this project.

Stephen Little and Eli Bortz at the University of Notre Dame Press did
a great job of guiding *Abandoned Tracks* through to completion. Thanks especially to Eli, who picked up this project in midstream and ushered its way to publication. Matthew Dowd, managing editor of the press, skillfully guided the final steps of the process.

Washington & Jefferson College provided vital support in allowing me to spend several sabbaticals working on this project. I would like to thank the college for this time, which offered me the opportunity to research, reflect, and write. A Kenneth M. Mason, Sr., Summer Grant for Faculty Research from the college also allowed me to explore and document numerous sites throughout the county.

My final thanks go to my wife, Debbie, who has patiently endured my obsession with all manner of railroads for many years. For this and other reasons too numerous to mention, this book is dedicated to her.

Washington, PA
June 2017

Introduction

The Underground Railroad has become a hot topic over the last several decades. New books on the subject appear regularly, reenactors portray the escape of famous fugitive slaves such as Henry "Box" Brown (so called because he mailed himself to freedom in a box), and dozens of local historical societies have focused their attention on stations and conductors in their vicinity. This renewed interest in the "Liberty Line" has occurred at both the popular and scholarly levels, and reflects the "discovery" of the vital role that African Americans played in the Underground Railroad. Once depicted largely as passive passengers or bystanders, African Americans have only recently been recognized as the biggest risk takers on the "railroad," whether they dared to flee slavery or to aid fugitive slaves.[1] Works ranging from Faith Ringgold's juvenile novel *Aunt Harriet's Underground Railroad in the Sky* to Fergus M. Bordewich's monograph *Bound for Canaan* portray this new understanding of the Underground Railroad. The establishment of the National Underground Railroad Network to Freedom under the auspices of the National Park Service in the late 1990s likewise attests to this surge of popularity. Perhaps the opening in 2004 of the National Underground Railroad Freedom Center in Cincinnati best illustrates contemporary interest in the Underground Railroad. When Oprah Winfrey not only helps to sponsor the center but also introduces its video, you know that the Underground Railroad has achieved contemporary fame. Colson Whitehead's 2016 Pulitzer

Prize–winning novel, *The Underground Railroad*, which topped several best-seller lists, attests to the continuing popularity of this venerable institution.[2]

The Underground Railroad strikes a deep chord with most Americans. Virtually everywhere I have spoken on the topic of the local Underground Railroad in southwestern Pennsylvania, people have asked if I am aware of such-and-such house, where they have seen a secret hiding place or heard about a tunnel leading to the exterior. At least north of the Mason-Dixon Line, even people who do not watch the History Channel find something about the Underground Railroad fascinating and compelling.

I have gone on quite a few wild goose chases in response to tips from enthusiastic audience members. Although southwestern Pennsylvania has a documented Underground Railroad history, the purported stations I was shown have turned out on inspection to have been built after the Civil War or to have had no connection that can be documented to abolitionists and the Freedom Train. I vividly recall a former student whom I encountered working at a local office supply store some years ago. When I told this student that I was not teaching that semester but instead was on sabbatical re-searching the local Underground Railroad, his face immediately lit up. He asked if I was aware that his fraternity at Washington & Jefferson College had once been a stop, volunteering that he had even been shown the base-ment room where fugitive slaves had been hidden. Intrigued, I said that I was not aware of this and asked what fraternity he belonged to. He replied that he was a Fiji—a Phi Gamma Delta. Wanting to be certain that I had the location of the Fiji house right, I asked him if the Fiji house was adjacent to Mellon Hall, a dorm that is the architectural twin of his fraternity. He indi-cated that it was.[3] I told him that I saw one major objection to the notion that he had been shown a genuine Underground Railroad hiding place—namely, that the cornerstone for Mellon Hall bears the date of 1948. His fraternity house must have been built within a year or two of Mellon. Per-haps his fraternity did in fact once help fugitive slaves (its charter dates prior to the Civil War), but clearly no fugitive slaves found shelter in a building constructed after World War II. As this example illustrates, the Underground Railroad has a rich imagined history.

Even in cases where there is a well-documented connection to the Un-derground Railroad, legend and myth have often overshadowed what I will call the "real" history of the Underground Railroad. Dr. F. Julius LeMoyne is the only truly national figure to emerge from Washington County's Un-derground Railroad history. A physician in Washington, Pennsylvania, some twenty-five miles southwest of Pittsburgh, he conducted an extensive correspondence with such well-known abolitionists as Arthur Tappan and John Greenleaf Whittier and was once nominated to be the vice-presidential candidate for the abolitionist Liberty Party. The National Park Service has recognized his Greek Revival house on East Maiden Street as one among a select company of several dozen national Underground Railroad sites. Solid evidence links LeMoyne to the Underground Railroad.

Visitors to his house, however, are regaled with a story rather than the history of his actual involvement in the Underground Railroad. The story that docents tell goes like this: On one occasion, probably in the 1850s, six runaway slaves made it to LeMoyne's substantial stone house. Before arrangements could be made to pass the fugitives along to the next "station" on the railroad, a soldier appeared at the door, armed with a search warrant. In the absence of Dr. LeMoyne, who was apparently out making a house call, Mrs. LeMoyne told the slaves to hide under her bed on the second floor. Meanwhile, she hurriedly donned a nightcap, climbed into bed, and instructed one of her children to close the door. The soldier searched the entire house before coming back to the closed bedroom door. Feigning illness, Mrs. LeMoyne begged him not to disturb her rest and pleaded that no lady should be seen in bed by a stranger. The soldier, apparently touched by this appeal to gentility and feminine modesty, ultimately ceased his entreaties to open the door and left the LeMoyne house without his quarry. Quick thinking had saved the day. The six fugitives left soon thereafter and made their way safely to Canada.[4]

Generations of visitors to the LeMoyne house have apparently been told and accepted this story, but to me it is a problematic one that raises profound questions about how the history of the Underground Railroad is conveyed. Although it is a charming, lovely story, full of drama, courage, and resourcefulness, I am highly skeptical of it. For starters, there is no written historical evidence to support it. Of course, the lack of written evidence does not always mean that a story is suspect. Students of the Underground Railroad have often had to rely on oral history more extensively than students of other aspects of American history. With the notable exception of William Still in Philadelphia, few stationmasters kept detailed records of their activities, and even fewer passengers recorded their journeys on the Underground Railroad.

In LeMoyne's case, however, the lack of written evidence to support the story of the slaves under the bed is surprising. Late in her life, the youngest of the LeMoyne daughters, Madeleine LeMoyne Reed, who lived to be one hundred, told two historians of her family's involvement in the Underground Railroad . On separate occasions, Mrs. Reed recollected to Earle Forrest and Margaret McCulloch an incident in which the LeMoynes had hidden twenty-five slaves in the upstairs of the house. This was *the* incident that most clearly stood out in her mind about her family's house as a stop on the Underground Railroad. If the much more dramatic story of the slaves under the bed were true, one suspects that Mrs. Reed would have passed it along as the family lore about the Underground Railroad.[5] Although concealing twenty-five slaves was undoubtedly more of a feat than that of concealing six, there is no unexpected knock of a soldier at the door or other high drama in McCulloch's or Forrest's rendering of this family tradition. (The inclusion of a soldier in this story is also an improbable detail, since the military was not typically responsible for enforcing the 1850 Fugitive Slave Law. U.S. Commissioners, who authorized the recapture of fugitives by slave catchers, bore the main responsibility. Only in cases where a crowd threatened to rescue a captured fugitive—several notable cases of which occurred in Boston—did the military become involved.)[6] The story of the slaves under the bed does not seem to have come from the LeMoyne family. I suspect that it is a more recent invention that serves to dramatize the LeMoyne family's Underground Railroad activities.

The stories told about the LeMoyne house and the Fiji house neatly encapsulate the popular view of the Underground Railroad, what I will call the legend of the Underground Railroad. This legend goes far beyond the boundaries of Washington County and is national in scope. As Bordewich has commented, "Few aspects of the American past have inspired more colorful mythology than the Underground Railroad."[7] By far the most prominent element of this mythology is that the Underground Railroad typically involved dramatic escapes from the clutches of foulmouthed, whiskey-swilling slave catchers. The heroic counterparts to these villains were white abolitionists such as Julius LeMoyne, although they are usually depicted as kindly Quakers. The legend appeals to Americans' love of secrecy and clandestine places, locating the hiding places of fugitive slaves in secret compartments or in subterranean tunnels. The Underground Railroad is quite literally conceived of as an operation whose activities took place underground. Finally, the legend of the Underground Railroad feeds on a sense that important history transpired locally. It is an important event that happened here, in this place. Only one place can claim the historic legacy of Valley Forge or

Gettysburg, but countless localities throughout the northern United States can claim to be associated with the Underground Railroad. Local historians in virtually every Northern city, town, village, and crossroads have been eager to claim a piece of the Underground Railroad as their own. It is the rare northern locality that does not at least claim to have hosted a depot. Just as in many other places, local historians in Washington, Pennsylvania, have accepted and passed on the stories about the glorious days of the Underground Railroad not out of any desire to dupe their audience, but because they have undoubtedly been convinced that these legends were history. The repetition of these rumors and stories—some exaggerated, some distorted, and some completely imaginary—that have been passed down orally from generation to generation and from "experts" to visitors has made them into established fact in localities across the North.[8]

Although there are many reasons for the persistence of these local traditions, historical scholarship is not one of them. The verdict of modern historians about the nature of the Underground Railroad stands in sharp contrast to the local traditions shared by many northern communities. Historians have long recognized the legendary character of much of what has passed for the history of the Underground Railroad. Larry Gara's path-breaking book *The Liberty Line*, published in 1961, exposed many myths and legends about existing conceptions of the Underground Railroad. "Although the underground railroad was a reality," he conceded, "much of the material relating to it belongs in the realm of folklore rather than history."[9]

Gara contended that the existing scholarly and popular literature on the Underground Railroad was flawed on two counts. First, this literature greatly exaggerated and romanticized the role of white abolitionists in the Underground Railroad. This literature treated white abolitionists as the heroes of the Underground Railroad, whereas the fugitive slaves who took enormous risks to gain their freedom were treated as passive passengers. Gara also believed that the folklore had created the false impression that the Underground Railroad operated on a national level and was as efficiently organized as a railroad corporation that delivered large numbers of fugitives to the North. Like its metaphorical namesake, the Underground Railroad had its president, stationmasters, and conductors who transported fugitive slaves over well-orchestrated and well-maintained routes. In reality, Gara argues, it was a much more haphazard operation that helped a relatively small number of slaves. Furthermore, although the legendary Underground Railroad supposedly operated under a shroud of deep secrecy, relying on hidden tunnels and secret passageways, Gara pointed out that abolitionists publicly bragged about their complicity in helping fugitive slaves escape in the 1840s and 1850s while the Liberty Line was operating.[10]

The legend of the Underground Railroad, Gara argues, originated in the reminiscences of aging white abolitionists (typically Quakers) and their descendants that local historians recorded in the 1880s and 1890s. These reminiscences became the "history" of the Underground Railroad. Wilbur H. Siebert, a historian at Ohio State University, lent scholarly weight to this history when he published a profoundly influential book, *The Underground Railroad from Slavery to Freedom*, in 1898.[11] Although Siebert's work contained extensive factual information about the Underground Railroad, he also unwittingly included much material that had little historical basis. As historian David W. Blight put it, Siebert gathered "much truth" but also many "tall tales."[12] Even some of the former abolitionists whom Siebert contacted for their reminiscences expressed wariness about the tales of the Underground Railroad that were surfacing decades after the Civil War. As one said, "I am convinced that the number [of fugitives] passing over this line has been greatly magnified in the long period of time since this road ceased to run its irregular trains."[13] Nevertheless, Siebert crystallized the mood of the white Northern public in the Gilded Age as it looked back to the daring escapes and rescues that had taken place before the Civil War and captured the romance of the Underground Railroad for succeeding generations. Although Siebert may not have created the legend of the Underground Railroad, he validated it and gave it widespread circulation.[14]

The second major flaw that Gara identified in the legend of the Underground Railroad is closely related to the first. If the legend magnified the role of white abolitionists, it minimized that played by the fugitive slaves and black abolitionists. It ignored the most dangerous part of a fugitive's journey through the slave states and instead focused on the dangers faced by white abolitionists. Although the legend occasionally acknowledged the role played by the free black community in the North, it always did so in a secondary way. Of the more than 3,200 Underground operatives identified by Siebert, only 140 were black. The legend also conveniently overlooked the fact that many fugitives made their way to freedom in the North or to Canada without any organized assistance. Racism heavily tinted the legendary Underground Railroad, which depicted blacks as hopeless inferiors. It is probably no accident that Gara's book highlighting the active role

African Americans played in acquiring their own freedom appeared in the middle of the Civil Rights movement.[15]

Gara's debunking of the Underground Railroad legend won almost immediate acceptance among historians. His insistence that fugitive slaves were the primary authors of their own escapes and made the most dangerous part of their journey to the free states with minimal assistance made eminent sense. As Blight observes, "Most often, fugitive slaves fled on their own volition, with their destiny at the mercy of fate and the limits of their own courage."[16] Likewise, Gara's skepticism about the importance of white abolitionists in the Underground Railroad has won widespread acceptance. "Popular accounts often depict fugitives hiding in secret passageways under the homes of white abolitionists," Matthew Pinsker has written, "but anyone who stops to consider the issue will understand immediately why it made more sense for most runaways to stay within black neighborhoods." Historians of the Underground Railroad ever since Gara have approached their field with a critical eye.[17]

Gara also shaped the direction of subsequent scholarship on the Underground Railroad. The most notable trend since his work appeared has been the inclusion of African Americans as the authors of their own escapes and as agents on the Liberty Line in the free states. Charles L. Blockson broke new ground here with his July 1984 article in *National Geographic*, which introduced a popular audience to a new version of the Underground Railroad that featured African Americans as the prime movers in the institution. Blockson followed this article with several books on the Liberty Line nationally and in Pennsylvania.[18] The recovery of the black Underground Railroad continues to this day. Eric Foner's 2015 book *Gateway to Freedom* relates the discovery of new evidence detailing the activities of black activists in New York City in the 1850s.[19]

Ironically, however, Gara's work seems to have inhibited academic scholarship on the Underground Railroad for decades. (After his initial appearance in *National Geographic*, Blockson's works were published by relatively obscure, nonacademic publishers.) Gara's scathing critique of the legendary aspects of the Underground Railroad was such a tour de force that the topic seemed to be exhausted. The result was a long period of scholarly neglect of the Underground Railroad. For example, the leading scholars of fugitive slaves, John Hope Franklin and Loren Schweninger, mention the Underground Railroad only twice in their comprehensive 1999 study

Runaway Slaves. They contend that the vast majority of plantation rebels hid out for several weeks in the vicinity of their home to avoid beatings or to negotiate better treatment. (Slave owners anxious to bring in a valuable harvest were willing to overlook past violations of plantation discipline to obtain needed workers.) Only a tiny minority of these rebels ever sought to escape slavery permanently. As Franklin and Schweninger observed, the one or two thousand slaves who did escape each year represented a "mere trickle" out of the millions of slaves who remained in bondage. In large measure because of Gara, Underground Railroad scholarship seemed to have hit a dead end until the twenty-first century. Only in the last fifteen years have scholars shown renewed interest in the topic.[20]

Despite widespread agreement among scholars about the legendary character of the Underground Railroad, scholars have had comparatively little influence on popular conceptions of the Liberty Line. Popular audiences still fixate on the hidden tunnels and secret passageways conjured up by the metaphor "the Underground Railroad." Tours of the LeMoyne House continue to feature the story of the six slaves hidden under the bed. Perhaps this should be expected. Most Americans are consumers of history and seldom consult historians about the current status of historical issues. Films such as *Gone with the Wind* have reached audiences in the tens of millions and shaped their perceptions of slavery and the Civil War, whereas even best-selling historians such as James McPherson can only hope for sales in the hundreds of thousands—and that on very rare occasions.[21] Still, a huge gap exists between how historians understand the Underground Railroad and how the public at large sees it. This chasm between historians and the public may be one of the largest in American history. Why has historical scholarship had so little impact?

One reason, as noted above, stems from the very success of Gara's interpretation of the Liberty Line in the world of scholarship. Gara so thoroughly debunked the legend of the Underground Railroad that historians subsequently saw little reason to pursue inquiries in the field. The widespread acceptance of Gara's interpretation led to a long period of scholarly neglect, and scholars consequently had little to say about the Underground Railroad when it resurfaced as a popular topic in the early 1990s. Thus popular lore about the Underground Railroad circulated pretty much unaffected by Gara's 1961 critique and even by the republication of his book in 1996.

Beyond the long silence of professional historians, a second factor may also help to explain the ongoing discrepancy between historical and popular understandings of the Underground Railroad. The core of this explanation is that the Underground Railroad has become part of our national mythology or even part of the "American psyche," in Gara's words, that is "accepted on faith as a part of America's heritage."[22] As Blight has observed, "The Underground Railroad is one of the most enduring and popular threads in the fabric of America's national historical memory."[23] It has helped to define who we are as a people and who we want to be. Like many national myths, it has acquired great symbolic power. In a country founded upon the ideal of liberty, the Underground Railroad has become one of the fundamental symbols of freedom for many Americans. As Blight explains, the Underground Railroad embodies Americans' desire to hear a story about "a journey of risk and success that lifts our spirits and makes us proud."[24]

The basic outlines of that story owe much to Harriet Beecher Stowe's phenomenal best-seller *Uncle Tom's Cabin* (1852), which outsold every book but the Bible in nineteenth-century America and enjoyed theatrical success well into the twentieth century.[25] Eliza's escape with her young son from her Kentucky plantation, across the ice-packed Ohio River and then through Ohio (aided by a network of kindly Quakers) to the ultimate safety of Canada, became the escape with which virtually all nineteenth-century Americans were familiar. Thus Stowe's *fictional* story provided the archetype for *historical* accounts featuring villainous slave catchers, heroic fugitives, and saintly conductors. *Uncle Tom's Cabin* established the Underground Railroad as the subject of a uniquely American morality play in which the forces of good and evil confront each other.

The Underground Railroad legend appeals to Americans' imaginations for a darker reason as well. The legend offers whites feel-good stories of racial harmony and cooperation that suggest that the Underground Railroad mitigated, even if it did not solve, America's racial problems. The legend absolves them of guilt. Narratives of fugitive slave escapes emphasize the freedom gained without raising questions about the prejudice and difficulties that faced those who escaped. These narratives also ignore the millions of slaves who were left behind. Just as the Underground Railroad solved the problem of freedom for those who escaped, the legend implicitly claims that the Thirteenth Amendment solved America's racial problems once and for all. The story of the Underground Railroad is at bottom a story about race relations in America.[26]

The Underground Railroad thus might well be regarded as one of America's foundation myths along with the First Thanksgiving and Valley

Forge. Foundation myths are based on the need to believe in "an ennobling past," as Blight puts it. They identify heroes and villains, good and evil, and reveal core values and beliefs. They sometimes bear only a tenuous connection to history. They are anchored in belief and memory, not historical scholarship. Such myths, once they have taken root, display great resilience and are not easily modified.[27]

However, myths and symbols do change, sometimes in dramatic fashion. The Confederate battle flag is a case in point. Although protests have been waged for decades against flying the Confederate flag at Southern state capitols, they had been only marginally successful. The protests were met invariably with the claim that the flag represented "heritage, not hate." This picture changed very rapidly after a white supremacist murdered the pastor and eight parishioners of a historic black church in Charleston, South Carolina, in June 2015. The South Carolina legislature voted to remove the Confederate flag from the state capitol less than a month later. For more than fifty years this staunch symbol of the Confederacy, white Southernness, and resistance to desegregation had flown in Columbia, South Carolina, but it was taken down in a remarkably short period of time.[28]

Additionally, historians have affected how the public perceives selective aspects of the Underground Railroad. The primary example here concerns quilts as secret signs for travelers on the Underground Railroad. Initially published to great acclaim in 1999, *Hidden in Plain View: A Secret Story of Quilts and the Underground Railroad,* by Jacqueline L. Tobin and Raymond G. Dobard, purported to show that fugitive slaves had used quilts to display hidden messages to aid them on their journey.[29] An anonymous reviewer for Amazon.com touted the book as a "unique piece of scholarship, oral history, and cultural exploration that reveals slaves as deliberate agents in their own quest for freedom."[30] Early readers were equally enthusiastic in their reviews of the book. "A MUST for every quilt history and black history library," reads the caption from one response. Another wrote that it was "a fascinating, inspiring book."[31] When historians began to delve into *Hidden in Plain View,* however, they found that it was riddled with historical errors both large and small. Quilt historians such as Leigh Fellner pointed out that the quilts described in the book did not exist until after the Civil War. Giles R. Wright noted that the only evidence cited in the book was the oral testimony of a quilt maker named Ozella Williams, from whom Tobin had purchased a quilt. The small number of slaves who did escape from Charleston, Wright observed, probably made their escape by boat instead of trekking through the Appalachian Mountains. Historians of slavery and the Underground Railroad weighed in, observing that the escape route from Charleston to Cleveland depicted in the book defied logic. Perhaps most devastating of all, Fellner pointed out that no African American who claims the "quilt code" as part of a family oral history legacy can identify an ancestor who escaped via the Underground Railroad.[32]

This historical criticism has been telling on readers' responses posted on Amazon.com. Reviews are now often headed by warnings such as "Questionable," "Not History," "Caveat Emptor—An Interesting Fiction," and "Book Creates a new American Myth." As one reader commented, "I recommend this book only if the reader understands it is complete fiction, being peddled as fact." A number of reviewers explicitly cited historians to buttress their views. As this book goes to publication, while 45 percent of readers continue to rate *Hidden in Plain View* highly on Amazon.com, 23 percent give it the lowest possible rating. Well-informed readers have been amply warned by historians that this book is a highly fallible guide to the Underground Railroad. Historical criticism has arrested a myth in the making.

Abandoned Tracks has two aims and, ideally, two audiences. The first aim is to bring the light of historical scholarship to bear on the Underground Railroad in one locality for a popular audience. Just as historians have collectively made a difference in exposing the Underground Railroad quilt myth, I hope that *Abandoned Tracks* will join other recent historical works in distinguishing the difference between legitimate history and the myths, legends, and collective memories that enshroud popular perceptions of the Underground Railroad. The broad aim is to bridge the gap between historical scholarship and a popular audience. Although the arguments laid out by Larry Gara and David Blight are well known to historians, they have received little recognition beyond scholarly circles. I will beg historians' indulgence for highlighting the legends that circulate in Washington County and many other localities about the Underground Railroad.

This book thus seeks to rescue the real history of the local Underground Railroad—to separate the history from the legend, to distinguish between the actual and the imagined. It constitutes an extended analysis of the evidence and questions about that evidence. What is the evidence? How reliable is it? What are the sources? Are there multiple sources that independently confirm a site's authenticity? My examination reveals that Washington County has some sixty claimed Underground Railroad sites that range from the extremely well documented to the highly probable, the likely, and highly unlikely, and the spurious. (The appendix lists all of the sites I have unearthed for Washington County and evaluates the evidence for each site.) To date, very few studies have offered a critical analysis of Underground Railroad sites and a typology for those sites.[33] In a field where legends often have been spun out of thin air, it is important to ground this history on the known facts. I hope that a "real" story and understanding will emerge from my explorations and be as compelling as the legends.

The second aim of *Abandoned Tracks* is to contribute to and clarify the ongoing scholarly debate about the extent, effectiveness, and nature of the Underground Railroad. As Pinsker has observed, "any study of the Underground Railroad must begin by coming to terms with elusive judgments about its fundamental nature and scope of operations."[34] At the heart of this debate is the question of whether the Underground Railroad should be considered mostly as a legend and myth or whether it should be regarded as a highly organized venture whose network had an impressive reach, even if it did not stretch across the free states. This debate is far more subtle than the debate that Gara opened with Siebert fifty years ago; it is a debate about nuances and emphases. But one pole of this debate is still defined by scholars who follow Gara and are inclined to be skeptical of claims made about the Underground Railroad. David Blight and Peter Hinks are examples of scholars who define this end of the spectrum. They do not doubt the existence of the Underground Railroad, but they think the claims made about it have often been influenced by wishful thinking. In his musings about the Underground Railroad, Blight repeatedly reminds readers of the tensions between legitimate history and the temptation to believe the long-held myths about the Freedom Train. The burden of his message is to be on guard against falling for the myths. We should celebrate the Underground Railroad, but, as he puts it, "we should do so with a cautious understanding of the relationship between legitimate history and the enduring collective memory and abiding mythology surrounding the Underground Railroad."[35]

At the other end of the spectrum are scholars who are well aware of the legendary aspect of the Liberty Line but think that too much attention has been given to criticizing myths and legends. Foner, for example, thinks Gara's sweeping revisionism went too far in questioning the legitimacy of the Underground Railroad.[36] Such revisionism has deflected attention away from the real people who escaped from slavery and the real people who assisted them on their road. Acknowledging that the symbolism of the Underground Railroad has often become detached from its moorings in reality, Pinsker points out in his survey of Pennsylvania that the state witnessed almost two thousand documented cases of escape. The Underground Railroad was a reality in the Keystone State. David G. Smith, in his study of fugitive slaves in south central Pennsylvania, likewise believes that scholars have exaggerated the mythological elements of the Underground Railroad and ignored evidence of real escapes. Historians such as Keith Griffler, who studied the operations of the Underground Railroad in the Ohio Valley, and J. Blaine Hudson, who examined Kentucky, have concluded that these regions saw considerable traffic. Cheryl LaRoche likewise argues for significant traffic in African American communities in the North. Stanley Harrold has written an illuminating study of fugitive slaves in the Washington, DC, area. Bordewich's popular history *Bound for Canaan* also suggests that the Underground Railroad was highly organized and assisted a large number of fugitive slaves.[37]

One way to resolve or at least make better sense of this debate is through the use of local studies. As Griffler has commented, few local and regional studies of the historical context for the Underground Railroad existed until the turn of the twenty-first century. Until recently, most local histories focused instead on dramatic rescues, colorful personalities, and escape routes, with little regard for context or chronological development.[38] Renewed scholarly interest in the Underground Railroad in the twenty-first century has resulted in a growing number of historical examinations of the institution in a microcosm. By examining abolitionism and vigilance committees at the local level, historians have become better positioned to perceive subtleties and distinctions that previous grand interpretations have overlooked. The local studies that have appeared since 2000 suggest, I would argue, that the Underground Railroad varied significantly from region to region, thereby accounting for some of the discrepancies in historical literature about the national institution. The antebellum North was not a monolithic region. It is readily apparent, for example, that southwestern Pennsylvania had far fewer potential fugitive slaves than the tobacco-growing regions of Virginia around Washington, DC, that Harrold has studied. The mountainous regions of western Virginia (what is now West Virginia) had significantly fewer slaves than the area around Washington, DC. Support for abolitionism also varied greatly even within Pennsylvania, ranging from high levels in the Philadelphia region to low-to-moderate levels in the rest of the state.[39]

David Smith's study of the fugitive slave issue in south central Pennsylvania is of particular importance in providing a context for this study of

Washington County in southwestern Pennsylvania. Like Washington County, Adams, Cumberland, and Franklin Counties were largely rural and lay just north of the Mason-Dixon Line. They constituted a middle ground between Dixie and the "Yankee" North (New England and the Upper Midwest) in which attitudes about slavery, abolitionism, and fugitive slaves were highly contested. Both south central and southwestern Pennsylvania experienced the transition from slavery to freedom after the American Revolution subsequent to Pennsylvania's passage of a gradual abolition law. Both regions had been reluctant converts to abolitionism, evading the law into the 1820s by keeping even the grandchildren of slaves in bound labor. Both had growing free black populations that tended to congregate in small towns such as Gettysburg and Washington. Both saw a growing number of fugitives fleeing to their borders beginning in the 1830s.[40]

Important differences also separated these two rural regions in Pennsylvania. The size of nearby slave populations had important implications for local traffic on the Underground Railroad. South central Pennsylvania lay to the north of Maryland counties that had a large slave and free black population. It was a major escape route for all slaves east of the Appalachians. Although Washington County was also a border county, the slave population of nearby western Virginia was significantly smaller. The western border of the county was shared with counties in Virginia's northern panhandle, while the Mason-Dixon Line lay less than thirty miles to the south. Although slavery was a marginal presence in these Virginia counties (typically no more than 5 percent of their population), slaves did take advantage of their proximity to a free state to run away. Ethnic and religious backgrounds also played a significant role in attitudes about abolitionism and fugitive slaves. South central Pennsylvania had a large German population that proved largely indifferent to abolitionism but also a sizable Quaker minority that was sympathetic to it. The predominant Scotch-Irish Presbyterians who settled Washington County proved far more receptive to abolitionism. Washington County became the first in western Pennsylvania to organize an antislavery society, one that remained active until the Civil War. Despite the presence of Quakers, the south central Pennsylvania counties were unable to sustain an organized abolition movement. Thus, ironically, counties that were lukewarm in their support for abolition witnessed substantial traffic by fugitive slaves while Washington County's comparatively well-organized abolitionists helped substantially fewer.[41]

By drawing comparisons with Smith's study and other recent local studies, *Abandoned Tracks* seeks to add to the historical understanding of the Underground Railroad in a regional setting. Southwestern Pennsylvania and Washington County in particular have received little scholarly attention. Although R.J.M. Blackett has written an article about the Underground Railroad in Pittsburgh and devoted considerable space to it in his 2013 book *Making Freedom*, there has been no book-length study of the institution in Pittsburgh. Nor have there been any extensive studies of other southwestern Pennsylvania localities. *Abandoned Tracks* seeks to begin to fill that void.[42]

As will be readily apparent, *Abandoned Tracks* is highly sympathetic to the point of view of skeptics of the Underground Railroad such as Gara, Hinks, and Blight. It offers numerous examples of how local historians and collective memory have distorted or magnified historical incidents into something that they were not. There is a real history to the Underground Railroad in Washington County, but as in so many other places, it has been covered up by a heavy layer of romantic lore and greatly exaggerated. My hope is that *Abandoned Tracks* may serve as a useful guide for others investigating the legacy and meaning of the Underground Railroad.

Washington County, Pennsylvania, offers an excellent case study of the tensions between the legends and history of the Underground Railroad. Unlike many other localities in western Pennsylvania, which have only yellowed newspaper clippings from the twentieth century to document their Underground Railroad heritage, Washington County has a wealth of primary documents. These include the extensive correspondence between Julius LeMoyne and his abolitionist counterparts ranging from Lewis Tappan, the wealthy New York merchant who became a major figure in the American Anti-Slavery Society, to Lewis Woodson, an African American who became one of Pittsburgh's leading abolitionists. They include the register in which slave owners were required to record the birth of children born to slaves, which documents the evolution of slavery and freedom in the county. Several surviving autobiographical accounts from Underground Railroad agents offer personal perspectives on abolitionist activities. Washington County is also notable for having several well-documented African American Underground Railroad operatives. One of these, Howard Wallace, wrote an autobiographical pamphlet that traces the network of safe houses used in the eastern part of the county to convey fugitive slaves to freedom.

The local newspaper for the county seat also has relatively complete files that date back to the early 1800s. Several other short-lived newspapers, such as the *Washington (PA) Patriot*, an abolitionist paper, help provide a context for the local Underground Railroad. In addition, several abolitionist petitions from county residents to Congress requesting the abolition of slavery in the District of Columbia remain extant.

Washington County also witnessed events of national significance with regard to the Underground Railroad. An incident in the county involving a kidnapped slave ultimately resulted in the passage of the nation's first fugitive slave law in 1793. It was the scene of at least one capture of a fugitive slave and several attempted recaptures. As noted previously, the county also was home to one individual who achieved national prominence as an abolitionist: Julius LeMoyne. Washington County became the first west of the Appalachians to organize an abolition society. And although it is not clear if John Brown of Harper's Ferry fame was stealing slaves out of nearby Virginia in his visits to the county in the 1840s, his discussions with abolitionists in the western part of the county are well documented. Theodore Dwight Weld, one of the most famous abolitionist lecturers, spent several weeks in the county delivering a series of speeches. Weld's lectures, LeMoyne's leadership, and an active free black population made Washington County the vanguard of abolitionism in the western part of the state.

Abandoned Tracks sets the story of the Underground Railroad's origins, development, and scope in a local and national context. The first chapter begins with the settlement of Washington County in late colonial times, when Pennsylvanians and Virginians began pouring over the Appalachians, sometimes with their slaves. It then examines the slow death of slavery in the aftermath of Pennsylvania's passage of the Act for the Gradual Abolition of Slavery in 1780 and the growth of free black communities. Knowledge of the slow and painful transition from a place where virtually every black person was enslaved to one where the free black population constituted a sizable minority is vital to understanding the development of the Underground Railroad. Chapter 2 examines the development of local abolitionism in the 1820s and 1830s as part of the background of the Underground Railroad. It also traces the evolution of the local black and white Underground Railroads and examines the connections between them. Chapter 3 is devoted to an analysis of the realities and legends of the Liberty Line in the county. Although evidence supports the idea that the county had a loosely organized Underground Railroad, this chapter points out that this evidence has often been misinterpreted or misread. The concluding chapter discusses the "routes" so authoritatively described in local histories. It argues that the local Underground Railroad was a much more haphazard affair than these histories would indicate. Finally, the appendix lists some sixty sites in Washington County, evaluates the evidence for each of them, and categorizes each site based on that evidence. The categories range from sites that are indisputably authentic to those that are probably spurious.

CHAPTER ONE

The Twilight of Slavery

SLAVERY AND THE SETTLEMENT OF SOUTHWESTERN PENNSYLVANIA

The earliest indications of Underground Railroad activity nationally appeared in the 1780s in Philadelphia, where a large Quaker population opposed slavery, a substantial free black community could assist runaway slaves, and influential spokesmen such as Benjamin Franklin headed an antislavery organization. Washington County, on the frontier some three hundred miles to the west, could claim a few Quakers in the 1780s, but the tiny minority of blacks in the county were all enslaved, and the local elite was far more likely to own slaves than to argue that all men were created equal. It would take four decades before conditions were ripe in Washington County for the gestation of the Liberty Line. This chapter analyzes how the roadbed was laid for the Underground Railroad there.

The development of the Underground Railroad in Washington County was profoundly influenced by the early settlement of the region in the decade before the American Revolution. Of primary importance was the fact that a significant number of the county's first white settlers were slaveholders. No Underground Railroad could operate effectively as long as slavery was an accepted institution locally and the vast majority of blacks in the county was held in bondage. Eventually acute tensions would arise there between the owners of human chattel and the proponents of human freedom who claimed that the American Revolution invalidated the institution of slavery.[1]

The Ohio Country, as southwestern Pennsylvania was first known, was initially contested by the French and British during the 1750s. The first blacks to arrive in the area accompanied the disastrous Braddock expedition of 1755 and the successful Forbes expedition of 1758, which drove the French out of the area. The vast majority of these black participants were slaves who served as teamsters, drovers, and servants, but at least one, Tom Hyde, was a free soldier.[2]

The French and Indian War did not end the contest for the Ohio Country. Both Pennsylvania and Virginia claimed the upper Ohio Valley as their own on the basis of their colonial charters. As settlers began streaming into southwestern Pennsylvania in the late 1760s and early 1770s, it was not at all clear which colony's claims would hold up. Virginia's claim was particularly strong in the area west of the Alleghenies and south of the Ohio. This dispute was not settled until 1780, when the two states agreed to establish the western boundary of Pennsylvania by extending the Mason-Dixon Line to five degrees west of the Delaware River. Once the western boundary had been settled, Pennsylvania created Washington County in 1781. The county initially included all of current-day Greene County and parts of Allegheny and Beaver Counties.[3] (See Map 1.)

Virginians, however, comprised the majority of the county's early inhabitants. These Virginians had brought slaves with them to what they had called Yohogania County, Virginia.[4] Along with a smaller number of slave owners from Maryland and Pennsylvania, they gave what was to be Washington County a high concentration of slaves relative to Pennsylvania. Although no one was apt to confuse Washington County with Virginia's Tidewater region because of its slaves, about 6 percent of white families in the county owned slaves in 1782, when the first registration of slaves took place. The county's white population at the time is estimated to have been about 16,000 people, so the 417 slaves in Washington County constituted about 2.5 percent of its population.[5] In Pennsylvania as a whole, slaves accounted in 1780 for slightly more than 2 percent of the population—far less than the neighboring states of Delaware (19 percent), New Jersey (7.2 percent), and New York (10 percent).[6] The 146 slave-owning families in Washington County in 1782 held an average of about three slaves per family. Slaveholders such as Herbert Wallace of Fallowfield Township, who owned twenty slaves, were quite exceptional. Only six other individuals owned ten or more slaves. Fallowfield Township residents Francis Wallace, John Hopkins, and James Innis owned eleven, ten, and eleven slaves, respectively.

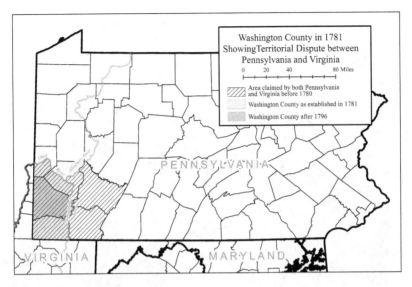

Map 1

William McMahon and John Tinnell, both from Hopewell Township, owned thirteen slaves and eleven slaves, respectively, while John and George Wilson from Strabane Township owned eleven. Nearly half of the county's slave owners—sixty-three of them—possessed only one slave.[7]

Slaveholding in the county was initially concentrated in several townships. (See Map 2.) Half of the county's slaves lived in the eastern townships along the Monongahela River.[8] One of those townships, Fallowfield, featured the most slaveholders (28) as well as the slave owners who owned the largest number of slaves in the county. The residents of this township collectively owned 109 slaves—26 percent of all the slaves in the county. Hopewell Township in the western part of the county was home to 21 owners of a total of 62 slaves. Strabane Township, in the center of the county, was another early stronghold of slavery. There, 19 owners held 52 people in bondage. The town of Washington, which was carved out of Strabane in 1788 and became the county seat, held the vast majority of these slaves. Many of the prominent men of the early town, such as William Hoge and Absalom Baird, owned slaves. Hoge and his brother John permanently influenced racial patterns in Washington by giving their slaves lots in the area of East Walnut Street and North College Street, a neighborhood that

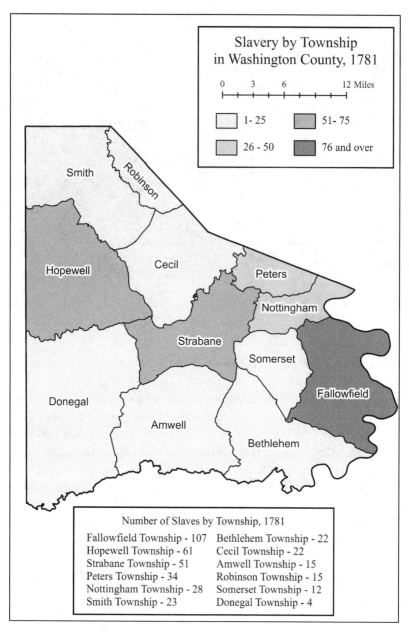

Slavery by Township
in Washington County, 1781

0   3   6   12 Miles

☐ 1- 25   ☐ 51- 75
☐ 26 - 50   ■ 76 and over

Smith

Robinson

Hopewell   Cecil

Peters

Nottingham

Strabane

Somerset

Donegal   Fallowfield

Amwell

Bethlehem

Number of Slaves by Township, 1781

Fallowfield Township - 107   Bethlehem Township - 22
Hopewell Township - 61   Cecil Township - 22
Strabane Township - 51   Amwell Township - 15
Peters Township - 34   Robinson Township - 15
Nottingham Township - 28   Somerset Township - 12
Smith Township - 23   Donegal Township - 4

Map 2

remains predominantly black today. Architectural historians believe that one of the cabins built by the former Hoge slaves is still standing today.[9]

Despite their relatively small numbers, slave owners exercised disproportionate power and influence in Washington County. The mere fact of owning slaves marked one as a person of some means. In 1775, for example, a slave cost between fifty and seventy-five pounds sterling, the equivalent of a year's earnings for many artisans.[10] More than two-thirds of slave owners were ranked among the wealthiest 10 percent of Washington County's population.[11]

The first county elections in 1781 gave Virginians a substantial majority of the county offices, and slaveholders continued in positions of leadership well into the 1790s. For example, David Bradford, of Whiskey Rebellion fame, purchased slaves upon his arrival in the county from Maryland. His nemesis, John Neville, the federal collector of revenue for western Pennsylvania, was a Virginian who owned more than a thousand acres of land and eighteen slaves in 1790. James McFarlane, a Revolutionary War veteran and casualty of the Whiskey Rebellion, also owned bondsmen. Not all of these slaveholders were Southerners. Thomas Scott, the first congressman from the region elected under the Constitution, was a native of Pennsylvania and owned slaves. His fellow Pennsylvanian, Colonel George Morgan, was also reputed to be a slave owner; an Indian agent and Revolutionary War soldier, he owned what is said to have been the largest private estate west of the mountains, Morganza. County historian Earle Forrest appears to have erred, however, in contending that Morgan owned many slaves after he moved to Washington County in 1796 from New Jersey. The 1800 and 1810 censuses do not show Morgan owning any slaves, though the 1810 census does indicate that Morgan had nine free persons unrelated to his family living on his estate. These may well have been African Americans who were working for Morgan as indentured servants or "twenty-eight-year servants"— servants who were bound to work until they reached the age of twenty-eight. If so, it may explain why Forrest believes that there was a slave burial ground on Morgan's property. Morgan clearly made use of black labor at Morganza, as he advertised the sale of an indentured African American man who had seven years to serve on his indenture in 1814.[12]

Slavery in Washington County resembled slavery in much of the rest of the northern states where the institution was of marginal importance. Slave labor clearly did not rest on the cultivation of staple crops such as tobacco as it did in the Chesapeake. At least through the end of the American

Revolution, settlers in western Pennsylvania struggled for subsistence, and slaves were likely to have been put to work clearing land, planting crops, building houses and barns, and helping to provide other necessities of life. As R. Eugene Harper has observed, the rapid settlement and economic development of western Pennsylvania between 1783 and 1800 meant that agriculture ceased to be the only economic activity, although it remained an important one. The appearance of towns such as Washington, Canonsburg, and Parkinson's Ferry (later Monongahela) made for a much more diverse occupational structure in which artisans, laborers, millers, lawyers, and other professionals had a niche. Slavery continued to exist in Washington County not because labor was needed to cultivate large plantations, but rather to provide domestic or farm help. As Harper has commented, the ownership of slaves also conferred status on the owner.[13]

Slaves in Washington County were sold as property at least through the eighteenth century. Only a few of these transactions were recorded, so it is difficult to arrive at an estimate of the volume of this traffic. Only three slave sales appear in the deed books of the county; there were undoubtedly others that were not recorded. In the first transaction, Alexander Mc-Candless sold a female slave for sixty pounds in 1781. In the second, dated 1784, Samuel Bealer sold "Hen and a Negro child born of said wench named George" to Seshbezzar Bentley for 100 pounds and twenty gallons of "mercantable whiskey." In the last sale recorded in the deed books, Reason Pumphrey obtained seventy to one hundred pounds apiece for three slaves in 1795.[14]

Slaves were also bequeathed to wives and other inheritors of property. The inventory of Edward Griffith's estate, dated May 19, 1778, reads in part as follows:

A Negro Woman named Sall	88 pounds
A Negro Garl named Esther	64 pounds
A Negro Garl named Siddis	54 pounds
A Negro Boy named Harry	54 pounds

The presumption of white Washington County in the late 1700s was that any black person was in fact a slave. It was probably for this reason that a "Negro man named Yara" went to the county court to have a paper issued certifying that he was "free and as such may be employed by any person."[15]

THE GRADUAL ABOLITION OF SLAVERY

Two developments changed the prospects of slave owners in Washington County. The first was the agreement signed in 1780 by Pennsylvania and Virginia designating the boundaries between the two states. Although this line was not run until 1785, it soon became clear that Yohogania County, Virginia, would disappear, and that most of the land initially claimed by Virginia north of the Mason-Dixon Line would become a part of Pennsylvania. (In the end, only the panhandle between the Ohio River and the western border of Pennsylvania remained part of Virginia.) In 1781 Washington County effectively supplanted Yohogania County.[16]

The second development was Pennsylvania's passage of the Act for the Gradual Abolition of Slavery in 1780. Secured primarily through the efforts of the Quakers, the act—the first of its kind in the United States—technically did not free a single slave. A compromise between humanitarians who wanted to end slavery and slave owners who wanted to keep their property, the abolition law specified that the children born to enslaved mothers after 1780 were to gain their freedom at the age of twenty-eight. (This was the origin of the term *twenty-eight-year servants*.) Every representative of adjacent Westmoreland County, which at the time included Washington County, voted against the 1780 act. Since Washington County was created after the 1780 act establishing the Pennsylvania–Virginia boundary, a special law had to be passed in 1782 extending the provisions of the abolition act to the county. A subsequent law, passed in 1788, required that slave owners register the children born to slave mothers to ensure that these children were ultimately freed.[17]

These laws amounted to a death sentence for slavery in the state—but, as Gary Nash has written, it was a death sentence with a "two-generation grace period." Under the 1780 act, it was entirely conceivable that a slave born before 1780 could have lived a long life and still been a slave in 1847, when Pennsylvania finally abolished slavery outright. Children born to slaves after 1780 could expect to spend the majority of their lives as the servants of a white master. In Washington County, a child born as late as 1817 to a slave for life would not have become a free person until 1845. The 1780 act did, however, have a telling effect on slavery in the state and in the county. After reaching a peak of about 6,855 slaves in 1780, the number of slaves in Pennsylvania fell sharply. In 1790 the state had 3,760 slaves; in

1800, it had 1,706 slaves; and by 1810, there were only 795 slaves left. The number of slaves fell much more rapidly than the operation of the 1780 act alone would have suggested. The act called the legitimacy of the institution into question by openly condemning slavery for depriving blacks of the "common blessings that they by nature were entitled to" and thereby encouraged slaveholders to free their slaves.[18] The act also prompted slaves of less-sensitive owners who showed no inclination to manumission to run away. Fugitive slaves amounted to three-fourths of the number of manumitted slaves in Philadelphia in the 1780s.[19] Finally, the 1780 act discouraged slaveholders from settling in the state because it prohibited the entry of slaves into the state on a permanent basis. Any slave who was brought into the state and resided there for more than six months became a free person under the provisions of the law. Conversely, the 1780 act caused owners committed to the institution of slavery to leave the state. After its passage, some of the "best families" of the area reportedly left for Kentucky and other territories where slavery remained unchallenged.[20]

These acts gradually undermined slavery in what had been one of the state's largest slaveholding counties. In 1782, when the first registration of slaves was mandated in Washington County, 417 slaves were held there. Of these, 376 resided within the final boundaries of the county. (Parts of the original county were hived off to form all of Greene County and portions of Allegheny and Beaver Counties.) The number of slaves declined to 217 in 1790 and to 76 in 1800. Part of this decline, particularly between 1782 and 1790, reflected the migration of slave owners unhappy with the Gradual Abolition Act to Kentucky. Another dramatic drop-off occurred between 1814 and 1820. An 1814 census of the county listed thirty-five slaves, but by 1820 only five slaves remained. The rapid decline between 1814 and 1820 likely reflects many deaths in an aging slave population whose life expectancy was about forty years. Of the thirty-five slaves listed in 1814, fourteen were forty or older. The year 1820 witnessed the second-to-last entry in the county's slave registry, recording the birth of a child of a Washington County slave or twenty-eight-year servant. By 1830, only one slave remained in Washington County. The 1840 census reported that the number of slaves in the county had actually increased to two.[21] And in 1845, James Henderson of Morris Township made the last entry in the Washington County Slave Record—a child born to a Kentucky slave—before the end of slavery in Pennsylvania in 1847.[22]

Table 1. Slavery and Freedom in Washington County (Current Boundaries)[1]

Year	Total Population of County	Slaves	Percent Slaves	Free Blacks	Percent Free Blacks
1782	16,300 (1784 est.)	376	2.307	0?	0?
1790	23,982	217	.904	9	.04
1800	28,298	76	.269	340	1.20
1810	36,289	36	.099	570	1.57
1814		35			
1820	40,038	5	.012	742	1.85
1830	42,784	1	.002	885	2.07
1840	41,279	2	.005	1,113	2.70
1850	44,939	0	0	1,559	3.47
1860	46,805	0	0	1,726	3.69

[1] R. Bell, "Black Persons in Early Washington County," 1–4, 8; Ewing, "Washington County Slave Record"; Harper, *Transformation of Western Pennsylvania*, 8, 12–13; Forstall, *Population of States and Counties*, 139.

Washington County's response to the questions raised by the Gradual Abolition Act was a mixed one. Like other Pennsylvania counties that shared a border with slaveholding Virginia or Maryland, it held onto slavery longer than the rest of Pennsylvania. (Delegates from neighboring Westmoreland County to the east had vehemently opposed the 1780 act.) The predominance of early settlers from Virginia and Maryland likewise gave slavery a legitimacy that it lacked elsewhere in the state. A begrudging acquiescence toward the 1780 abolition act seems to have characterized the attitude of most slave owners who stayed in the county. But a hardcore minority ignored and even attempted to subvert the law. Slave running across the ill-defined border between Pennsylvania and Virginia continued for years after the passage of the act.[23]

Some slave owners did come to question the morality of slavery and freed their slaves. Charles Stuart was the first one known to have acted on his misgivings about slavery. In May of 1788, he set Edward Huggins, his "mulatto man indented unto me during life," free from his service and had Huggins's legal freedom recorded in the county deed books.[24] Four years later, Neal Gillespie became the second resident of the county to manumit a slave, his "Negro man Slave named Harry." James Edgar, a judge of the county court, provides additional evidence on this issue. Edgar had registered a five-year-old slave named Hannah in 1782. In 1796, Edgar freed Hannah from her status as a lifelong slave, declaring, "I am under the serious conviction that involuntary servitude beyond a just compensation for maintenance and education is incompatible with a sense of duty to God and my fellow creatures." It was Edgar, however, who defined the terms of "just compensation." He declared that Hannah would be freed when she attained her twenty-seventh birthday, approximately in 1805.[25]

The transition from slavery to freedom was neither neat nor clear cut, as the experience of the slaves of Dr. Charles Wheeler illustrates. Wheeler arrived in Washington County in 1774 after serving as a surgeon in Lord Dunmore's War and purchased a 345-acre farm in what eventually became West Pike Run Township in the eastern part of the county. In 1782, in compliance with the Gradual Abolition Act, he registered four slaves with the county court: Nero, age thirty-four, Daniel, age nineteen, Rachell, age sixteen, and Rose, age nineteen. Wheeler's slaveholdings gradually decreased, but there is no evidence available to explain why. In the 1800 census he is listed as owning two slaves and having four "other free persons" (i.e., free blacks) living in his household. By the 1810 census, Wheeler held only one slave but had ten free blacks living on his farm. The presence of these "other free persons" living in Wheeler's household suggests that the end of slavery brought not outright freedom but instead a quasi-dependence on the former owner.[26]

Wheeler probably freed at least one of his slaves. He stipulated in his will, executed in 1808, that twenty-five pounds be given to "black Rachel" and fifty pounds be given to "black Daniel"—presumably two of the slaves he had registered in 1782. Wheeler also gave fifty-pound bequests to four other free blacks living on his farm. Wheeler considered himself a benign owner. In explaining these bequests, he commented, "The above black people was raised under my roof. I therefore hope they will consider the intent of the small bounties bestowed them by an indulgent master and to apply the same discreetly to their interests." Wheeler did not, however, bestow emancipation on his remaining slave in this will. This slave is likely to have been Rachel McGude, who appears on the 1814 county tax list as a fifty-year-old slave living in Pike Run Township. The "Rachell" whom Wheeler registered in 1782 would have been about forty-eight in 1814—close enough to fifty, given the uncertainty of slave birth dates. What became of Rachel after Wheeler's death in 1813 is unclear. Wheeler's wife, Elizabeth, who outlived him by some twenty-five years, does not appear in the 1820 census, so it is not clear if Rachel became Elizabeth's property.[27]

Black people who remained slaves grew increasingly restive with their status. Surviving local newspapers from the late eighteenth and early nineteenth centuries are full of advertisements for slaves who had absconded from their owners. Advertisements for runaway slaves began appearing in the *Pittsburgh Gazette* as soon as it began publishing in 1786.[28] The first known instance of an attempt to run away from slavery in Washington County occurred in 1795, as the following newspaper advertisement attests:

TWENTY DOLLARS REWARD
RUNAWAY from the house of James SEATON, living on Little Whitely in Washington County, on the Night of Sunday the 6th of December last,
A NEGRO WENCH
About two or three and twenty years of age, named CATE, very black, short, well made, and very active. The wench is the property of JENNETE PRATHER. Whoever takes up the said Wench, and delivers her to CHARLES PRATHER, at the mouth of the Buffaloe, shall receive the above award.
Washington, January 4th, 1796[29]

Another advertisement from Canonsburg, dated October 5, 1803, offered an eight-dollar reward for the return of Priss, described "as a likely negro wench . . . aged 15, about 5 feet, 6 inches high, slim-made, with a handsome face, a proud walk, and haughty appearance." The advertiser presumed that Priss would try to make it to nearby Raccoon Creek, where her sister lived.[30] Female runaways seem to have been particularly troublesome. On January 17, 1814, John Cooper of Fallowfield Township cautioned readers of the *Washington (PA) Reporter* "against harboring my negro girl ANNE as her negro man, THOS. FARIS, has made a practice of taking and stealing her. I am determined to put the law in force against him, or any person who will harbor her without a pass from me. She has a child about 5 months old." Most commonly, advertisers offered rewards for the return or apprehension of their property. Thomas H. Baird of Washington promised to give ten dollars to anyone who caught James Ross, a "runaway negro fellow" whom Baird characterized as "a thief and liar." The preceding advertisements would suggest that these fugitives were hiding out locally and not seeking freedom in distant places. In short, we are not looking at the genesis of the Underground

Railroad here. The advertisement that Zephaniah Nook placed in November 1815 may be an exception. He offered a reward for eight slaves who had run away while staying at Workman's Tavern about a mile east of Washington. It is not clear if these slaves resided in Washington County, nor is it clear if any of these advertisements ever brought about their intended results.[31]

The white population of Washington County became bitterly divided over the question of abolishing slavery in the 1780s and 1790s. The Washington Society for the Relief of Free Negroes Held in Bondage, formed in 1789, illustrates just how touchy the subject was in Washington County. It was an offshoot of the Pennsylvania Society for Promoting the Abolition of Slavery, and for the Relief of Free Negroes Unlawfully Held in Bondage (PAS), initially founded in 1775 and reorganized after the Revolutionary War in 1787. The nation's first abolition society, the PAS attempted to use legal means to whittle away at the institution of slavery. The Quaker elite and other well-to-do founders of the PAS, including Benjamin Franklin, challenged slave ownership by filing lawsuits based upon violations of Pennsylvania's abolition law; they did not advocate direct action against slavery, as their more radical successors did in the 1830s. The Washington Society proved to be even more conservative than its parent body, dropping all reference to abolition in its name. This name change suggests that members were more concerned about the kidnapping of free blacks than with the weightier issue of abolishing slavery. At least two members, David Bradford and Thomas Scott, were slaveholders or the owners of twenty-eight-year servants.[32]

The local society formed in response to the plight of a slave named John Davis. Davis's owner had brought him from Maryland to Washington County before the passage of the 1780 Gradual Abolition Act. The owner, however, had not registered Davis as a slave by the end of 1782 as was required under the new law. Under its terms, Davis should have become a free man. Davis's owner apparently disposed of this legal nicety when he moved to Virginia in 1788 and took Davis with him. There he rented Davis's services out to a Mr. Miller, probably for a year. Davis's friends in Washington County decided to take matters into their own hands. They went to Virginia and rescued Davis from slavery. Fearful that he would have to pay Davis's owner for his lost property, Miller hired three men to abduct Davis; they kidnapped Davis from Washington County in 1788 and carried him back to Virginia as a slave.[33]

The men who organized the Washington Society for the Relief of Free Negroes Held in Bondage regarded the abduction of someone they regarded as a free man as an outrage. Led by Alexander Addison and David Reddick, both attorneys, the society pressed for Davis's legal rights. It successfully argued before a Washington County court that the kidnappers, who were identified as Francis McGuire, Baldwin Parsons, and Absalom Wells, should be indicted, but they had fled to Virginia, which refused to give them up. The society then enlisted the aid of Pennsylvania Governor Thomas Mifflin. In a memorial in May 1791 to Mifflin, the society stated that "a crime of deeper dye is not to be found in the criminal code of this state, than that of taking a Freeman and carrying off with intent to sell him, and actually selling him as a slave." Despite Mifflin's pleas that Davis and his abductors should be returned to Pennsylvania, the Virginia governor refused to yield either party. He claimed that Davis was nothing more than a fugitive slave and that no federal statute covered extradition proceedings.[34]

The Davis case ultimately had national significance for resolving legal disputes between states in the newly formed Union and led to the passage of the Fugitive Slave Act of 1793. Although the recently adopted Constitution specified that neither people charged with a crime nor persons "held to service or labor" could escape justice or bound servitude by fleeing to another state, Congress had not passed any enabling legislation as of the date of Mifflin's request. Thus the Davis case had relevance for the return of fugitive slaves and the extradition of criminals. Governor Mifflin appealed to President George Washington for help in resolving the extradition issue; Washington in turn directed the matter to Congress's attention. Congress responded by passing the Fugitive Slave Act of 1793. As its title suggests, the law dealt primarily with this issue of runaway slaves and only secondarily with the issue of extraditing the kidnappers of free blacks. Thus, ironically, the 1793 law made it difficult to bring accused criminals across state lines, but offered very little protection to blacks whose captors accused them of being fugitive slaves. States below the Mason-Dixon Line got most of what they wanted from the new law. It did not protect Davis, who remained a slave. It did protect his kidnappers, who remained free in Virginia.[35]

The efforts of the Washington Society to bring Davis's kidnappers to justice thus backfired and actually encouraged the practice of stealing free blacks. Under the 1793 law, slave owners or their representatives did not need a warrant to seize an alleged runaway. They had only to convince a local judge that the person in custody was a slave. The law did not require jury trials and did not permit the supposed runaway to call witnesses in his defense. It also established a hefty fine of five hundred dollars for anyone who was convicted of aiding a runaway slave. In Pennsylvania and in the Ohio Valley, free blacks had few rights and often became the victims of kidnappings.[36]

The Washington Society for the Relief of Free Negroes Held in Bondage fell into disfavor locally for reasons that are not clear. Perhaps the society's intervention in Davis's case caused a backlash. More likely, its successful use of the 1780 act to free several Washington County blacks who had been held in bondage illegally provoked the enmity of local slave owners. In any case, the society's actions in the local courts proved deeply unpopular. Public pressure forced a number of the eleven original members to resign. As one of the remaining members wrote to James Pemberton, the president of the PAS, "We have the prejudice of the people, the Disapprobation of the magistrates fals [sic] records and corrupt officers to contend with." Helping blacks who should have been freed because their owners violated the 1780 act was apparently too much antislavery activity for many Washington County residents.[37]

Even the small successes of the Washington Society caused its members regrets. Alexander Addison, a lawyer who had pressed Davis's case and been instrumental in founding the local society, complained that the few slaves whom the society had succeeded in freeing because of violations of the 1780 act seemed incapable of making good use of their liberty. He lamented, "With the best intentions, we seem to produce only practical mischief. Removing the fear of a master, the only restraint of which their debased and untutored minds were conscious, without being able to fix upon them the check of honour, the Laws or Religion; we loose them to unprincipled licentiousness, idleness and every concomitant vice. We seem to deliver them up to the controul of Satan and their own lusts, and make them more the children of Hell, than before they were of misery." These comments, it is helpful to remember, came from someone who ostensibly was a friend of African Americans. Addison's remarks help to illuminate why the combination of public pressure and futility caused the Washington Society for the Relief of Free Negroes Held in Bondage to fold by 1794.[38]

Some former members of the society, however, continued their commitment to the legal rights of local blacks. Joseph Pentecost took on the case of Lucy, "a negro woman" who filed suit against her owner, "Reazin Pumphrey," as his name appears in court documents, in 1799. Pumphrey had arrived in Washington County from Anne Arundel County, Maryland, in 1772, bringing with him four slaves. He registered six slaves in 1782 to comply with the slave registration act, but Lucy was not among those he registered. Lucy sued Pumphrey for five hundred dollars for unlawful detention. She claimed that she had been Pumphrey's slave in 1782 and had been living in Washington County, but that Pumphrey had failed to register her. Therefore Lucy should be set free and was entitled to damages. The jury awarded Lucy one dollar in damages for the seventeen years she had spent as Pumphrey's slave while she was entitled to her freedom.[39]

David Reddick, an attorney who has been identified as "the head of the Washington County movement," also continued to champion the cause of local African Americans who had been illegally held in bondage. Reddick helped file a suit funded by the Pennsylvania Anti-Slavery Society on behalf of two women, Lydia and Cassandra, who had been brought as slaves into Washington County from Maryland by their owner, Samuel Blackmore, in 1782. Blackmore had not registered his slaves within the six months required by Pennsylvania's Gradual Abolition Act. When the case went to trial, Blackmore claimed that he thought he had moved to Virginia, not Pennsylvania. The Pennsylvania Supreme Court did not buy his explanation and ruled in 1797 that Lydia and Cassandra were free women.[40]

Pentecost and Reddick, however, represented a distinct minority. Evasions of Pennsylvania's abolition laws continued in Washington County into the 1820s. Slaveholders in the county kept the grandchildren—not just the children—of slaves as servants until the age of twenty-eight. The Washington County Negro Register contains numerous instances in which the children of twenty-eight-year servants were registered so that they could be forced to work until they too attained the age of twenty-eight. A typical entry reads as follows: "Thomas Ward of Somerset Township enters of record, a female negro child named Susannah, born the tenth day of Septemr. 1805 of Rachel a negro woman entered by Frederic Cooper in march 1789—a slave until she arrives at the age of twenty eight years."[41] Not until 1826 did the Pennsylvania Supreme Court rule that this practice was unconstitutional. These grandchildren would probably have been listed in the census not as "slaves" but as "servants," even if they were slaves in fact. Other evasions of the 1780 Gradual Abolition Act continued into at least the early 1830s. A state senate committee in 1833 found that some whites in the southwestern counties were buying slaves in Virginia and emancipating them—and then forcing them to work as indentured servants for seven years. Local courts sometimes required black children who were bought as slaves in another state to serve their new owners until they reached the age of twenty-eight. Whites were thereby able to take advantage of the cheap labor of people in quasi-slavery who had very few legal rights.[42]

The case of Mary, who is simply described in court documents as "a Negro woman," illustrates this subterfuge of granting an out-of-state slave freedom, only to deny it by indenturing that person for seven years in Pennsylvania. Her owner, John Cooke, had freed Mary in Berkeley County, Virginia. She apparently accompanied him when he moved to Washington County about 1800, and in February of that year Cooke used the power of the local courts to force her to become his indentured servant for nearly seven years. Supposedly Mary entered into this agreement "with my own free and voluntary will and accord without any persuasion or compulsion," but it is difficult to believe that no compulsion lay behind Mary's action. Her reason for signing her mark to this document, she stated, was that "John Cooke has not had service from me sufficient to compensate him for the trouble and expenses he has had with me and I am desirous to make the said John Cooke full compensation." Mary promised henceforth to make amends and to be a true and faithful servant. The court document hints at the kinds of troubles that Mary had previously caused Cooke. Mary vowed that she would not "absent myself from my said masters service day or night during said term, or play at cards, or any other unlawful game, and will not give away or destroy my said masters goods and chattels." Mary, however, continued to be a vexatious servant for Cooke. On August 16, 1802, he sold the balance of Mary's term as an indentured servant to Joseph Pentecost on the stipulation that "she shall not come on John Cooke for her maintenance for the future." Probably this was the same Joseph Pentecost who had supported Lucy's case for freedom.[43]

The motivation behind maintaining indentured servitude for the county's African Americans can be understood quite easily: indentured labor was cheap. One Irish immigrant to Pennsylvania estimated that an indentured servant cost one-eighth that of a free laborer. The supply of white indentured servants, however, dried up in the nineteenth century as European immigrants took advantage of cheaper transatlantic fares to purchase their own passage and to arrive in America as free people. White farmers and rural artisans in Washington County who were able to purchase the indentured labor of blacks therefore benefitted from the breakdown of slavery. Although many of them could not have afforded to purchase a slave, they could afford to hire an indentured black servant. Furthermore, they continued to treat their bound black labor much as owners had treated their slaves and indentured servants before the American Revolution.[44]

Slavery's presence thus lingered a long time in a supposedly "free" county north of the Mason-Dixon Line. Although the children born to slaves after 1780 were technically servants, they were being sold as if they were slaves. The pervasive assumption in newspaper advertisements for the sale of "twenty-eight-year slaves" was that they were property. The following advertisement appeared in the *Reporter* on February 25, 1811:

FOR SALE

A FRAME HOUSE, two stories high, with a kitchen and three excellent lots, in the town of West-Boston, Washington County, Pa.

Also, a stout healthy negro wench, fourteen years of age, a servant till 28. For terms enquire of

ISAIAH STEEN

Such servants were advertised for sale in the pages of the *Reporter* as late as 1825:

PUBLICK SALE Will be sold at the house of John Fleming in Washington on Wednesday next [March 30, 1825] at two o'clock in the afternoon the unexpired time of a mullatto woman named Margaret (born 15 Nov. 1803) and her Lucinda (born 24 Apr. 1824), also a mullatto, late the property of John Hoge, Esqr. dec'd. (The said Margaret and Lucinda will not be separated.)[45]

Margaret and Lucinda were sold to John Dagg for eighty dollars. An 1823 advertisement similarly offered an eighteen-year-old "young woman of colour" for sale for the remainder of her servitude. Of the 232 children born to slaves who were registered between 1788 and 1825, 104 were born after 1800. Even though Washington County had only five slaves in 1820, a substantial number of the county's black population was still bound labor subject to being sold well after that date.[46]

While slavery lingered in Washington County into the 1820s, it is clear that by the 1830s it was a dying institution there, just as it had all but disappeared in the Commonwealth of Pennsylvania.[47] Only one slave was listed in the county's census report for 1830. The Pennsylvania Supreme Court had put an end to the practice of indenturing the grandchildren of slaves four years earlier, and by 1830 advertisements for the sale of slaves and in-dentured black servants had ceased to appear in local newspapers. The end of such advertisements reflects the fact that there were fewer servants for sale and perhaps hints that the moral climate of the county was changing. Simi-larly, advertisements for fugitive slaves had disappeared from the newspa-pers of south central Pennsylvania by the late 1820s. David Smith attributes this absence to changing local sentiment and the fact that slavery had virtu-ally disappeared in Adams, Cumberland, and Franklin Counties.[48]

An affidavit made to Gabriel Bleakeney's will reflects the changing temper of the times in Washington County. In his 1824 will, Bleakeney, a Revolutionary War veteran and a farmer in Amwell Township, had be-queathed his slave Betsy to the wife of his good friend John Hoge, one of the founders of Washington. On his deathbed, however, Bleakeney changed his mind and freed Betsy because of her kindness toward him.[49]

It should not be blithely assumed that the lot of freed slaves was a happy one. The case of Dido Munts serves as a cautionary tale. Munts had been the slave of the Reverend John Clark and his wife Margaret. When Clark died, he freed Munts and willed a substantial sum to Jefferson College in Can-onsburg with the stipulation that part of this sum be used to maintain her in her old age. In March 1838, John Holmes, who apparently lodged her, presented a claim to the trustees of the college for her support. The commit-tee handling this claim acknowledged the college's obligation to "pay a competent sum for the support of the above named Dido Munts." It paid Holmes $110 for her room and board. The following year, however, the col-lege decided that her upkeep was too expensive and authorized her removal to "the Poor House as soon as practicable."[50]

THE GROWTH OF FREE BLACK COMMUNITIES

The gradual emergence of free black communities in Washington County after 1790 paralleled the slow demise of slavery. These communities grew because of the gradual emancipation of slaves locally and the migration of manumitted slaves from the South, primarily Virginia. (Although the law was applied unevenly, manumitted slaves were required to leave Virginia, typically within a year of being freed, or risk re-enslavement.[51]) The federal censuses give the major outlines of this story. In 1790, 217 slaves resided in Washington County but only nine free blacks. Significantly, all nine of these free blacks lived with white families. By 1800, a major transformation had taken place. The slave population had dropped to 76 and the free black population had risen to 340. Of the free blacks, 251 were living with black families and apart from the direct supervision of whites. In short, the earliest free black communities took shape in Washington County around 1800 and grew substantially thereafter. As the number of slaves dwindled to insignificance by 1830, the number of free blacks continued to grow. In 1810, there were 570 free blacks; in 1820, 742; in 1830, 885; in 1840, 1,113; and in 1850 there were 1,559 free blacks in the county. On the eve of the Civil War this population had grown to 1,726, or 3.7 percent of the county's population.[52]

Free blacks initially stayed close to the farms where they had been slaves or indentured servants, but over time they tended to congregate in villages and towns. Thus townships along the Monongahela River, where slavery had initially been concentrated, continued to have a relatively large black population. In 1830, Pike Run Township had 92 black residents and Fallowfield Township 74. The southern and western townships had just a sprinkling of black residents. Washington, the county seat, proved to be the biggest magnet for free blacks. Five black families totaling 41 people were living in Washington in 1800. This number nearly doubled, to 82, between 1810 and 1820 and rose by 1830 to 122. By 1850 Washington had 235 blacks among its population of 2,662, or about 9 percent of its population. Nearly two-thirds of the borough's African Americans had been born in Pennsylvania, but more than a quarter had been born in a slave state, 41 of them in Virginia.[53]

Maria Cooper was one of those Virginians. Born into slavery, probably about 1816, she lived near Front Royal in Warren County. She and her children were freed in 1851. Cooper's owner, Ruhannah M. Buck, had apparently established a close relationship with Cooper and took particular care to ensure that Cooper was not only freed upon her death, but also given sufficient money to establish herself in a free state. (An 1806 Virginia law stipulated that emancipated slaves had to leave the state within a year or face the prospect of re-enslavement.) Upon Buck's death, her executors immediately gave Cooper, her six children, and one grandchild their freedom papers. They bought a new wagon, two horses to pull that wagon, and various equipment for the horses and wagon. They also advanced $300 of the $800 Buck had willed to Cooper so that she could buy a house when she had left the state of Virginia.[54]

Cooper's motives for moving to Washington, Pennsylvania, remain unknown, although she apparently chose this destination before she left Warren County. When she passed through Uniontown and Brownsville, Pennsylvania, residents encouraged Cooper and her family to settle in these towns, but she continued along the National Road to Washington, probably in the fall of 1852. So far as is known, no blacks from Warren County had preceded Cooper to Washington. Perhaps the town's reputation as a place that was congenial for blacks drew her there. Washington's substantial black population may also have been an inducement.[55]

At least initially, Cooper found life in Washington to her liking. Her family met with a warm reception, and her two elder daughters found ready employment as domestic help at wages of $1.50 per week. Trained by her former mistress to read and write, Cooper reported back to the executors of the estate that she could easily have found positions for her youngest daughters as well but wanted them to be able to take advantage of free public schooling. She rented a three-room house at a decent price and found food quite affordable. She was able to make some money by taking in laundry. Cooper's initial optimism soon soured, however, when the horses purchased for her proved to be virtually worthless for hauling coal and other materials and a drain on her meager financial assets. She eventually had to purchase a new horse by borrowing money. Even more significantly, the executors of the Buck estate proved recalcitrant in forwarding the $500 balance that had been willed to her. Burdened financially by illnesses that led to the deaths of two members of her family, and pressed by her creditors for money, Cooper pleaded in letter after letter to be given the $500 that was due her. Not until 1859 did the executors finally desist from excuses and pay the money that was owed to Cooper—no doubt in part because a young white attorney, David S. Wilson, became her advocate. She promptly bought a house (probably the one she had been renting) in Washington's small black neighborhood for $575. Cooper had made friends and put down roots in Washington, which offered a small but supportive black community, white friends sympathetic to injustices, free public education, and steady employment.[56]

The Skinner family offers another example of a black family in Virginia that relocated to Washington, Pennsylvania, after being forced to leave Virginia. Harriet Skinner was born free in Loudoun County and lived about five miles from Harper's Ferry. She married a slave and had ten children by him. She purchased his freedom in 1849, so the family was required to leave the state within a year. Interestingly, her husband was required to assume her last name on the certificate of freedom issued to him. The family took ten days to travel by wagon over the National Road to Washington in 1850. Armstead Skinner, the youngest of the children who came to Pennsylvania when he was nine, could offer no reason, in a late nineteenth-century newspaper interview, for why his family decided to come to this city in southwestern Pennsylvania.[57]

As was true across the North, greater economic and social opportunities in urban areas led Washington County's black population to leave the countryside for the city.[58] Lacking the capital to buy land, rural blacks faced the prospect of working under the close supervision of whites and of social isolation. As Nash has commented, "For newly freed blacks, moving to the city was a logical way to obtain work, to find friends and sociability, to begin or perpetuate a family—in short, to build for the future."[59]

While the economic opportunities may not have been great, there were opportunities. Of the forty-two black men whose occupations were listed in the 1850 census for the borough of Washington, more than three-fourths appear as day laborers who probably performed menial jobs. The remaining nine individuals had learned a skill or trade such as carpentry, barbering, or coopering. One owned a grocery store. About one-quarter of the borough's black population had succeeded in acquiring their own homes by 1850. By contrast, only about 8 percent of black households in Philadelphia owned property in 1837. A similar occupational pattern emerges from Monongahela City, which had an African American population of 75 persons out of a total of 977. Ten of the seventeen black adult male heads of households are listed as laborers, but Monongahela also supported two farmers, two wagoners, a schoolteacher, and several tradesmen. Rural townships showed much less occupational diversity. In Fallowfield Township, for example, five of the six black heads of household are listed as laborers; only one apparently owned the land needed to be designated a farmer. Hopewell Township in the western part of the county offered more opportunities for land ownership, as five African Americans had succeeded in acquiring land. Still, 76 percent of its black heads of household were laborers. The only other occupation listed for an African American in Hopewell Township was that of a boatman— probably one who made his living on the nearby Ohio River.[60]

The small towns of Washington County also offered institutions that could seldom be found in the countryside. Churches are the primary example. The African Methodist Episcopal (AME) Church became the core of the black community in Washington County. Methodism attracted black congregants for several reasons. First, its founder, John Wesley, held well-known antislavery views. Second, Methodists disdained well-crafted sermons in favor of church services that were full of spontaneity and emotion. They also imposed a discipline that influenced the private lives of struggling but aspiring whites and blacks far more than rival denominations. For Richard Allen and other African American leaders of early Methodism, Wesley's church "seemed a perfect system for lifting up an oppressed people and healing the suffering experienced by slavery." When white Philadelphia Methodists refused to accord equal status to black congregants, Allen, a former slave himself, decided in 1794 to build a church that would minister exclusively to his people. Although Allen remained officially within the fold of the Methodist Episcopal Church until 1816, when he organized the AME Church, the seeds of separation had been sown long before.[61]

In the town of Washington, the St. Paul AME Church was founded in 1818, just two years after the formation of the AME Church nationally. The impetus for the organization of the local church came from George Boler (some accounts say Bolden), a black barber who was the exhorter in the local Methodist Church. African Americans had been attending this church since it was built in 1801 but were relegated to the balcony. By 1810 there were enough black members to form a class. Such classes met during the week at the home of a member and were intended to aid in the quest for salvation. A second class had been added by 1819. Boler headed the first class, which met at his home, while Joseph Reynolds headed the second. Boler wrote to Philadelphia requesting that a black minister be sent to serve Washington's black Methodists. The Reverend David Smith arrived in Washington in 1820 in response to this request. Shortly thereafter, the congregation built a church on a lot between Chestnut and Walnut Streets in the black neighborhood at the east end of town. That more than half of Washington's eighty-one blacks joined youth and adult classes at St. Paul's testifies to the importance of the church in the black community. The establishment of a separate church reflected the growing wealth and independence of the black community—and probably also reflected the desire to be free of white supervision. As Gayraud S. Wilmore has commented, the black church was "the one impregnable corner of the world where consolation, solidarity, and mutual aid could be found and from which the master and the bossman—at least in the North—could be effectively barred."[62] Another AME church, Wright's Chapel, was organized in Washington in 1843.[63]

The expansion of black churches in Washington County paralleled national developments. Between 1836 and 1846, AME churches proliferated across the North, increasing from eighty-six to nearly three hundred.[64] Two AME churches appeared in the eastern part of the county in the 1830s and 1840s. (See Map 3.) William Paul Quinn, who had been present at the

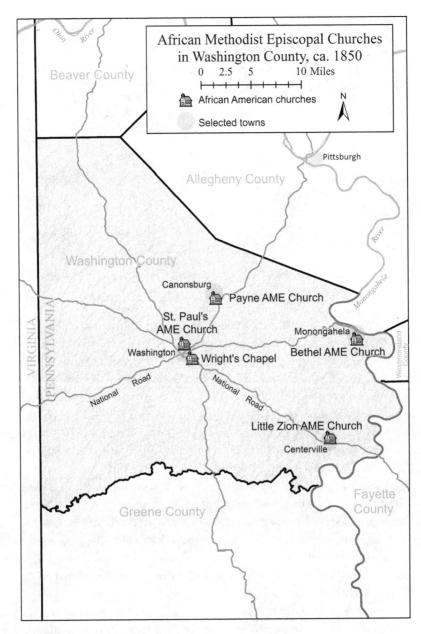

African Methodist Episcopal Churches in Washington County, ca. 1850

0   2.5   5   10 Miles

African American churches

Selected towns

N

Map 3

1. Fallen grave marker in Little Zion AME Church graveyard, Centerville, PA

founding of the AME Church in Philadelphia and became a major force in the church, helped to organize the Bethel AME Church in Monongahela in 1833. The Reverend Samuel Clingman served as the first pastor of the church, and Bowman and Ralph families were stalwart members of this church for several generations. The first building occupied by the church stood at the corner of Geary and Fair (now Sixth) Streets. The church moved to its current location on Main and Seventh Streets in 1871.[65]

The other antebellum black church in eastern Washington County was the Little Zion AME Church in West Pike Run Township, founded in 1844 by Augustus R. Green. It was unique in Washington County in that it was a rural church. Abraham Lowdrake hosted meetings of this church at his home until 1850, when the congregation erected a log building. In 1880 the congregation built a frame church northeast of Centerville. Among the members were William Wallace, a major figure in the local Underground Railroad, and William Ralph from nearby Monongahela, who served briefly as the pastor of the church.[66]

The Payne AME Church in Canonsburg dates to the early 1830s. The church initially met in private residences. After it formally organized, Reverend Clingman became the pastor of the church. By 1843, the church had evidently found a permanent home. A letter written by Daniel Arnet, James Brown, and F. L. Chambers, all of whom lived in the Canonsburg area, called for a countywide meeting of African Americans in the Canonsburg AME Church in that year. The congregation built a new church in 1853 or 1854 in the west end of town.[67]

The slow demise of slavery, the emergence of free black communities, and the establishment of institutions independent of white control all helped to create the roadbed for the local Underground Railroad. As David Smith has commented, "A strong free black population was an important component to successful aid to fugitive slaves."[68] By 1830 a fugitive slave could find a refuge in the small but established communities of free blacks in towns such as Washington, Canonsburg, and West Middletown. The growth of radical abolitionism in the 1830s among a small but dedicated minority of whites in Washington County enabled a growing number of fugitive slaves to find a safe haven either in the county or in Canada. The next chapter examines how this minority took up the cause of abolitionism.

CHAPTER TWO

Radical Abolitionism and the Arrival of the Underground Railroad

The origins of the Underground Railroad in Washington County are shadowy. While the local and regional origins of aid to fugitive slaves are obscure, it is nearly certain that this aid came from African Americans. Although no organized network to assist fugitive slaves existed until the 1810s at the earliest, the growing free black communities in the borough of Washington and surrounding rural areas probably provided aid out of compassion and sympathy from their initial establishment in the early nineteenth century. County historian Earle Forrest contends that "the free Negroes in this section always gave aid to members of their race trying to reach Canada." He points to a black gunsmith named Tower or "Tar" Adams—so called because of a common mispronunciation of "Tower"—as the founder of the local Underground Railroad. Advertisements offering rewards for the capture of fugitive slaves appeared in the *Washington Reporter* as soon as it began to be published in 1808, indicating that slave owners perceived the area as one in which their slaves might seek refuge. As Keith Griffler has observed, what became known as the Underground Railroad was a black monopoly in the Ohio Valley in the first few decades of the nineteenth century. Not until the late 1830s would white abolitionists begin to participate substantially in the Liberty Line and help make it an organized, interracial network instead of the work of isolated African American activists.[1]

Washington County's involvement in the Liberty Line came several decades after it began elsewhere. At the national level, Quakers and free blacks organized the predecessor of the Underground Railroad in the Philadelphia area in the 1780s and 1790s. George Washington in 1786 was one of the first to complain that an organized effort to help escaping slaves existed in Philadelphia. Washington had a personal basis for this complaint, having lost one of his own slaves. The Philadelphia area, however, remained for decades the only place in the country where an organized system for assisting fugitive slaves existed. The uniqueness of this area stemmed from its large Quaker population (absent elsewhere) and the city's large free black population.[2]

Wilbur Siebert, in his pioneering study of the Underground Railroad, dates the first signs of that network in western Pennsylvania to the War of 1812. Although he cites no evidence, Siebert offers the explanation that soldiers and sailors returning from that war brought the news to the slave states that black bondage did not exist in Canada. African American sailors comprised perhaps as much as one-tenth of the crews of American naval ships on the Great Lakes. Black veterans of the War of 1812 reported that Canada provided a safe haven for slaves and refused to return them to the United States. These reports led to a small but growing number of blacks to use western Pennsylvania as an escape route to Canada. The experience of one such person, James Adams, indicates that Buffalo, New York, had already become an important crossing point into Canada by 1824. After escaping from slavery in western Virginia, Adams made his way to Buffalo. A friendly boat captain checked the streets of Buffalo to make sure that no handbills had been posted for Adams's capture. Although Adams obtained assistance occasionally from sympathetic whites, his journey to freedom suggests that there was no organized network of helpers available to runaway slaves in Ohio in the mid-1820s.[3]

Newspaper advertisements provide indirect evidence that fugitive slaves found a safe haven in Washington County by the War of 1812, particularly in the county seat of Washington. Advertisements offering rewards for the capture of fugitive slaves appeared in the *Washington Reporter* almost from its inception. Most of these advertisements assumed the runaways were making a break for freedom. Slave owners from counties in the nearby Virginia panhandle, and from as far away as Baltimore and Front Royal, Virginia (the original home of Maria Cooper), perceived Washington County as a possible destination for their runaway slaves as early as 1810. Hezekiah Conn of Front Royal believed that his slave Gim, who ran away in 1816, had "bent his course towards Pennsylvania or Ohio." At least one slave owner suspected that his slave had found refuge in Washington, Pennsylvania. Moses Shepherd of nearby Ohio County, in the panhandle of

Virginia, offered a fifty-dollar reward in 1814 for the return of a slave named Ben, who "was lately seen in the borough of Washington." He described Ben as being "six feet high, about 30 years of age, stoops when he walks, is fond of liquor." Blair Moran from nearby West Liberty, Virginia, placed the following advertisement in the *Reporter* on July 25, 1814:

$20 REWARD

Ran away, on Friday the 30th of May, a negro boy named Jacob, about 18 years old; 5 feet six or seven inches high; well made; is very black; has a middling broad nose, and somewhat red-eyed but a handsome boy. . . . He took with him two coarse shirts, one pair of linen trousers, one pair of fulled linsey, coat of fulled linsey, also, though not made for him; it is old fashioned and must be too large for him. . . .Whoever apprehends said boy, and delivers him in Wheeling jail, shall have the above reward.[4]

Not all of these advertisers believed that these fugitives intended to find a safe haven in the free states. In 1813, a twenty-nine-year-old slave named Andrew escaped from his owner in Charlestown, in neighboring Brooke County, Virginia. Samuel Bray had purchased Andrew on the Eastern Shore of Maryland and intended to take him to Kentucky. Bray believed that the runaway would attempt to return to the Eastern Shore, where he apparently had family. In offering a reward, Bray warned readers that Andrew was a "cunning, artful fellow, and will no doubt try to pass as a freeman."[5]

Because what eventually became known as the Underground Railroad began locally before the construction of the first railroads in the United States in the late 1820s, it makes sense to refer to the early efforts of African Americans in Washington County to hide fugitive slaves and to pass them on to safety in other communities as the "Underground Road"—the term used by perplexed slave hunters for the mysterious mechanism by which their property disappeared. The term *Underground Railroad* was not widely used until the 1840s. Several authors have offered explanations for the origins of the term. Although these authors differ with regard to place and time, they follow a pattern similar to a story set in 1831. The story centers on Tice Davids, a runaway slave from Kentucky. Davids's owner was so close to capturing him that Davids had no choice but to jump into the Ohio River and swim for safety. Despite marking the spot where Davids had climbed out of the water on the northern shore, the slave owner, after crossing the river in a rented skiff, could find no sign of Davids. Furthermore, no white

Ohioan had seen Davids. When asked what had become of his slave, the owner reputedly replied that "the nigger must have gone off on an underground road." A remarkably similar story is told about a slave owner who pursued a runaway slave to Columbia, Pennsylvania, only to lose all trace of him.[6] Later, as railroads became a familiar fact of everyday life, the expression was modified to become "underground railroad."

The opening in 1818 of the first federally financed highway to the west, the National Road (or National Pike), meant a substantial increase in westward traffic through Washington County of slaves destined for sale at the Wheeling, Virginia, slave market. Most would ultimately be taken to the booming cotton lands of the Old Southwest. It also meant an increase in the number of fugitive slaves escaping locally. After the War of 1812, slave owners in the old tobacco belt of Virginia and Maryland capitalized on the high demand for slaves on the newly established cotton plantations of territories such as Alabama and Mississippi by selling their surplus slaves. The National Road, which connected Cumberland, Maryland, and points farther east to Wheeling, provided the easiest way for slave owners in western Maryland and northern Virginia to send their slaves to the Lower South. (See Map 4.) Slaves who were taken to or sold in Wheeling then were boarded on steamboats that took them to slave markets downstream in Natchez and New Orleans.[7]

The National Road through Washington County saw a good deal of this traffic in human beings. The all-weather highway, which was an engineering marvel in its day, ran some forty-five miles through Washington County. (Route 40 largely follows the National Road today.) After crossing the Monongahela River at Brownsville, it went northwest to Washington before veering off to the southwest and Wheeling. Coffles of slaves chained together were a common sight along the early National Road. As Thomas B. Searight, the author of a late-nineteenth-century history of the "Old Pike," commented, "Negro slaves were frequently seen on the National Road. The writer has seen them driven over the road arranged in couples and fastened to a long, thick rope or cable, like horses. This may seem incredible to a majority of persons now living along the road, but it is true, and was a very common sight in the early history of the road and evoked no expression of surprise or words of censure. Such was the temper of the times."[8] Benjamin Lundy, the Quaker abolitionist who spent some time in Wheeling in the 1820s, witnessed "'droves of a dozen or twenty ragged men bound for the West, chained together and driven through the streets,

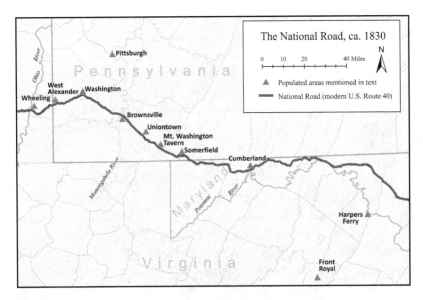

Map 4

bare-headed and bare-footed, in mud and snow,' by men with whips and bludgeons." John Deets, a wagon driver from Uniontown, Pennsylvania, similarly remembered seeing "scores of slaves" being driven through that town, "handcuffed and tied two and two to a rope that was extended some 40 or 50 feet, one on each side."[9]

One of the best-known fugitive slaves made this journey along the National Road to Wheeling in the early 1820s. Ironically, Josiah Henson, regarded by many as the model for Uncle Tom in Harriet Beecher Stowe's novel, made this trek as a loyal slave. Unaccompanied by his owner, Henson led eighteen unshackled fellow slaves, including his wife, to his owner's new home in Kentucky. His journey through Washington County is what may have given rise to the local legend that the fictional characters of *Uncle Tom's Cabin*, Eliza and her young son, Harry, actually stopped at Underground Railroad stations in the county.[10] Henson, however, never seems to have given any thought to escaping while traveling through Pennsylvania. Determined not to betray his owner's confidence in him, he even ignored the appeals of free blacks in Cincinnati to stay on the north side of the Ohio River rather than continue his assigned mission to Kentucky. Only after his owner, Amos Riley, reneged on a promise to allow Henson to purchase his freedom and then tried to sell him did Henson strike out for Canada with his wife and several small children.[11]

The traffic in slaves along the National Road also meant a substantial increase in reported escapes. In 1822, William Perry offered a $150 reward in the local newspaper for the capture of two slaves who had been chained together and made their escape about nine miles east of Washington on the National Road. He suspected that these two men, John Wells and George Tyler, would attempt to return to their former home in Fauquier County, Virginia. A year later, Thomas Talbot speculated that two male slaves who had run away from him could be hiding "in the neighborhood of Washington" but might "make for Virginia."[12]

Although many of these escapes along the National Road were clearly acts of self-liberation, there is reason to think that some of them involved the assistance of free blacks. Both black and white wagoners traversed this highway between Cumberland and southwestern Pennsylvania. The rigid racial barriers that separated black and white teamsters would have facilitated escapes. Black drivers ate at separate tables in the taverns along the road and occupied separate quarters. They could have easily concealed fugitives seeking freedom in the Keystone State in their cargoes. Unfortunately there is no hard evidence to support this speculation.[13]

Fugitive slaves clearly used the National Road as a highway to freedom, but it was a path fraught with danger. Searight concluded that many fugitive slaves had been captured along the Old Pike and returned to their owners. Searight pointed to Captain Thomas Endsley, a former slave owner who kept a tavern in Somerfield, Pennsylvania, which now lies under Youghiogheny River Lake, as being one of the most tenacious of these slave catchers. On one occasion Endsley subdued two fugitives but was unable to capture the third. Ironically, the man whom Searight identified as being the most noteworthy friend of fugitive slaves, William Wiley, lived in the same small community. Although fugitives could find help and shelter occasionally, they traveled the National Road for the most part at their own peril. On July 4, 1845, three white wagoners identified a black man walking along the road near Mt. Washington Tavern as a runaway. He was only able to escape by knifing one of his assailants, who died on the spot.[14]

The most famous case of a fugitive slave escape along the National Road in Washington County occurred in 1828. Christian "Kit" Sharp had fled from his Kentucky owner, Robert Carlyle, but Carlyle tracked Sharp down and captured him somewhere on the National Road between

Washington and West Brownsville in southeastern Washington County. Carlyle brought Sharp back to Washington and spent the night of January 31 there. The next morning, he set off on foot for Wheeling before daylight with his handcuffed slave in tow. Carlyle was murdered on the outskirts of Washington later that morning, his skull crushed by a blunt object. Sharp reported the crime and claimed that three unknown assailants had attacked his master. He was immediately suspected of the murder, however, because of the bloodstains on his clothing. Although Samuel McFarland, a prominent local attorney who later became a leader in the local Underground Railroad, defended Sharp, the jury convicted him of the murder. Sharp was executed on November 21, 1828.[15]

At least some residents of the county believed Sharp's story even after he had been convicted and hanged. They suspected that Tar Adams, the first identifiable figure in the local Underground Railroad, had in fact been one of the three assailants who attempted to help Sharp gain his freedom. Regardless of his involvement in the Carlyle affair, Adams is the first individual to emerge from the local Underground Railroad. According to Forrest, Adams had helped fugitives escape "even before the Underground was established." Forrest dates the organization of "the Underground"— by which he means the white Underground Railroad—to 1824. Perhaps it is merely a coincidence, but Jean Fritz, in her young adult novel about the Underground Railroad, *Brady*, named one of the black conductors Tar Adams. The setting for her novel is southwestern Pennsylvania.[16]

Tar Adams's life spanned the entirety of Washington County's Underground Railroad history. Born a free person in Maryland in 1788, Adams had moved to Washington when he was a young man and begun practicing his trade as a gunsmith while running slaves to freedom. Adams emerges as a larger-than-life figure in the stories told about him. According to Forrest, Adams was a wonderful runner, but often went around on crutches "as a blind to slave hunters." He was apparently fleet of foot even in his advancing years. One story related by Forrest has it that Adams was at a blacksmith shop on West Chestnut Street in Washington when a group of slave catchers passed by. Feigning lameness and hobbling on crutches, he overheard their inquiries about some fugitive slaves whom they were pursuing. Once out of sight of these pursuers, Adams dropped his crutches and took off like a bolt for West Middletown, where he knew the fugitives were staying. (Jean Fritz likewise has her fictional Adams drop his crutches when the need arises.) The sheriff, upon seeing Adams take off out of the corner of his eye, informed the slave hunters that further pursuit was useless because "the old darky leaning on crutches would reach West Middletown before they could." They laughed the sheriff's comment off as a joke, only to discover upon reaching West Middletown that, to their chagrin, the fugitives had escaped. The story in all likelihood is apocryphal—it seems difficult to believe that men on horseback could not catch up to a man on foot with a lead of several hundred yards over the twelve miles to West Middletown—but nonetheless wonderful. One suspects that Forrest has indulged in a bit of hyperbole in relating this story, but it certainly testifies to Adams's speed and to his involvement in the Underground Railroad.[17]

Another major player in the early days of the local Underground Railroad is William or Bill Asbury. A powerfully built, light-skinned former slave from Virginia, Asbury had arrived in western Washington County by 1830, when he appears in the census as "William Ashbury." According to the family legend, Asbury was so unruly that his owner eventually let him go free. Shortly after settling in Cross Creek Township, he became involved in the Underground Railroad. According to the historian of the Cross Creek Cemetery, Asbury "was, from 1837 until his death, head engineer on the 'Underground Railroad' from his residence to Pittsburgh." Reputedly Asbury and another free black led scores of slaves to freedom. He became so infamous among Virginia slaveholders that a reward of one thousand dollars was offered for his head in Wheeling. Asbury died of natural causes in Cross Creek on March 12, 1846, at the age of forty-seven.[18]

Doubtless other African Americans in Washington County hid runaways and assisted them on the road to freedom in the early days of the Underground Railroad, but their names are lost to history. As Larry Gara commented in 1961, previous historians of the Liberty Line regarded it as primarily a white organization and often ignored the participation of black Americans. The involvement of blacks has similarly been slighted in local treatments of the Underground Railroad. Although Forrest does mention Tar Adams, he devotes far more space to the exploits of white abolitionists. Adams is one of the few African American operatives whom Forrest identifies by name. Other historians of the county similarly had very little to say about black involvement in the Underground Railroad. There are probably several reasons for this neglect of black Underground Railroad agents. First, white historians simply may not have known about the activities of African American operatives. Second, blacks were probably less likely to have left behind written records of their activities, and they were not often sought out by earlier historians of the county. White participants also emphasized their own role in helping fugitive slaves escape, downplaying or ignoring the role of African Americans. The role of racial prejudice cannot be discounted either. As Gara has commented, whites were the heroes of the Underground Railroad legends, while blacks were often reduced to the role of passive passengers.[19]

However shadowy our information is about the origins of the local Underground Railroad, it is clear that by 1830 African Americans had developed a network of assistance in the county. The growth of the free black community, the organization of independent black churches, and a hard-fought measure of prosperity for a small minority of blacks made it possible to help fugitive slaves in a more systematic way than the spur-of-the-moment aid that had been available previously. Adams and Asbury represent the tip of an iceberg of unknown dimensions. As we will see, local African Americans later developed extensive networks to aid fugitive slaves in their quest for freedom. This black-organized Liberty Line probably preceded white involvement in the local Underground Railroad by several decades.

THE BIRTH OF RADICAL ABOLITIONISM

The development of the Underground Railroad among whites in Washington County was intimately connected with the growth of radical abolitionism—the belief that slavery represented such an enormous evil that its existence could no longer be tolerated in the United States. Although only a small fraction of whites in the county became abolitionists and even fewer of them participated in the Underground Railroad, the existence of an organized abolition movement that believed slavery was a national sin fostered white efforts to aid runaway slaves. Understanding the growth of radical abolitionism is crucial to understanding the subsequent building of the Underground Railroad.

After the disappearance of the Washington Society for the Relief of Free Negroes Held in Bondage in the mid-1790s, there seems to have been no organized antislavery activity among whites in the county until the 1820s. As was the case in other Northern communities, the post–Revolutionary War fervor to end slavery died out by the end of the eighteenth century. Renewed local concern about slavery may have stemmed the national debates over the expansion of slavery that ultimately resulted in the Missouri

Compromise. Occasioned by the request for Missouri's admission to the Union as a slave state, the debate over Missouri raised slavery as a major national issue for the first time since the Constitutional Convention of 1787. The compromise ultimately balanced the number of free and slave states by agreeing to the admission of Missouri as a slave state and of Maine as a free state. After hearing about the Missouri crisis, Thomas Jefferson wrote from his mountaintop home in Virginia that this news had awakened him "like a fire bell in the night" with fears for the future of the Union.[20]

The Missouri question aroused not only fears about the preservation of the nation but also concerns about the morality of slavery. The Pennsylvania gubernatorial race of 1820, pitting Joseph Hiester against William Findlay, reflected the divisions in the state. Findlay's supporters portrayed the contest as one between "Hiester & Slavery vs. Findlay & Freedom." The *Harrisburg (PA) Republican* castigated Hiester as a slaveholder who had voted against the state's abolition law and defended the institution at every turn, whereas it portrayed Findlay as a man who had sacrificed his self-interest by freeing a slave. Sympathetic to Findlay, the *Washington Reporter* reprinted the entirety of the *Harrisburg Republican*'s assault against Hiester and slavery and editorialized that slavery was "a shame to the heathen, a disgrace to the tyrant, and a curse to the free; the greatest perversion of our boasted liberties, and the blackest shame to our nation." Hiester, running as a Federalist, narrowly defeated Findlay in the contest.[21]

The Pennsylvania legislature showed new sympathy for the plight of fugitive slaves in wake of the Missouri controversy. In 1820 the legislature passed a law that prohibited local magistrates from "recognizing any matter arising from the national fugitive slave law." This marked the first instance in which a state deliberately challenged the Fugitive Slave Act. The legislature went even further in 1826 by declaring that anyone who attempted to seize an alleged runaway without a constable and a duly executed warrant would be guilty of kidnapping. The law made it much more difficult for slave owners to recover what they claimed was their property and offered legal protections to Pennsylvanians who assisted fugitive slaves.[22]

The first sign of renewed interest in abolitionism in Washington County appeared in 1823 or 1824, when about fifty people inaugurated the Western Abolition Society in Washington. Among those attending were many individuals who became noted abolitionists in Washington County, such as John McCoy, Thomas McKeever, and John Reed. The Reverend Andrew Wylie, president of Washington College from 1817 to 1828 and a

Presbyterian minister, gave the principal address at the meeting. Wylie called for improving the condition of free blacks and preventing the kidnapping of free blacks—goals similar to those of the earlier Washington Society. Wylie went beyond the old organization, however, in stipulating the need for a plan to oppose slavery in general. Still, Wylie's was no call for a revolution against slavery. This society, like its predecessor, was apparently short-lived. Although it held an annual meeting in 1830, no record of any meetings after that date exists. Another antislavery society, calling itself the "Abolition Society of Washington and Fayette Counties," also met once at the Baptist church in June of 1827 and again in 1830 in Washington, but no record of subsequent meetings of this organization has come to light.[23]

The 1820s, however, was a key period for the gestation of abolitionist sentiment locally. Several other abolition societies appeared in the county during this decade. One newspaper advertisement testifies to the existence of a society at Centerville, some eighteen miles east of Washington on the National Road, in 1826. This society, which may have been organized by the Quakers living in eastern Washington County, took a much more uncompromising stance on slavery. It resolved that it was "the duty of every friend to our country, to unite in proper measures for the abolition of so criminal, so disgraceful, and so dangerous an evil." Records indicate that West Middletown, some dozen miles to the west of Washington, also had an abolition society by 1827. In addition, a student antislavery group formed at Washington College under Wylie's presidency. Very little is known about these societies. Still another manifestation of growing abolitionist sentiments locally was the memorial that some twenty-four Washington Countians sent to Congress in 1829. Contending that slavery was the "greatest political and moral evil that affects our country," they petitioned Congress to end slavery in the District of Columbia.[24]

These fledgling abolitionist groups faced formidable opposition from local proponents of the colonization movement. Founded in 1816, the parent American Colonization Society (ACS) argued that the solution to America's racial problems lay in sending free blacks and slaves back to a colony in Africa. The ACS proposed dealing with the issue of slavery by encouraging slave owners to free their slaves, who would then be transported under ACS auspices to Liberia. A mixture of motivations lay behind this proposal. Some, such as the Quaker Benjamin Lundy, the leading abolitionist of the 1820s, saw colonization as a truly humanitarian movement for the benefit of the enslaved. However, a substantial part of the ACS emphasized the disadvantages of slavery for the white race rather than for those whom it subjugated. Many of the society's membership consisted of slave owners from the Upper South who wanted to rid the country of its free black population. Prominent slaveholders such as Henry Clay and James Monroe endorsed the ACS's scheme. Pennsylvania, however, claimed more members than any other state, and accounted for more than one-third of the organization's some 250 local auxiliaries. Although Pennsylvania's black population remained very small in the 1820s (about 3 percent of the population), the migration of free blacks and the exodus of fugitive slaves to Pennsylvania from the Upper South had led to a more visible black population and heightened white racial anxieties. Industrialization and European immigration had led to a deterioration of economic conditions for many white workers, who vented their frustrations on blacks. But Pennsylvania's elite also joined the state colonization society. From their perspective, the free black population represented nothing but problems. According to the leaders of the Pennsylvania colonization movement, "Pennsylvania's gradual abolition experiment had produced a free black class of vagrants, drunks, and criminals." The colonizationists believed that abolition would bring about a nightmare: "semi-savages," when freed, would invade the North and bring a racial plague in their wake. The ACS's blatant racist literature had considerable appeal to whites living north of the Mason-Dixon Line, particularly in areas such as Washington County that had seen a substantial influx of Southerners. The organization offered a solution to the problems of race and slavery that stood in sharp contrast to that proposed by abolitionists in Washington County: deportation instead of emancipation.[25]

Local proponents of colonization established a branch of the ACS in 1826. The Washington County colonization society temporarily ceased its activities around 1828 or 1829, apparently because antislavery groups in the county had become moribund. But when abolitionism gathered momentum again in the 1830s, there was no lack of colonizationists eager to debate them.[26]

BLACK ABOLITIONISM

The ACS's harsh racial tone had unintended consequences. Repudiating the ACS for its racism, free black leaders in cities such as Philadelphia and Boston strongly asserted that they belonged in America and had no desire to be sent to a colony in Africa. As Richard Allen, the founder of the AME Church, observed, "The land we have watered with our tears and our blood is now OUR MOTHER COUNTRY." Black leaders condemned "colonization as virtual war on African Americans." In Pittsburgh, they denounced the ACS as "intriguers" who wanted to deport black leaders from the country "so the chain of slavery might be riveted more tightly." Determined to defend their rights aggressively, African Americans began to devise a new strategy that insisted on racial equality in the North and an immediate end to slavery in the South. The new black activists linked racism and bondage.[27]

David Walker exemplified this new assertiveness among northern blacks. A free black from North Carolina who had moved to Massachusetts and become the owner of a used clothing store in Boston, Walker vented his frustration and anger in what became known as *David Walker's Appeal*, published in 1829. Although Walker castigated his fellow free blacks for their indifference to slavery, he also chastised whites for their complacency and warned that such complacency might ultimately lead to a violent rebellion against slavery: "Remember Americans, that we must and shall be free and enlightened as you are, will you wait until we shall, under God, obtain our liberty by the crushing arm of power? Will it not be dreadful for you?" Distributed openly in the North and clandestinely by black seamen in Southern ports, Walker's *Appeal* caused a furor in the South when its contents became known. When Nat Turner's Rebellion broke out in Southampton County, Virginia, in 1831, leading to the death of some fifty-seven whites, slave owners attributed the insurrection to Walker's influence. Walker's death under mysterious circumstances in 1831 did not silence his voice.[28]

This new, militant black abolitionism soon spread to Pittsburgh and southwestern Pennsylvania. As noted above, Pittsburgh blacks were vehemently denouncing the colonization movement by the early 1830s. The black convention movement of the early 1830s also spread the message calling for an immediate end to slavery and for recognition of black equality. The first of these conventions was held in Philadelphia in 1830 and marked the first time black leaders from around the country had met to discuss their situation. Black abolitionism grew substantially as a movement at the national level after this convention. African American communities in many Northern localities formed antislavery societies. John B. Vashon, a black barber and businessman, organized the Pittsburgh Anti-Slavery Society in 1833. Other African American abolition societies appeared not only in large cities such as Philadelphia and New York but also in much smaller localities such as Carlisle, Pennsylvania, and Troy, Michigan. Women's auxiliaries often appeared in parallel with the all-male antislavery societies.[29]

The outlines of black abolitionism in Washington County remain sketchy. Very little has been written locally about the subject, and what has been written focuses on the exploits of a few isolated individuals such as Tar Adams. The black communities of the county were far too small to support their own newspapers, and very few records from African American churches have survived. It is reasonable to surmise, however, that local leaders kept informed of national developments through their connections in Pittsburgh and through the network of AME churches. The few pieces of evidence available point to a substantial level of black organization in the county. On October 23, 1843, a committee of three men representing blacks from Canonsburg and vicinity invited Dr. F. Julius LeMoyne, a noted white abolitionist from Washington, Pennsylvania, to address a countywide convention of blacks at the Canonsburg AME Church. The immediate objective of this convention was to petition the state legislature to restore the right to vote to black males, a right that Pennsylvania's revised constitution of 1838 had taken away. Judging by the resolution passed at the meeting, much of the convention was devoted to black uplift and moral improvement. Resolutions called for the formation of temperance societies throughout the county and the encouragement of "education, industry, and every thing that pertains to our moral elevation."[30] The letter of Daniel Arnet, James Brown, and F. L. Chambers to LeMoyne suggests an extensive network connected blacks in the county.[31]

This network was far more radical than the resolutions passed at the Canonsburg convention might suggest. Arnet and Chambers served as subscription agents for Martin R. Delany's Pittsburgh abolitionist newspaper, the *Mystery*. Delany by the late 1840s had emerged as a national leader among American blacks. Born free in 1812 in Charles Town, Virginia, Delany was taken by his mother to nearby Chambersburg, Pennsylvania, so that he and his brothers could gain an education without fear of being imprisoned for acquiring literacy. Delany moved to Pittsburgh in 1831 to further his education. The young Delany lived briefly with John B. Vashon after his arrival in Pittsburgh and undoubtedly became involved in Vashon's antislavery activities. Delany soon made the acquaintance of other successful middle-class blacks in Pittsburgh such as Lewis Woodson and "Daddy" Ben Richard, whose daughter Delany ultimately married. They introduced Delany not only to the community of black abolitionists in Pittsburgh but also to the aspirations of self-help and improvement that they espoused.[32]

Delany's talent was recognized quite early by many. When LeMoyne asked Pittsburgh antislavery activist William H. Burleigh to send a black man to address the Washington Anti-Slavery Society's meeting on July 4, 1841, Burleigh proposed Delany. He introduced Delany as "a man who is as black as the ace of spades, and as fiery as Vesuvius." Burleigh commended Delany as a "really eloquent" speaker who could hold "an audience in close attention," although he cautioned LeMoyne that Delany could be "too vociferous and fiery." In the end Delany was unable to address the meeting because of a last-minute emergency. This acquaintance with LeMoyne later led Delany to study medicine with the Washington physician.[33]

The *Mystery*, the newspaper that Delany edited in Pittsburgh from 1843 to 1847 before he began to assist Frederick Douglass with the *North Star*, reflected the twin goals of abolitionism for the slaves and self-improvement for free blacks. The exhortation that appeared below the paper's masthead displayed Delany's abolitionist intentions: "Hereditary bondsmen! Know ye not who would be free, themselves must strike the first blow?" Scrutiny of the subscription agents for the one surviving copy of the *Mystery* reveals many names that have been identified with abolitionism and the Underground Railroad: Vashon, Philadelphia doctor James J. G. Bias, and the Reverend William Ralph from Monongahela in eastern Washington County. In addition to Ralph, Arnet, and Chambers, the following names from Washington County appear: Thomas S. Robinson, of Washington; James McAyeal, from Bavington; Ephraim Arnett, from East Bethlehem Township; and the Reverend Fayette Davis, a circuit rider for the AME Church in the county. In addition to Ralph, Robinson is known to have participated in the Underground Railroad; although none of the other names appear in local accounts of the Underground Railroad, they are certainly candidates for inclusion. The list of agents for the *Mystery* could easily be read as the network of black abolitionists in Washington County.[34]

IMMEDIATE ABOLITIONISM

The new brand of militant, black abolitionism that emerged in the late 1820s soon transformed white antislavery activities. As James Brewer Stewart writes, "Black abolitionism was the parent of the white crusade."[35] David Walker and other black activists, such as Philadelphia's James Forten, succeeded in gaining the ears of some sympathetic whites who had once championed colonization. The most notable of these converts was William Lloyd

Garrison, who until the late 1820s was writing for Lundy's Baltimore newspaper, the *Genius of Universal Emancipation*. Garrison became acquainted in Baltimore and Philadelphia with blacks who thoroughly resented the idea of expatriation and exposed him to Walker's *Appeal*. Garrison became a convert who dedicated the rest of his professional life to promoting racial equality and abolishing slavery. Adopting the message of black abolitionists that slavery could no longer be countenanced, Garrison emerged as the leading white crusader against the institution.[36]

First published on January 1, 1831, in Boston, Garrison's newspaper, the *Liberator,* inaugurated an era of radical and militant abolitionism among Northern whites. Unlike his predecessors in the Pennsylvania Anti-Slavery Society, who had called for gradual abolition, Garrison advocated the immediate end of slavery.[37] Garrison and his followers did not think that slavery would end overnight, but they did hope to see it disappear in the near future. They relied chiefly on "moral suasion"—the idea that appeals to the Christian consciences of slaveholders would cause them to release their bondsmen voluntarily. The proponents of moral suasion initially thought of themselves not as radicals, but rather as exhorters of Christian morality. However naïve this idea may seem today, Garrison and his followers expected that white Southerners would listen to them.[38]

Garrison's polemics against slavery, however, were not couched in persuasive tones. Unlike his predecessors, he denounced the institution as an unmitigated evil and slaveholders as devils incarnate. As the Boston minister Amos A. Phelps bluntly put it, "Slaveholding is a heinous crime against God and man."[39] By 1831 Garrison expressed "regret and shame for ever having said a moderate word about colonization." He had come to regard it "merely as a scheme" to remove the free black population. In contrast to most colonizationists, who regarded blacks as hopeless inferiors, Garrison offered a message of racial equality and brotherhood. For him there was to be no temporizing or compromising with slavery. It was a sin that had to be eradicated from national life without delay. Garrison vowed that he would be heard—and he was.[40]

Great Britain's emancipation of some 800,000 slaves in its colonies, chiefly in the Caribbean, also helped to gain adherents for Garrison's doctrine of "immediate emancipation." This British decision in 1833 gave immediatism an aura of respectability and practicality it had lacked before. It also added impetus to the efforts of American abolitionists. After all, if Great Britain, the symbol to most Americans of everything that stood opposed to liberty, had acted to end slavery, how could liberty-loving Americans continue to countenance the presence of slavery?[41]

Garrison's message thus resonated increasingly with a select group of Northerners in the early 1830s. Historians have long linked the religious revival known as the Second Great Awakening with the outburst of reform movements that appeared in American society beginning in the 1820s as the pace of economic development and industrialization quickened. Seen from this perspective, abolitionism was among a host of reforms inspired by evangelical Protestantism, such as temperance, that sought to deliver an increasingly materialistic society from the clutches of sin. Preaching the need for self-restraint, these reformers reached a wide audience in the middle-class North. Their effectiveness can be judged by the remarkable transformation in northern drinking habits that the American Temperance Society (ATS) achieved after its formation in 1826. Within a decade, the ATS had made a section indifferent to the perils of strong drink into one of abstainers—at least within the fold of middle-class Presbyterians, Baptists, and Methodists. Temperance and abolitionism shared a religious vocabulary that identified specified activities as sinful but had vastly different audiences in terms of their size. Whereas temperance attracted millions, abolitionism attracted a fraction of that number.[42]

The profound social and economic changes that followed in wake of rapid industrialization also inclined some groups of people toward abolitionism. Abolitionism was strongest in the industrial cities of Massachusetts (such as Lowell and Springfield) and those situated along the Erie Canal (such as Utica and Schenectady). According to Edward Magdol, skilled workmen, shopkeepers, craftsmen, and artisans formed the rank and file of antislavery's constituents. They comprised more than 50 percent of the membership of antislavery societies in these industrial towns that were hotbeds of abolitionism. Confronted by the new factory system and fearing the loss of economic independence, these men came to regard the slave system of the South—not the emerging factory system—as the greatest threat to their well-being. In effect, they projected their fears about growing inequality in the North onto the most potent symbol of dependence and degradation: slavery. These independent artisans increasingly identified themselves as being part of a "free labor" system. Thus, as Avery Craven has observed, abolitionists were responding to disturbing changes surrounding themselves more than to any changes in slavery. The only segment of the industrial workforce to share their perceptions were female textile operatives in places such as Lowell, who believed they understood quite well what it meant to be a slave. Male factory workers, on the other hand, were typically quite hostile to abolitionism.[43]

No single explanation can account for the reasons why individuals joined the antislavery crusade. Although many came from families that emphasized education and moral earnestness, this does not explain why some individuals fulfilled these expectations and others did not; Garrison, for example, also supported temperance, while his brother became an alcoholic. Individual family members responded differently to abolitionism just as they responded differently to temperance. What is clear is that a new humanitarian ethic permeated the sensibilities of those who followed the strictures laid down by such families. As Stewart comments, antebellum reformers "harbored unprecedented feelings of revulsion at the thought that people were physically abusing one another and subjecting one another to moral degradation. Seeing themselves as pathbreaking humanitarians, evangelical reformers had no tolerance for those who inflicted hardship on others, an attitude that not only prefigured abolitionism but also crusades against flogging, dueling, prostitution, and capital punishment."[44] Leading evangelists, such as Charles G. Finney, also taught that the earnest Christian should combat the world's evils. For those for whom slavery came to symbolize the abuse of power, the peculiar institution offered an inviting target.

THE WASHINGTON ANTI-SLAVERY SOCIETY

When antislavery activities resumed in Washington County in 1834, they had a very different tone, character, and message than previously. The organization of the American Anti-Slavery Society (AASS), founded in Philadelphia in December 1833, provided the impetus. The AASS spread Garrison's message of immediate abolitionism by recruiting agents, often young clergymen, and sending them out into the hinterland. Within five years the AASS claimed 1,300 local affiliates across the North and a membership of 250,000. The society's efforts transformed what had been a mild sentiment against slavery held by diverse individuals into a clearly articulated antislavery ideology that was organized into a national movement. As Fergus M. Bordewich writes, this "expanding array of antislavery societies . . . would provide the white rank and file of the Underground Railroad."[45]

An agent of the AASS visited Washington in May 1834 but did not meet with immediate success. A majority of local citizens, after hearing a three-day debate over the merits of abolitionism versus colonization, voted to resuscitate the old Washington Colonization Society. The AASS agent did, however, persuade a critical minority of townspeople to form an abolition society. The Washington Anti-Slavery Society held its inaugural meeting on July 4, 1834—the anniversary of the Declaration of Independence—and announced that its mission was "the immediate emancipation of the slave." The society elected Joseph Henderson as its first president.[46]

The organization of the Washington Anti-Slavery Society marked the first appearance of an AASS chapter west of the Allegheny Mountains and foreshadowed the county's role as a center of abolitionist support in western Pennsylvania. Once organized abolitionism took root, it grew. Washington County stands in stark contrast to Adams County and other rural counties in south central Pennsylvania, where efforts to establish a mass abolition movement failed. Despite the presence of a substantial Quaker minority in Adams County, agents of the AASS were unable to establish permanent chapters in that border county.[47]

Two developments stand out in the spread of abolitionism in Washington County after 1834. The first was the continued efforts of the AASS to organize auxiliaries in southwestern Pennsylvania. Appointed an agent in 1834, James Loughhead of Pittsburgh, one of Pennsylvania's delegates who attended the founding of the AASS, drummed up sufficient interest in West Middletown to establish an auxiliary there in 1835. Theodore Dwight Weld, who was to become nationally famous as an abolitionist lecturer, also sowed the seeds of abolitionism locally. Historian William Lee Miller regards Weld as the greatest of these preacher-abolitionists who devoted their energies to combatting slavery.[48] Weld had been expelled from the Lane Theological Seminary in Cincinnati in 1834 for his role in organizing debates over the sinfulness of slavery that radicalized the student body and in reaching out to blacks in the area. He and many other "Lane Rebels"—a majority of the student body who left Lane in protest—then went to the newly founded Oberlin College in northern Ohio. Although offered a teaching position at Oberlin, Weld decided to devote his energies to abolitionism. His speaking tours in northern Ohio were so successful that the AASS invited him to New York to train the society's lecturers and agents in 1835. The group that Weld trained, typically consisting of ministers, became known as the Seventy—the vanguard of radical abolitionism.[49]

Weld engaged in a heavy lecturing schedule. In 1835 he was invited to southwestern Pennsylvania to address the General Assembly of the Presbyterian Church. Weld persuaded a significant minority of the Presbyterian ministers who had gathered at Pittsburgh to adopt the abolitionist cause in several visits during 1835 and 1836. Weld's efforts were central to organizing abolitionist sentiment in heavily Presbyterian southwestern Pennsylvania. As one commentator has observed, Weld "did more than any other person for the abolition movement in Western Pennsylvania."[50]

Weld also traveled southwest to Little Washington, as locals sometimes referred to the seat of Washington County to distinguish it from the national capital. There he delivered nine lectures at the Methodist Church during a two-week stay in June 1835. The local Democratic paper, the *Examiner*, alluded to these lectures but did not name Weld. The *Examiner*'s anonymous correspondent expressed concern that casual observers might come to the erroneous conclusion that local Methodists had adopted the noxious doctrines of abolitionism en masse, but assured readers that the vast majority of that denomination remained dedicated to the sound doctrines of colonization. The rival Democratic local newspaper, *Our Country*, proved much friendlier to Weld, recognizing him as a "man of talent, a gentleman and a Christian." Its editor expressed surprise at how well attended Weld's lengthy lecture series was: "Although it might be supposed that our citizens would become wearied with such a prolonged series of discourses as Mr. Weld has been giving, yet so far from such being the fact additional interest appears to be excited by every succeeding lecture." Although the precise effect of Weld's lectures in Washington is difficult to gauge, he did not galvanize audiences in Washington County as he later did in upstate New York. In his 1836 speaking tours of western New York, he added hundreds of names to local abolitionist auxiliaries, rivaling the success of the religious revivals that had swept the area so often that it became known as the Burned-Over District. Washington County soil was not nearly as fertile for abolitionism as the industrial areas along the Erie Canal. However, it proved far more receptive to abolitionism than south central Pennsylvania.[51]

The second development that established a firm foundation for local abolitionism coincided with Weld's visit to Little Washington and may have grown out of it. This was the election of F. Julius LeMoyne, a middle-aged physician from Washington, as president of the Washington Anti-Slavery Society. Weld may have stayed with the LeMoynes while in Washington; he was at the very least a guest. Decades later Weld, in a letter to LeMoyne's daughter

Charlotte, praised Mrs. LeMoyne, whose "genial hospitality I vividly recall after the lapse of <u>almost</u> forty years."[52] In any case, LeMoyne made the society a force to be reckoned with after becoming president. The son of a doctor who had fled the French Revolution, LeMoyne (1798–1879) never quite fit into Little Washington. The writer Rebecca Harding Davis, who was born in Washington, offered the following unforgettable portrait of LeMoyne based upon her childhood memories: "He was as unlike the townspeople as if Neptune or Mars had put on trousers and a coat and gone through the streets. They were Scotch-Irish, usually sandy in complexion, conventional, orthodox, holding to every opinion or custom of their fore-fathers with an iron grip. He made his own creed and customs; he was dark, insurrectionary and French."[53] LeMoyne's fervent abolitionism made him stand out even more. Although as a college senior at Washington College he had debated the morality of slavery, he did not involve himself in the abolition movement until 1834. He maintained that he was never a convert to the abolitionist cause; he insisted instead that he discovered only at the age of thirty-six, while reading an abolitionist tract, that he was in full accord with the principles of antislavery. He was among the organizers of the Washington Anti-Slavery Society in 1834, became its president in 1835, and was reelected to that position the following year. LeMoyne turned an organization that during its first year had existed only on paper into an effective instrument of the abolitionist crusade. For good reason, Davis regarded him as "probably the truest representative of the radical abolitionist in this country."[54]

One of the first results of LeMoyne's leadership was the publication of an appeal in local newspapers to the county's citizens to advocate for the end of slavery. The Washington Anti-Slavery Society paid for an extra to appear in the *Washington Examiner*—a publication not known for its friendliness to the abolition cause. The society announced, "We advocate the immediate emancipation of the slave, because he is constituted by God as a moral agent, the keeping of his own happiness, is personally responsible for his own choice, and has the right to life, liberty, and the pursuit of happiness." The society sought to end slavery not through legislative action, but rather by endeavoring to "induce men to forsake this as every other sin, by speaking the truth in love."[55]

Opponents of abolitionism in Washington County did not greet LeMoyne's message with love. Popular stereotypes today have it that virtually every antebellum Northerner was an ardent friend of the slave, but this was not the case. Northerners in general and Washington Countians in

2. The LeMoyne House, Washington, PA

particular stigmatized abolitionists for their beliefs, not those who sympathized with slavery. One of the county judges called a meeting in 1835 to
protest antislavery agitation and to "express disapproval of the abolitionist
cause." A number of prominent citizens concurred and signed petitions
condemning abolitionists as troublemakers who were organized to inter-
fere with slavery and destroy the Union. Fears that this new abolitionist
assault on slavery would bring about disunion were commonplace throughout much of the North.[56]

Probably the best indication of the initial reception of abolitionism in
Washington County is the 1836 speaking tour of the Reverend Samuel
Gould, an agent of the AASS who had previously worked in Rhode Island
and was among the Seventy. Gould first tried to rally abolitionist sentiment
in nearby Fayette County but could find no churches open to him. Address-
ing a hostile crowd of whites at the county courthouse in Uniontown, he
gave up his attempt to speak when someone in the audience yelled out, "Tar
and Feathers," prompting Gould to leave the county for his personal safety.
Gould initially met with a much more favorable reception in Washington
County. In a whirlwind tour of the county, he delivered twenty-three ad-
dresses in June 1836. Gould was a very successful organizer; he established

AASS auxiliaries at Morris Township, Peters Township, Mount Pleasant, Cross Creek Township, Burgettstown, Florence, and Buffalo Township. Significantly, the rural townships and villages of the northern and western parts of the county had always had a very small black population, in contrast to the eastern townships where slavery had once been significant. Morris Township, along the southern border of the county, is the lone exception, but it too had always had a very tiny black population.[57]

As news of Gould's successes in rural Washington County spread, opponents warned him not to come to the town of Washington to deliver an address to the Washington Anti-Slavery Society. But Gould was not easily deterred and made his scheduled address on June 21. A mob gathered outside the Cumberland Presbyterian Church (the church of Samuel McFarland, one of the town's pioneer abolitionists) on West Wheeling Street where he was to speak. One representative of the restive crowd even made his way into the church, but LeMoyne repeatedly blocked his passage toward the speaker, much to the amusement of the audience of some five hundred people, and the young man retreated to the outside of the church. Once Gould began to speak, the mob pelted the church with stones, bricks, and eggs, some of which went through the windows. One of the stones struck Gould, but he was not badly injured. Gould's abolitionist friends were prepared for this onslaught. After Gould had delivered his lecture, they formed a square around Gould so that he could escape from the church. When the mob broke through the square, Gould made a hasty retreat to LeMoyne's home on nearby Maiden Street. LeMoyne had five of Gould's assailants arrested, an action that did not endear him to his neighbors. Town leaders, such as Judge Thomas H. Baird, who had advertised in the local paper for the return of a fugitive slave two decades earlier, and Burgess John R. Griffith, vilified the abolition movement shortly after this incident for intruding their "peculiar and offensive doctrines" on the public. They passed a resolution at a public meeting that characterized abolitionism as a movement that was "offensive to the great mass of our population." Gould had no doubt that the town fathers—"gentlemen of property and standing"—sanctioned the activities of the ruffians who attacked the church, noting that the rioters attended the meeting that denounced abolitionists. The five rioters were not tried after they agreed to pay for repairs to the church and to acknowledge being in the wrong.[58]

This hostile reception of abolitionism was hardly unique to Washington, Pennsylvania. Anti-abolitionist mobs engaged in a flurry of attacks on abolitionist speakers and leaders in the free states between 1834 and 1838. David Grimsted has identified forty-six such attacks during this period, the bulk of them occurring in 1835 and 1836. (He does not include the mobbing incident in Washington.) As was the case in Washington, Pennsylvania, leading officials (typically Jacksonian Democrats) and important towns-people often lent their tacit support to mobbings, even though they themselves did not participate. One of the most famous of these mobbings occurred in Boston in 1835, when a proslavery crowd led William Lloyd Garrison through the city with a noose around his neck. Garrison escaped unharmed, as did the Pittsburgh abolitionist John B. Vashon, whose home was mobbed in 1836. Elijah Lovejoy was not so fortunate. Determined to protect his printing press, which had been destroyed several times previously, Lovejoy decided to defend his new press with a gun and was shot to death in Alton, Illinois, in 1837.[59]

Gould's tour seems to have both polarized the county and solidified the abolitionist cause. Although some residents of Monongahela on the eastern border of the county mobbed Gould when he subsequently appeared there in 1836, others, disturbed by the violation of Gould's right to free speech, organized a protest meeting. As in other Northern communities, citizens who had once at best been indifferent to the plight of slaves came to see matters differently when mob action threatened the rights of whites. They also became disgusted by the violence associated with mobs. West Middletown held an "indignation meeting" to condemn the treatment of Gould in Washington and the subsequent resolution castigating abolitionism. That the abolitionists held their ground and defended themselves seems to have been crucial to establishing a permanent base for abolitionism in the county.[60]

Gould's second appearance in Washington, on July 4, 1836, proved decisive in deterring the mobbing of abolitionist speakers. Apprehensive about holding a meeting in a public place, LeMoyne invited Gould to speak to the Washington Anti-Slavery Society's annual meeting at his house on Maiden Street on the anniversary of American independence. In anticipation of trouble, LeMoyne stocked it with a dozen hickory clubs and instructed his young son to topple the beehives that resided on his third-floor balcony onto the street below if the need arose. Although some rough elements attended to protest the meeting, *Our Country* reported that the "unusually large" assembly—"one of the largest ever convened in the borough of Washington"—consisted of "ladies and gentlemen of the highest respectability."[61] When Luther Day read from the Declaration of Independence, a hostile member of the crowd yelled, "Stop that, we don't want to hear any more of that damned stuff." Even some of those who had gathered to see the abolitionists routed had to laugh at this detractor's failure to recognize the source of the doctrine that all men are created equal, and the crowd slowly dissipated. Young Frank LeMoyne never got the opportunity to see what a hive of angry bees would do. Public ridicule and embarrassment led the opponents of abolition to abandon further use of mobs. Significantly, the mobbing of Gould proved to be the last violent incident in the history of abolitionism in the county. Although abolitionism remained an unpopular cause, it was met subsequently with indifference, not violence. Furthermore, having exposed themselves to danger, the abolitionists hardened their resolve to place their cause before personal safety or convenience. The mobbings that took place in Washington County in 1836 may have even inadvertently advanced the cause of abolitionism by creating sympathy and admiration for those who were willing to face danger on behalf of the slave.[62]

The Washington Anti-Slavery Society under LeMoyne's leadership adopted several other tactics to attack slavery. One was to debate local colonizationists, who came from some of the most respectable ranks of society. The president of the local chapter, T. M. T. McKennan, was a Washington resident and attorney who served as the area's congressman for much of the 1830s. The president of Washington College at this time, the Reverend David McConaughy, was likewise a colonizationist. So was John Grayson, the publisher of the Democratic newspaper the *Washington Examiner*. As local historian Joe Smydo has concluded, the ranks of colonizationists included some of the most respected gentlemen in Washington.[63] LeMoyne countered that sending American blacks to Liberia was no solution. "I once thought that we might promulgate abolition without disturbing col'n [colonization]," LeMoyne confided to his colleague Dr. Joseph Templeton, "but I find that is idle. We must find the strong man and cast him out." LeMoyne, like James G. Birney, an Alabama slave owner who became a convert to abolitionism, believed that colonization served as nothing more than an "opiate to the consciences" of Americans. Moreover, LeMoyne concluded that the doctrines of colonization caused men to forget their humanity: "Those who can be instrumental in exiling their brethren on account of their color—feel but little interest in their enjoyment of their rights here—and care but little whether they are enslaved or not—Colonisation principles harden mens [sic] hearts."[64]

Unfortunately, colonization represented the polite and acceptable way of opposing slavery. To a degree that is difficult to appreciate today, this debate with colonizationists was *the* debate of the era.[65]

The Washington Anti-Slavery Society engaged in several heated debates with local colonizationists. LeMoyne's initial foray into public debate occurred in 1834 at West Middletown, a small but important village along the turnpike between Washington and Wellsburg, Virginia, on the Ohio River. LeMoyne persuaded a critical mass of the audience that only immediate abolitionism could solve the national problem of slavery. LeMoyne's argument, along with the organizing efforts of James Loughhead, served as a catalyst for the formation of an antislavery society in West Middletown. In the best remembered of these local debates, LeMoyne pitted himself against four colonizationists in a weeklong series of debates held in 1837. By all accounts, the colonizationists outnumbered the abolitionists attending these debates, but LeMoyne held his own.[66]

The colonizationists did win several local converts. Beverly R. Wilson, a black mechanic and Methodist preacher from the borough of Washington, went to Liberia in 1834 to see firsthand what conditions were like there. He reported in a letter to the ACS, dated March 4, 1834, from Monrovia, that Liberia "bids fair for a good country."[67] He maintained this high opinion of prospects for American blacks when he returned to the United States a year later. In a letter addressed to the "Free People of Color," Wilson argued that "Liberia for eligibility of situation is not often excelled." Wilson advised his audience that "if you desire liberty, surely Liberia holds out great and distinguished inducements. Here [in the United States] you can never be free." Wilson concluded his address by noting that he intended to return to Liberia within a month. The *Examiner* pointed out Wilson's local connections and approvingly noted his address.[68]

Franklin Chambers was probably the most important local African American to emigrate to Liberia. A barber in Canonsburg, Chambers had become increasingly frustrated by the lack of opportunities for blacks and restrictions on their freedom. He and his family left for Liberia in 1860.[69]

Peaching Herring, referred to in one local account as "Peachy Herron," a black man from West Middletown, proved to be the poster boy for local abolitionists. Herring and his family joined a colony and moved to Liberia in 1860. After spending several years there, Herring "became disgusted with the evils and abuses" and decided to return to the United States. Both he and his wife died at sea during the voyage home, and their child died of a mysterious malady in New York. Abolitionists in Washington County contended that Herring and his family had been poisoned to prevent them from exposing the actual conditions in Liberia.[70]

The relationship between local abolitionists and colonizationists is a complicated one. Despite LeMoyne's harsh words for colonizationists, he worked with them extensively in local civic matters. Smydo has argued that tensions between local abolitionists and colonizationists were less sharp than has been widely depicted, and that a great deal of cooperation existed between them. Even as they disagreed over how best to end slavery, LeMoyne and Congressman McKennan, who was elected on the Anti-Masonic ticket in 1830 and later reelected as a Whig, could serve amicably on the boards of local institutions such as Washington College, the Washington Female Seminary, and the Franklin Bank. Thus, while LeMoyne denounced colonization in general, he never named any specific individuals who supported the colonization movement. The two men were far from alone in putting aside their differences over the question of slavery to cooperate in building up the town. Names prominent on the rosters of the two rival organizations show up again and again on the boards of local institutions. Smydo argues that efforts to promote local development were far more important to these men than disagreement over slavery.[71]

The Washington Anti-Slavery Society's other tactic for winning adherents involved participating in a national petition campaign in 1835. Organized by the AASS, the campaign sought to end slavery in the one place where most Americans agreed that Congress had the authority to act: Washington, DC. Petitions signed by thousands of signatories flooded Congress when it convened in December 1835.[72] Washington County contributed three petitions to this flood in February 1836. Congressman McKennan introduced two petitions from the men of Washington County and one signed by "sundry females" of Washington Borough on February 29, 1836. McKennan did not necessarily agree with these petitions, but in keeping with tradition, he introduced them on behalf of his constituents. Unfortunately these petitions cannot be found.[73]

This barrage of antislavery petitions incensed the South. An outraged James Henry Hammond, a representative from South Carolina, demanded in 1836 that these objectionable antislavery petitions be rejected outright. The House, in May 1836, voted to table all abolitionist petitions without reading or taking any action on them. This tabling of constituent petitions soon became known as the "gag rule," which remained in force until 1844.

This silencing of citizens' rights to petition Congress won converts to the abolitionist cause. Miller observes that "as it was made apparent that the defense of slavery included an abrogation of civil liberty, including civil liberties of free states, the opinion opposed to the 'slave power' began to grow." Although the petition campaign was an abject failure and slavery remained legal in the national capital until 1862, antislavery advocates convinced many white Northerners that their rights were inextricably linked to those of the slave. It became increasingly apparent that the only rights that mattered to slave owners were those pertaining to the ownership of slaves.[74]

Among those who objected to this denial of fundamental American rights were 163 men from Washington County who sent two petitions to Congressman McKennan in 1838. Observing the House resolution denying abolitionist petitions with "astonishment and alarm," they claimed that the gag rule violated their right as citizens to petition the government and their representative's right to free speech. They regarded it as "an assumption of authority at once dangerous and destructive to the fundamental principles of republican government" and asked that Congress immediately rescind it. It would be interesting to know which, if any, of these signatories had not previously signed petitions requesting the abolition of slavery in the nation's capital. Unfortunately none of the earlier abolition petitions can be located. It can readily be discerned, however, that the gag rule petitions came from areas of the county that had notable abolitionist support: the borough of Washington and the village of West Middletown. Moreover, several of the petitioners are well known to students of local abolitionism. The names of Julius LeMoyne, Alexander Sweney,[75] and Samuel Mounts, all prominent members of the Washington Anti-Slavery Society, show up on the petition from the borough. Matthew McKeever, the only other abolitionist from Washington County apart from LeMoyne whom Siebert identified as a local Underground Railroad agent, and his brother Thomas appear on the West Middletown area petition. Locally, at least, the gag rule controversy drew a reaction from areas that were already committed to abolitionism. The threat to civil liberties may have prompted the neighbors of existing abolitionists to sign petitions, but it did not apparently engage those who were previously hostile to or indifferent to the movement.[76]

Also noteworthy is that women contributed some 40 percent of the signatures to this petition drive nationally and often organized the petition campaigns. Their participation in this movement marked a new public role for women that expanded greatly during the life of the abolitionist movement. Discussing the rights of African American slaves led inexorably to a discussion of the rights of women for pioneers of the women's rights movement such as Angelina Grimké and Elizabeth Cady Stanton. As Grimké observed, "The investigation of the rights of the slave has led me to a better understanding of my own."[77] In 1848 the women who attended the Seneca Falls Convention, organized by Stanton and Lucretia Mott, would issue a Declaration of Sentiments demanding their full rights as American citizens.

Women from Washington County participated in at least two of the petition drives to abolish slavery in the national capital. One petition, which has not survived, was sent by women from Little Washington. The surviving petition, introduced by Congressman McKennan in 1838, was signed by 118 women predominantly from the West Middletown area. It asked Congress to abolish slavery and the slave trade in the District of Columbia. "We are impelled to make this petition from a sense of the duty to our country to mankind and to God," they observed. "Our hearts recoil when we consider the miseries the oppressed sons of Africa are forced to endure." Only if this evil "in the heart of our free and independent government" ended could there be any hope of eradicating slavery on that national level. Although historian Beth Salerno was able to locate only one female antislavery auxiliary in western Pennsylvania (in Pittsburgh), it is clear that the female abolitionists of Washington County were highly capable organizers.[78]

Washington County stands out as a hotbed of abolitionism based upon the number of signatures per capita that were gathered in these petition campaigns. No county in western Pennsylvania sent more petitions than Washington during the Twenty-Fifth Congress (1837–1839). During the Twenty-Fifth through Twenty-Eighth Congresses, Washington County sent an estimated fifty to sixty petitions to Congress with 3,800 signatures.[79] In fact, only two counties in Pennsylvania equaled or exceeded Washington County in terms of per-capita signatures on abolitionist petitions, and nationally, only New England, the Burned-Over District, selected counties in the Western Reserve of Ohio, and a few counties in Michigan exceeded Washington County in number of signatures. The county can readily be identified on a map of U.S. counties that reflects the relative number of signatures gathered.[80]

By fighting off mobs, debating colonizationists, and launching numerous petition campaigns, the radical abolitionists of Washington County established a firm foothold in Washington County by the late 1830s. Agents of the AASS, including Theodore Dwight Weld and Samuel Gould, provided the initial impetus in organizing auxiliaries dedicated to the new doctrine of immediate abolition. Local leaders then emerged and saw to it that these antislavery chapters continued. Of these local leaders, Julius Le-Moyne was clearly the most prominent. His feistiness, energy, and dedication made him the recognized leader among local abolitionists. He proved himself such an adept proponent for the cause that he was soon in demand as a speaker. Sometimes these labors took him no farther than nearby Canonsburg, some eight miles away, where he spoke at the invitation of local abolitionist William H. McNary. LeMoyne had to deliver his speech from the street because no church or school was willing to give him permission to speak. But LeMoyne soon expanded his activities far beyond the local level. In January 1837 he attended the first statewide convention of the AASS in Harrisburg and was elected president of the state organization. Between 1837 and 1840 he traveled as a lecturer not only throughout southwestern Pennsylvania, but also into Ohio and beyond. In addition, he began corresponding with the Quaker poet John Greenleaf Whittier, James G. Birney, Arthur and Lewis Tappan, and many other well-known abolitionists. Weld considered LeMoyne his "honored friend" and enjoyed the hospitality of the LeMoynes during his stay in Washington. Birney likewise stayed at LeMoyne's house when he passed through the town. By 1840 LeMoyne had established a national reputation in abolitionist circles.[81]

CENTERS OF ABOLITIONIST SUPPORT

The abolitionist societies that formed in Washington County in the 1830s provided the organizational framework and the core of white support for the local Underground Railroad. Although many abolitionists shrank from abetting the escape of people considered to be another man's property, the ranks of known Underground Railroad operatives were drawn from the membership lists of these societies.

Three significant centers of white abolitionism can be identified in Washington County. (See Map 5.) The first of these was the county seat, Washington. It is difficult to estimate membership in this branch because no list has survived. However, judging by the number of signatures on the gag rule petition, perhaps seventy-five individuals identified themselves as abolitionists in the borough. LeMoyne was clearly the leading figure here, but he had substantial help. Samuel McFarland, a local attorney, emerged as an able

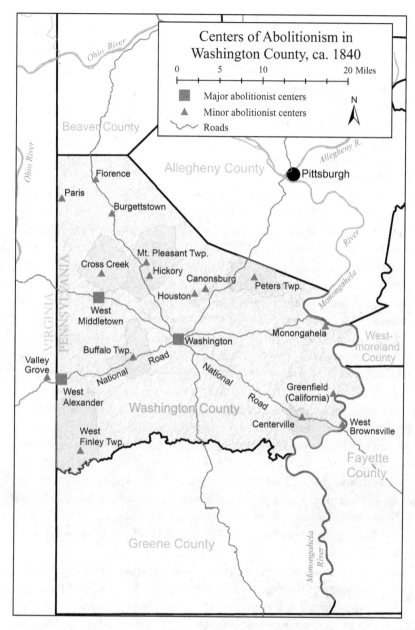

Centers of Abolitionism in Washington County, ca. 1840

0   5   10   20 Miles

■ Major abolitionist centers
▲ Minor abolitionist centers
⌇ Roads

N

Ohio River

Beaver County

Allegheny County

Pittsburgh

Allegheny R.

Ohio River

Florence

Paris

Burgettstown

Mt. Pleasant Twp.

Cross Creek

Hickory

Canonsburg

Peters Twp.

Houston

Monongahela

West Middletown

VIRGINIA

PENNSYLVANIA

Buffalo Twp.

Washington

National Road

Monongahela

Westmoreland County

Valley Grove

National

National Road

West Alexander

Washington County

Greenfield (California)

West Brownsville

Centerville

West Finley Twp.

Fayette County

Monongahela River

Greene County

Map 5

lieutenant. When LeMoyne's health began to deteriorate in the mid-1840s, McFarland assumed leadership of the local antislavery society. Overshadowed by LeMoyne in most local histories, McFarland was a national figure in his own right. In 1856, the Radical Abolition Party nominated Gerrit Smith as its presidential candidate and McFarland as its vice-presidential candidate. A number of other names crop up repeatedly as antislavery activists in Washington: Dr. Joseph Templeton, Alexander Sweney, George K. Scott, Patterson Scott, and Robert Lattimore, all signers of the gag rule petition and prominent advertisers in the anti-slavery newspaper that LeMoyne published in the late 1840s.[82]

The second center of abolitionism was the society organized in the fall of 1834 in the small village of West Middletown in the western part of the county. According to a Mrs. Woodburn, who was a little girl before the Civil War, slave owners took to calling the village "Helltown" because of its intense abolitionist sentiments.[83] Here the leading abolitionists came from the McKeever family: William, reputedly the first abolitionist in the western part of the county, and his two sons, Thomas and Matthew. In the 1820s, Thomas McKeever had been one of the original members of the Western Abolition Society, the existence of which indicates that a core of support already existed in the village. He may have learned his hatred of slavery from his father, who, according to one anecdote, was in 1830 so outraged at seeing a coffle of slaves being driven through the village by lashes and curses that he ran out of his house. He then "poured forth his righteous indignation" on the drivers of the manacled slaves and followed the coffle for the better part of a mile, all the while continuing his denunciations. When the drivers threatened violence if he did not desist, McKeever offered his bared chest and claimed that only a bullet through his heart would silence him. The drivers feared the consequences of injuring him and instead endured his condemnation of their "wicked business" as long as he accompanied them.[84]

Support for abolitionism in West Middletown went far beyond the McKeever family. As indicated above, the village and surrounding rural areas sent at least two petitions to Congress, one from the men demanding the rescinding of the gag rule, the other from the women calling for the abolition of slavery in Washington, DC. More than two hundred individuals in this largely rural area signed these petitions. In addition, the longtime pastor of the local Presbyterian church, Samuel Taggart, sometimes devoted his sermons to the evils of slavery. One of these sermons, "The Power For and Against Oppressors," was published as a pamphlet in 1839 and distributed by local antislavery societies. Although West Middletown is remembered as being fervently abolitionist, Taggart's experience would suggest that at the very least local Presbyterians were divided on the slavery question. (The McKeever family belonged to the Disciples of Christ Church.) Taggart's uncompromising pronouncements from the pulpit ended up splitting the congregation. Disaffected members at first refused to support the church financially. Asked later if it was true that he had vowed to continue to preach against slavery even if it meant living on bread and water, Taggart replied, "No, I never said that. I did say that I would preach on if I had to live on buttermilk and potatoes—not a bad diet for a good old Irishman." Eventually some thirty members who could not stomach Taggart's abolitionism left the church in 1844 to form the Patterson's Mill Associated Presbyterian Church and hired a pastor from the South.[85]

The historical memory of abolitionism in West Middletown was also shaped by a notable visitor to the antebellum village: John Brown of Harper's Ferry fame. When he first arrived in West Middletown in the winter of 1842, Brown came as an obscure buyer of wool and sheep representing the firm of Perkins & Brown of Akron, Ohio. For the better part of a decade, Brown made periodic rounds among the sheep farmers in the western part of the county, including Matthew McKeever. According to McKeever's recollections, Brown bought some thirty sheep from him in 1842. McKeever later gave Brown two hundred sheep on shares for four years, ultimately netting $2,400 when the sheep were sold. McKeever may have been one of the few individuals ever to profit from a business arrangement with Brown, who had failed at a number of businesses and had declared bankruptcy in 1842.[86]

At night, however, Brown's discussions with abolitionists such as Matthew McKeever and a local miller, James McElroy, turned from sheep to slavery. Half a century after Brown was hanged in 1859 for attempting to start a slave insurrection in Virginia, McElroy's son, James Jr., recalled, "I well remember that Brown would come over to our house in the evening after riding all day in the neighborhood buying wool. Our men neighbors would gather in, mostly to listen to talk between Brown and my father on the abolition of slavery. Brown was desperately in earnest and very bitter in his denunciation of slavery and the apologizer for it."[87] Memories of this abolitionist martyr's rants against slavery in the homes of ordinary West Middletown residents made it easy to forget the local Presbyterians who wanted nothing to do with antislavery sentiments.

Other notable abolitionist visitors to West Middletown included Abby Kelley Foster and her husband, Stephen Symonds Foster (not the famous composer). Raised as a Quaker in Massachusetts, Kelley became a convert to Garrisonian nonresistance and took up a career as an agent for the AASS. In this capacity, she shocked many by speaking to "promiscuous audiences"—meaning an audience consisting of men and women. (Angelina Grimké similarly aroused great consternation in 1837 when she addressed mixed audiences.) An "Abby Kelleyite" became a term for any woman who had gone beyond the bounds of propriety. Kelley went on an extended speaking tour in the mid-1840s. She married Foster, a fellow abolitionist, in 1845 in New Brighton in Beaver County, Pennsylvania, just north of Washington County. The newly married couple delivered lectures on three consecutive evenings in a West Middletown church. Mrs. R. C. Jones, then a schoolgirl, remembered attending the lectures with her classmates in 1846 and hearing Kelley denounce famous luminaries from Virginia such as Washington and Jefferson for stealing the "God-given rights" of their slaves. Unlike other localities where Kelley was often jeered at and harassed, West Middletown offered her a cordial reception.[88]

A third nucleus of abolitionism was the village of West Alexander and surrounding rural areas in western Washington County and neighboring Ohio County, Virginia. (West Alexander is about ten miles southwest of West Middletown.) The first manifestation of abolitionist sentiment in this region came from just across the border, in the community of Valley Grove, Virginia. In 1839, John Gilmore took the lead in drafting a petition to Congress requesting that slavery be abolished in the District of Columbia and that the further expansion of slavery be stopped. Born in Ireland in 1796, Gilmore had been brought to the United States as a young child by his parents and become a prominent man in his community, sufficiently so to become a justice of the peace. Gilmore's farm, just north of the National Road, stood about a mile from the Pennsylvania border and slightly more than that from West Alexander. (Although one account in the *Washington (PA) Observer* places Gilmore's barn in Pennsylvania, all of the available evidence indicates that it was actually in Virginia.) Twenty-two of Gilmore's neighbors signed this petition, including George and Peregrine Whitham. Unable to gain the support of their congressman to present the petition, Gilmore had former president and current member of Congress John Quincy Adams perform this duty.[89]

The rest of Ohio County was incensed by the petition. Although the county had only 211 slaves in 1840 (less than 2 percent of its population), any talk of imposing restrictions on slavery rankled. The other justices in the county demanded that Gilmore resign his office. A huge mass meeting held in Wheeling, the county seat, repudiated, in the words of the *Wheeling Gazette*, "the idea that the citizens of Ohio County would tolerate the circulation of such petitions within their county." The *Gazette* went on to dismiss those who had signed the petition as a few "miserable fanatics and Abolitionists living close to the dividing line between Pennsylvania and Virginia," hinting that most of these deluded individuals lived on the other side of the line. Gilmore, however, stood firm in the face of this verbal onslaught and refused to give up his office. "A compliance with your request," he answered, "would be a dangerous precedent, establishing the principle that a difference of opinion amongst the members of a court on a political or moral question is a sufficient cause to justify the majority to require the minority to resign."[90]

Two years later, in 1841, Gilmore held a meeting at his barn where like-minded individuals adopted a set of antislavery principles. Gilmore, John Emery, and S. Mayes Bell read a draft of the resolutions agreed upon, which twenty-five individuals signed. These men became the nucleus of antislavery activities in the northern panhandle, and Gilmore's barn became their accustomed meeting place, if for no other reason than that it was one of the few spaces available to them. Their request to hold a "free soil" meeting in Wheeling in 1844 was denied. Although invited to attend this meeting, Salmon P. Chase, an abolitionist lawyer from Cincinnati who would later become Lincoln's secretary of the treasury, was unable to do so. Chase did speak that same day at Bridgeport, Ohio, across the Ohio River from Wheeling, but was reluctant to cross into Virginia because of threats against him. Chase instead provided an address that was read by Bell at Gilmore's barn. When he had finished reading Chase's remarks, Bell proclaimed, "Today we plant the banner of Free Soil on Virginia Hills, and may we yet live to see Virginia a free State."[91]

West Finley Township, just south of West Alexander, also witnessed significant antislavery activity beginning in the mid-1840s. West Finley Township lies in the southwestern corner of Washington County and at the time shared its western border with Ohio County, Virginia. Kenneth Mc-Coy's farm, off of what is now Old Brick Road, became the headquarters of the West Finley abolitionists. The other known members of this society were John Henderson, James and Alexander Sprowls, Robert and Isaac Sutherland, and John McCoy, Kenneth's son.[92]

The village of West Alexander was clearly a hotbed of abolitionist sentiment. The Free Presbyterian Church of West Alexander, the only Presbyterian church in the country doctrinally opposed to slavery, not only served the antislavery inhabitants of the village but also provided a link between the abolitionists of Ohio County and West Finley Township. The McCoy and Sutherland families from West Finley Township joined this church, as did the Whitham families from Ohio County. Foremost among the ranks of West Alexander residents was Dr. Samuel McKeehan, whose house—a known Underground Railroad stop—still stands at the corner of Liberty Road and the Old National Pike.[93]

Several other areas of the county witnessed some abolitionist activity. One of these was in eastern Washington County, where signs of abolitionist activity appeared in the Greenfield (later California), Williamsport (Monongahela), and Centerville/West Brownville areas. Evidence for antislavery activism in the Greenfield area comes from an 1843 letter to LeMoyne written by Job Johnson, Salathiel Williams, William Morgan, Andrew Gregg, Samuel Rothwell, and Jefset Maxon (spelling unclear). This group invited LeMoyne to deliver a lecture that they hoped would energize their neighbors on behalf of abolitionism. "As this subject is now to some extent being agitated in this neighborhood," they wrote, "we believe good may be done." Abolition proved contentious in the Greenfield Methodist Church, which split in two over the issue. Apart from Job Johnson, who later operated a stop on the Underground Railroad, little is known about this antislavery society.[94]

Antislavery societies also probably existed in the Monongahela and Centerville areas. In 1837, James Miller of Finleyville, Pennsylvania, asked LeMoyne to come to Monongahela, then known as Williamsport, to help organize an antislavery society there. The mobbing of Reverend Gould in Williamsport a year earlier may have been the impetus behind this invitation. Evidence for the existence of an antislavery society in the Centerville and West Brownsville area comes from an 1837 letter written by Joseph Miller to LeMoyne, inviting him to deliver a lecture on the subject of abolitionism. Miller's use of "thee" and "eighth month" indicates that he was a Quaker.[95]

The farming communities and villages of northwestern Washington County also formed auxiliaries of the AASS. The auxiliaries that Samuel

Gould helped to organize in Peters Township, Mount Pleasant, Cross Creek, Burgettstown, Florence, and Buffalo Township all fall into this category. Apart from these, virtually nothing is known about the individuals who joined these chapters. However, many of these branches donated money regularly to the Pittsburgh headquarters of the Pennsylvania Anti-Slavery Society's Western District. LeMoyne served as president of the Western District's twenty counties.[96]

Religious affiliation played an important determinant of antislavery tendencies in the county. In particular, the stance of the Presbyterian Church on slavery and abolitionism during the Second Great Awakening had a profound effect on Washington County. Although the contribution of Presbyterians nationally to the abolitionist cause was "modest and should not be exaggerated," in the opinion of Andrew Murray,[97] their contributions locally were quite important. Theodore Weld's success in gaining converts to abolitionism at the Pittsburgh General Assembly of Presbyterians in the mid-1830s had a profound effect on southwestern Pennsylvania. Settled largely by Scotch and Scotch-Irish Presbyterians, Washington County (and southwestern Pennsylvania in general) had one of the highest concentrations of Presbyterians in the United States. In 1850, the county was home to forty-eight Presbyterian churches, second in Pennsylvania only to neighboring Allegheny County. Those churches claimed some 21,000 members out of the county's population of nearly 45,000.[98]

Presbyterians were far from united on the question of slavery, just as they were divided over matters ranging from theology to the education of ministers. Different branches of the Presbyterian Church adopted different positions on slavery. Mainstream Presbyterians (the Presbyterian Church of America) had taken a seemingly uncompromising stand in 1818 by unanimously denouncing slavery as "utterly inconsistent with the law of God." However, the church subsequently shrank from taking action on that declaration of principles. Although Presbyterians had far less of a presence in the South than Methodists and Baptists, southern members of the church still comprised an important constituency. According to one estimate, Southern Presbyterians owned some 70,000 slaves in 1850. What is more, perhaps one-third of Presbyterian ministers in the South owned slaves. As the debate over slavery sharpened in the 1820s, the presence of southern slaveholders and northern conservatives among the membership effectively muted the Presbyterian Church on the issue of slavery, and the national church beat a slow retreat from its 1818 declaration. Unlike other denominations, the

Presbyterians did not split into regional branches over the issue of slavery until the Civil War. When the Presbyterian Church split into the New School and Old School in 1837, the primary issue was whether to liberalize Calvinistic theology. Even though most Southern congregations joined the Old School, which held to a strict interpretation of Calvin, neither school harbored significant abolitionist tendencies. In Washington County, the twelve Presbyterian churches that belonged to the Presbyterian Church of America sided with the Old School, and very few Old School Presbyterians joined the ranks of abolitionists. LeMoyne resigned his membership in the First Presbyterian Church of Washington when the minister of that congregation denounced abolitionism in a sermon.[99]

The only body of Presbyterians to adopt abolitionism wholeheartedly was the Free Presbyterian Church. Frustrated by the refusal of the New and Old School churches to bar slaveholders from membership in the church, the Free Presbyterians organized their own synod in 1847. Only sixty-five churches joined this synod, the vast majority of them in southern Ohio. Presbyterian minister John Rankin, whose house stood high on a hill above the Ohio River in Ripley, welcomed many fugitive slaves from the Kentucky shore and served as the model for the abolitionist in *Uncle Tom's Cabin* who helped Eliza gain her freedom. Only one Free Presbyterian church formed in Washington County. In 1849, the Rev. Joseph Gordon led some members of the West Alexander Presbyterian Church with staunch antislavery convictions into the Free Presbyterian Church. Ultimately this church attracted 163 members from the village of West Alexander and surrounding rural townships, at least three of whom have documented links to the Underground Railroad.[100]

Two local groups of Presbyterians that originated in secessions from the Scottish Presbyterian Church also had abolitionist leanings. The first of these, the Covenanters, refused to accept the Restoration of Charles II to the English throne in 1660 on grounds that the church should be independent of the state and eventually organized as the Associate Reformed Presbytery. The second group, the Seceders (eventually the Associated Synod), left the Scottish Kirk in 1733 in protest against the policy of allowing landowners to bestow a living on a minister without the approval of a congregation. Thus both the Seceders and Covenanters sought to protect local congregations against unwanted outside interference. The Scottish dissenters were heavily represented in the emigration from Scotland and northern Ireland to western Pennsylvania in the middle and late eighteenth century.

Of Washington County's forty-eight Presbyterian churches in 1850, twenty-one came from an Associate Reformed or Associate background.[101]

The Covenanters and Seceders both took early stands against slavery and maintained those stands. The Seceders, for example, declared in 1811 that all slaveholding members must free their slaves if they wished to remain in good standing with their church. Jane Grey Swisshelm, the Pittsburgh-born antislavery advocate and writer, took her conviction that slavery was incompatible with Christianity from her Covenanter pastor, John Black. Because the Covenanter and Seceder churches were small, closely knit, and predominantly in the North, it was not difficult for them to maintain an antislavery stance. The broad agreements between these two groups on slavery and other matters showed when they merged to form the United Presbyterian Church in 1858.[102]

Of the eighteen whites who participated in the local Underground Railroad for whom a religious background can be established, eight were members of Associate and Associate Reformed churches in 1850. The number sharing this background is even greater if the three operatives from Washington County's lone Free Presbyterian church are included.[103]

The only other denomination that contributed significantly to the ranks of local Underground Railroad agents was the Disciples of Christ, whose origins lie in Washington County. The Disciples likewise came out of a Seceder Presbyterian background. Soon after arriving in western Pennsylvania from Ireland, Thomas Campbell ran afoul of local Seceders for failing to observe strict standards in those he allowed to take Communion. He left the Presbyterian fold and led his followers in 1809 into a nondenominational Christian Association of Washington (Pennsylvania) that sought to avoid doctrinal controversy. His son Alexander soon assumed leadership of the movement. Although the Campbellites believed in baptism by full immersion and allied themselves for a time with the Baptists, Alexander Campbell disagreed with the Calvinist beliefs of Baptists. Ultimately, the younger Campbell's followers joined forces in 1832 with a similar movement in Kentucky to form the Disciples of Christ. Campbell settled in Bethany, Virginia, several miles from the Pennsylvania border. The Disciples finessed the issue of slavery by allowing local congregations to determine their own policies. Locally the Disciples had a pronounced abolitionist flavor. Four members of the West Middletown Disciples of Christ congregation, just a few miles from the Virginia border, had prominent Underground Railroad connections, and Matthew McKeever married into the Campbell family.[104]

The ranks of antislavery activists coming out of other denominations are thin. Only one came out of the Baptist Church and only one out of the Methodist Church. Conceivably other Methodists were participants, for the Greenfield Methodist Church, which served what is now the California area in eastern Washington County, split over the issue of slavery. Job Johnson led those who desired a church that would take an abolitionist stance to form a new Methodist congregation. Local Methodists on the whole, however, were not very receptive to abolitionism. At the 1841 Pittsburgh Conference of the Methodist Episcopal Church, the one minister noted for his dedication to the antislavery cause was in danger of being "tried for his abolition sins" and suspended from the church.[105]

Quakers played a fairly small role in Washington County abolitionism. Although the Friends established four meeting houses in eastern parts of the county in the late 1700s, the Quaker presence slowly dwindled as members died or moved to the Salem area of eastern Ohio. Quakers did assist with establishing an abolition society at Centerville in 1826 and arranging for abolitionist lectures in that area in the late 1830s. By the late 1830s, however, so many Quakers had left Washington County that they did not play a significant role in the crusade to end slavery. Two of the Quaker meetings had totally disbanded by the early 1840s, and by 1851 only one family was attending the Pike Run Meeting. The Westland Meeting continued to serve a few families until it closed its doors in 1864. Howard Wallace, the son of an African American Underground Railroad conductor, credited his Quaker neighbors for their willingness to contribute materially to the cause, but Quakers were not prominent contributors to abolitionism locally.[106]

The one exception to this generalization was Amos Griffith, who might be regarded as the last Quaker in the county. It was Griffith who was on hand to close the Westland Meeting. Griffith clearly had abolitionist credentials. He was one of a handful of Washington County residents who subscribed to an antislavery publication in 1847 and was apparently also personally acquainted with John B. Vashon, one of the leading African American figures in Pittsburgh abolitionism. How Vashon and Griffith came to be acquainted is a mystery, but their relationship must have been a close one, as the 1850 census shows Vashon's half-sister Virginia living with Griffith's family.[107]

Assessing the strength of the abolitionist movement in Washington County is a difficult task. By many measures it was very successful. It bears repeating that the Washington Anti-Slavery Society was the first white abolitionist organization west of the Allegheny Mountains and least a dozen auxiliary antislavery societies were established in small villages and rural townships in the county. The petition campaigns of the 1830s involved hundreds of residents from the county in the antislavery crusade. These campaigns were so successful in obtaining signatures that Washington County is clearly identifiable on a national map for its participation in these campaigns. When viewed in this context, Washington County stands out not just in Pennsylvania but along the entire border region between North and South.

Washington County also differed substantially from the counties of south central Pennsylvania for the strength of its abolitionist organizations. Washington County and these counties west of the Susquehanna River shared many traits. They were rural counties that once held substantial numbers of slaves, at least for the Keystone State. They were located in border regions on the boundary between the free and slave states. Yet whereas Washington County was successful in establishing an organized abolition movement, the south central counties of Adams, Franklin, and Cumberland were not.[108]

By other measures, however, Washington County did not represent the vanguard of abolitionism. Abolitionism clearly had deeper roots in New England and in parts of the Upper North settled by New Englanders, such as the Western Reserve of Ohio. These areas sent in many more antislavery petitions per capita than Washington County. The contrast between Weld's reception in Washington County and Utica, New York, could not be starker. His two-week speaking tour of Washington County in June 1835 did not result in a flood of converts to abolitionist ranks. No antislavery auxiliary organized in the county in wake of his visit. However, in Utica, located on the Erie Canal in central New York, Weld achieved spectacular success early in 1836 in conducting an antislavery revival comparable to the religious revivals led by Charles G. Finney, his mentor. Six hundred people joined the ranks of the Utica Anti-Slavery Society alone, and hundreds of others did so in surrounding towns and villages. Utica became the antislavery stronghold of central New York.[109]

Abolitionism in Washington County also appears to have suffered from declining enthusiasm in the 1840s. One gauge of the depth of abolitionist support is the weekly newspaper that LeMoyne founded in 1845, the *Washington Patriot*, a four-page weekly. LeMoyne selected a Pittsburgh newspaperman, Russell Errett, as editor of the paper, which served as the political organ of the Liberty Party, the antislavery party organized in 1839.

Errett solicited advertisements from many individuals whose names appear in connection locally with abolitionism and the Underground Railroad. Dr. Joseph Templeton of Washington took out many advertisements for his patent medicines. George S. Hart, a Washington attorney, and Job Johnson, an attorney from Greenfield, Pennsylvania, also supported the paper. Errett even drummed up supporters in Pittsburgh for his enterprise. James R. Reed, a watch and clock maker, and James McMasters, who owned the Eagle Livery Stable on Liberty Street, placed ads in Errett's paper. McMasters's stable often housed fugitive slaves fleeing north from Washington County.[110] Errett edited this paper for slightly more than four years before apparently concluding that Washington was too small of a market to support an antislavery paper and himself. The *Washington Patriot* folded, and Errett moved on to become editor of a Pittsburgh newspaper and eventually entered politics as a Republican.[111]

Errett was not the only one to feel frustrated by the lack of support for the abolitionist cause in Washington County in the 1840s. M. H. Urquhart, a traveling agent for an antislavery publication, could only find fifteen subscribers willing to pay for this newspaper in all of Allegheny, Fayette, and Washington counties in southwestern Pennsylvania. Six of these subscribers hailed from Washington County: Job Johnson, Cox Beazel, George Hornbeck, Amos Griffith, William McKee, and Dr. F. J. LeMoyne. In a letter written from Little Washington on February 11, 1847, Urquhart lamented to his superior, "Since my last I have been traversing a region rather barren of abolitionism."[112]

Russell Errett would have agreed that abolitionism was not a paying proposition locally. Only in West Alexander and perhaps in West Middletown can abolitionism be said to have been the sentiment of a majority. As historian Robert Brewster commented, "The Washington Society for the Detection of Horse Thieves received much more newspaper space than did the abolition societies."[113]

Urquhart's frustration and the lack of newspaper coverage, however, need to be put into perspective. Enthusiasm for the abolitionist cause understandably diminished after the 1830s, when fervent expectations of immediate change in the institution of slavery were first raised. Disillusion and disappointment were the natural fruits for many early enthusiasts when they discovered that the South had no inclinations to recognize the moral wrong of slavery. By the 1840s, only the staunchest abolitionists could muster the faith to believe that their efforts would one day prevail.[114]

3. Masthead of the *Washington Patriot*, LeMoyne's abolitionist newspaper. The Learned T. Bulman '48 Historic Archives & Museum, Washington & Jefferson College.

Explaining why Washington County occupied an intermediate ground in regard to abolitionism between south central Pennsylvania and areas settled by Yankee Protestants is more difficult. To state the obvious: Washington County was not New England, upstate New York, the Western Reserve of Ohio, or other areas settled by New Englanders. By virtually any measure, abolitionism was far stronger in these areas than it was in this southwestern Pennsylvania county. It is useful to reiterate the point that those most receptive to the message of abolitionism came from where the great revivals of the 1820s were the strongest—New England, the Burned-Over District of New York, and other places where the forces of the market revolution and industrialization were the strongest. If scholars are correct in identifying industrialization as a key cause in the formation of abolition societies in factory towns such as Lynn, Massachusetts, and Utica, New York, then it stands to reason that abolitionism would have far less appeal in Washington County and the border counties of south central Pennsylvania. The Industrial Revolution that threatened the independence and livelihoods of skilled workers in the factory towns of New England was barely on the horizon in antebellum Washington County. Commercial cities such as Albany, New York, saw much weaker abolitionist movements. Industrialization split some communities. Pittsburgh manufacturers such as Charles Avery were drawn to abolitionism whereas bankers and merchants were not.[115]

Although the National Road enhanced commercial possibilities in southwestern Pennsylvania, making the town of Washington a major stopping point and supply center, it did not lead to a fundamental economic transformation. One enterprising individual founded the Hayes Carriage Factory, but it was a small-scale operation that bore little resemblance to the textile factories of New England, which employed several hundred hands each. Nothing resembling a working class appeared in antebellum Washington. Improved transportation instead allowed the county to become one of the nation's leading sheep-raising areas. (Sheep had replaced distilling whiskey as the major source of economic livelihood.) Agriculture remained the principal occupation for 75 percent of the county's workforce as of the Civil War, and economic continuity meant a fairly small audience for abolitionist doctrines. Only in the 1880s did Washington experience an industrial boom following the discovery of cheap oil and natural gas. South central Pennsylvania likewise remained predominantly rural as of the Civil War.[116]

If the reasons for differences in abolitionism stand out in sharp contrast between Washington County and the Upper North, they are muted at first glance when looking at Washington County and south central Pennsylvania. They shared many characteristics: they were border areas where slavery had once exerted a significant influence and where commercial agriculture thrived. So why did a sustained abolitionist movement take root in Washington County, whereas it did not in south central Pennsylvania? The clearest difference that emerges between these counties stems from religion and ethnicity. David Smith argues that the German population of south central Pennsylvania posed a significant obstacle to solidifying a mass abolition movement. Germans, who comprised nearly 50 percent of the population of Adams County and were predominantly Lutheran, voted overwhelmingly Democratic and were decidedly hostile to abolitionism. Despite a sizable Quaker minority in south central Pennsylvania, organized abolition could not get off the ground. The Scotch-Irish Presbyterians who formed the dominant ethnic group in Washington County proved far more receptive to the abolitionist message. Although only a minority of Presbyterians joined the movement, they made a crucial difference. In Washington County, the Free Presbyterians, dissenting Presbyterians, and offshoots such as the Disciples of Christ provided a critical mass for the growth and endurance of radical abolitionism.[117]

This Scotch-Irish Presbyterian background helps explain why Washington County and, to a lesser extent, neighboring Allegheny County, stand out in relation to not just south central Pennsylvania but also the rest of Pennsylvania and border North. (Allegheny County, where Pittsburgh is located, also sent in a large number of antislavery petitions to Congress.) These two counties were the core of Scotch-Irish settlements in the commonwealth, which distinguished them from counties both near and far.[118]

If the local abolition movement remained small in comparison to New England and a rather barren field for traveling agents such as Urquhart, it is still important to recognize the achievements of those who joined the ranks of antislavery activists beginning in the 1830s. Unlike the previous antislavery societies founded in the county, the members of those established in the 1830s were still sponsoring pamphlets, debating colonizationists, corresponding with abolitionists elsewhere, and sending delegates to national antislavery conventions up until the Civil War. Some of their more radical members had also begun to assist the growing trickle of fugitive slaves that made its way to Washington County on the road to freedom.

THE FOUNDING OF THE LOCAL UNDERGROUND RAILROAD AMONG WHITES

Although the arrival of radical abolitionism in Washington County can be pinpointed with some precision, the beginnings of extensive white involvement in the Underground Railroad are much vaguer. The earliest claim among white abolitionists in Washington County would place their participation in the 1820s, when antislavery societies made a sporadic appearance. Responding to a reporter's inquiry in 1880, Matthew McKeever of West Middletown recollected that he had been a conductor for some forty years. Since the Underground Railroad ceased to operate at some point during the Civil War, this claim would put the beginnings of his career as an operative in the early to mid-1820s. McKeever's activities, however, would appear to be an isolated example. As Bordewich notes, through the 1820s it was only in southeastern Pennsylvania that an organized network of people to help fugitives escape slavery existed.[119]

Probably it was not until the mid- to late 1830s that local whites began to participate in the Underground Railroad in Washington County— shortly after the Underground Railroad had begun to develop networks that linked most of the North. Wilbur H. Siebert provides indirect evidence that the Underground Railroad took shape in Washington County in the late 1830s. He observes that fugitive slaves began arriving in western New

York from Ohio and Pennsylvania during this period. Many of the Underground Railroad routes through the county led to northwestern Pennsylvania and northeastern Ohio and ultimately to western New York. More broadly, the 1830s marked the true appearance of what became known as the Underground Railroad nationally. The establishment of the Liberty Line was intimately connected with the spread of radical abolitionism because the local chapters of the AASS provided the structure for the Underground Railroad. They brought like-minded individuals together locally and put them in touch with abolitionists in nearby communities and across the North. "Only after western abolitionism emerged as a consolidated movement," Keith Griffler writes, "did anything approaching the customary picture of the Underground Railroad begin to coalesce"—a network of operatives from the boundary line with slavery to Canada. Although the AASS never sanctioned breaking the law and had many members who never even contemplated assisting a runaway, the organization had, as Bordewich observes, a symbiotic relationship with the Underground Railroad.[120]

The AASS also brought sympathetic whites together with the black activists who had previously provided the only organized aid for fugitive slaves. White participation and the greater resources of the white abolitionist community greatly expanded the scope of the lines initially developed by African Americans. By 1840 a biracial alliance had been forged to create a network that encompassed much of the North.[121]

Julius LeMoyne's career as an abolitionist offers some hints about the formation of the local Underground Railroad. Although it would be a mistake to suppose that LeMoyne represents the entirety of the local Underground Railroad, far more is known about him than any other individual. Even in his case there are frustrating gaps in the evidence, but the major outlines of his involvement are known.

LeMoyne in 1835 was an obscure, small-town doctor who had only recently become a convert to abolitionism; by 1840 he had become a nationally known figure in the abolitionist movement who was almost certainly an activist in the Underground Railroad. What led him to join a movement that involved abetting the escape of people considered to be another man's property?

LeMoyne's situation needs to be understood in the context of the struggles faced by abolitionists nationally. By the late 1830s it had become apparent that, despite the spread of abolitionist societies throughout the North and a vast propaganda effort, the campaign to persuade Southern owners to free their slaves had been a resounding failure. Moral suasion had not succeeded. Instead, the South had hardened its stance on slavery. John C. Calhoun of South Carolina in 1837 proclaimed that the South's peculiar institution amounted to a "positive good" that had rescued American slaves from the barbarity and heathenism of Africa. Whereas Thomas Jefferson had once apologized for slavery as a "necessary evil," Southerners in the 1830s rallied behind the propaganda line that slavery was a benevolent institution. It became clear to abolitionists that there could be no meaningful dialogue with the South, which had responded to petitions to end slavery in the national capital by instituting the gag rule and by denying the right of petition.[122]

The 1837 murder of abolitionist editor Elijah Lovejoy by a proslavery mob in Alton, Illinois, marked a pivotal turning point for many Northerners in the debate over slavery. Now nearly forgotten or relegated to a footnote, the incident at the time electrified communities across the North. Hundreds of Northern churches commemorated the abolitionist editor who died trying to save his press as a martyr to the abolitionist cause, and thousands of Northerners who had once been indifferent to abolitionism began to see a bond between the denial of free speech and slavery. It was the Lovejoy murder that prompted John Brown to vow that he would see the end of slavery. At a meeting called to mourn Lovejoy's death at the Hudson, Ohio, Congregational Church, Brown proclaimed, "Here before God in the presence of these witnesses, I consecrate my life to the destruction of slavery." It was Brown's first known public statement about slavery. Although the careers of thousands of other abolitionists were not nearly as dramatic as Brown's, they too began a reassessment after Lovejoy's death. It became apparent to many of them that a new strategy was needed to combat this oppressive institution over an extended period of time.[123]

One sign of this reassessment was a transformation of attitudes toward fugitive slaves. A reformer from southern Pennsylvania wrote in 1837 that "public sentiment has undergone a salutary change [on the subject of runaways]." A sympathetic crowd of abolitionists attended the trial of a fugitive slave to exert pressure on the judge, who eventually ruled in favor of the fugitive.[124]

Abolitionists could not, however, agree upon a common strategy for fighting slavery and fell to fighting bitterly among themselves in the late 1830s. Three major factions can be identified. William Lloyd Garrison and his followers concluded that the United States would be forever tainted by its association with slavery and advocated the secession of the free states from the Union. The Garrisonians advocated not just abolitionism but also women's rights and rejected all manner of authority, including that of the national government itself. Garrison pushed the doctrine of abolitionism to its logical conclusion: if slavery was immoral because it rested on arbitrary power and force, then other social institutions such as marriage were also immoral because they too rested on coercion. It is no accident that abolitionism gave rise to the women's rights movement and to reformers such as Mott and Stanton.[125]

LeMoyne distanced himself from the Garrisonians. Although he was committed to providing a sound education for his daughters, as is evidenced by his role in founding the Washington Female Seminary, he was not an advocate of women's rights. Significantly, the organizers of the Pennsylvania Anti-Slavery Society had not invited women to attend its inaugural meeting in Harrisburg in 1837. When the abolitionist movement split in two in 1840, in large measure over the issue of women's rights, LeMoyne joined the more conservative of these factions. For him, the abolitionist cause was controversial enough without adding the equally controversial cause of women's rights. Rebecca Harding Davis may have been right in calling him a "radical" so far as his abolitionism was concerned, but LeMoyne held rather conventional ideas about the appropriate spheres of men and women. LeMoyne and his collaborators in the Washington Anti-Slavery Society took the unusual and controversial step of inviting black speakers to address the society, but so far as can be determined never invited women to do so.[126]

The second faction of the fragmented abolitionist movement, led by LeMoyne's friend James G. Birney, sought a political solution to the problem of slavery and organized the Liberty Party, the first national antislavery party, in 1839. Recognizing that slavery was deeply embedded in the existing Democratic and Whig parties, Birney hoped to offer Americans who saw slavery as the ultimate national sin a clear political choice. At its inaugural convention, the party nominated Birney as its presidential candidate.

The third faction, led by Lewis Tappan, a wealthy New York merchant, continued to adhere to the cause of moral suasion that had dominated abolitionism in the 1830s. It regarded Garrison and his feminist, anarchist followers as dangerous fanatics who would deflect reformers from the true national problem of America: human bondage. The final rift between Tappan's followers and Garrison's group came at the 1840 convention of the AASS. Both sides attempted to control the convention, but Garrison's forces prevailed and left the abolitionist movement permanently divided. The losers at the convention soon formed the American and Foreign Anti-Slavery Society, headed by Lewis Tappan.[127]

LeMoyne initially cast his lot with the adherents to the founding doctrine of moral suasion. When the Liberty Party formed in 1839, he received its nomination to be its vice-presidential candidate in the 1840 election. However, LeMoyne declined the nomination. His reasons for doing so are revealing. "The anti-slavery reformation is emphatically a religious enterprise," he insisted. If the movement went into politics, it would be left open to the charge that "we have lost our first confidence in strict moral means, and that we are now compelled to resort to means which we at first overlooked, if not repudiated." The end of slavery was to be achieved by persuasion, not coercion.[128]

Yet within a year LeMoyne had followed his friend Birney in joining the Liberty Party. We do not know what prompted his decision. It may have been the fractious dispute at the 1840 convention that left a clear dividing line between the "radical" Garrisonians, on the one hand, and the "conservative" political and moral suasion camps, on the other. Perhaps, as a relative latecomer to the abolitionist cause, LeMoyne took longer to conclude that moral suasion alone had not made a dent in slavery other than hardening the lines between North and South. In any case, he concluded that politics might serve as a lever to pry the nation from slavery. In the 1840s, he would run three times (unsuccessfully) as the Liberty Party's candidate for the governorship of Pennsylvania. Some measure of abolitionist sentiment in the county can be gleaned from the fact that LeMoyne won just eighty-five votes from local voters when he ran for governor in 1841.[129]

LeMoyne's reasons for becoming an Underground Railroad operative were almost certainly connected to his decision to abandon moral appeals as a means to end slavery. Assisting fugitives certainly did not fall within the scope of moral suasion; it was one thing to lecture on the evils of slavery and to send petitions to Congress, but it was quite another matter to break the law. LeMoyne was far from alone among white abolitionists by the early 1840s in concluding that assisting runaway slaves constituted a practical way to end slavery for at least a small number of individuals. David Grimsted argues that abolitionists of many stripes became enthusiastic about "slave theft" once the potential of moral suasion had come to a dead end in the late 1830s. Because slave owners were guilty of "man-stealing," abolitionists were justified in "property-stealing." Helping fugitive slaves also gave abolitionists an opportunity to act on their beliefs instead of just holding meetings and sending petitions. The Underground Railroad held a fascination for the "spice of both personal danger and meaningful action."[130]

A second potential reason for LeMoyne's participation in the Underground Railroad was his growing belief in racial equality. Under his leadership, the Washington Anti-Slavery Society grew increasingly receptive to black voices and concerns in the 1840s. Although it may hardly sound radical today, the society took the extremely unpopular step of inviting three black speakers to address it. Ready enough to denounce the evils of slaveholders, many abolitionists saw no double standard in barring black speakers from their meetings and black persons from their homes, except as servants. This invitation to black speakers suggests that LeMoyne was beginning to develop a vision of human equality that was comparatively rare even among white abolitionists. LeMoyne similarly accepted invitations from blacks to speak at their organizations, including one at nearby Canonsburg. He also accepted Martin Delany as a medical student. LeMoyne's dedication to racial equality earned him immense respect among African Americans in western Pennsylvania. Forced to decline LeMoyne's invitation to address the Washington Anti-Slavery's July 4, 1842, meeting, Lewis Woodson, writing from Allegheny, Pennsylvania, apologized, "Your great benevolence and abundant labour in behalf of my wronged and oppressed race, has given you claims upon my services superior to any man in this commonwealth."[131]

LeMoyne was also willing to listen to African Americans. Faced with a dilemma when the Liberty Party fractured in 1848, he reluctantly attended the Free Soil convention in Buffalo in August of that year. The Free Soil Party represented a dilution of abolitionist principles for LeMoyne since its platform called for opposition to the expansion of slavery and not to the institution itself. Abolitionists also found it difficult to stomach the party's nominee for president, Martin Van Buren, the former Democratic president who was often dubbed a "doughface." Only a personal visit to LeMoyne's hotel room by Frederick Douglass persuaded LeMoyne to support the Free Soil ticket.[132]

LeMoyne's evolving stance on the question of interracial marriage also reflected his growing commitment to racial equality. In 1836 he had placed a notice in a local newspaper to deny that he had ever advocated interracial marriage between poor whites and blacks. He dismissed reports circulating locally as "false and injurious," saying that "I do not now, nor ever have entertained such a sentiment." He charged that "persons of some standing" had been circulating this rumor "doubtless with the purpose of prejudicing the public mind against the cause of the poor and oppressed in our land." By 1841, however, LeMoyne had changed his position significantly. He voiced strenuous opposition to a bill pending in the state legislature to outlaw interracial marriages.[133]

Finally, and perhaps most importantly, LeMoyne became acquainted with African Americans from Pittsburgh and western Pennsylvania who are known to have connections to the Underground Railroad. As president of the Pennsylvania Anti-Slavery Society's Western District in the late 1830s, he attended meetings with Vashon, Woodson, and John Peck, who became a member of the executive committee in November 1838. If LeMoyne had not already made the acquaintance of George W. Boler, the African American barber who was instrumental in organizing the AME church in Washington, he did so at meetings of Western District antislavery society.[134]

If LeMoyne is any indication, the route that led to the Underground Railroad for whites in Washington County ran through radical abolitionism and the formation of antislavery societies beginning in the mid-1830s. These societies became committed to the belief that slavery was an evil that had to be eradicated from the United States. When it became apparent by the late 1830s or early 1840s that persuasive means alone would not lead to the abolition of slavery, individuals such as LeMoyne entered politics and put their beliefs into action by helping fugitive slaves. Some of them became committed to the ideal of racial equality. It would not be surprising if contact with black abolitionists led whites to discover the Underground Railroad, just as it is highly probable that most of the fugitives who traveled through Washington County on this line were put aboard by black conductors.[135]

During the 1840s and 1850s the black and white abolitionists of Washington County collaborated to construct a network of safe houses for fugitives from slavery. In some cases this network provided the means by which fugitives were able to flee to the security of Canada. It also provided a hiding place for many slaves who ultimately made Washington County their home.

CHAPTER THREE

The Legendary Underground Railroad in Washington County

Ever since the publication of Larry Gara's *The Liberty Line* in 1961, scholars have been acutely aware of the legendary aura surrounding the Underground Railroad. As Gara wrote, "Few other legends in American history have gained the almost universal acceptance and popularity of the underground railroad. The romance and glamour of the institution have helped endear it to Americans, especially in the North. The legend of the underground railroad tells of intrepid abolitionists sending multitudes of passengers over a well-organized transportation system to the Promised Land of freedom. The fugitives were often hotly pursued by cruel slave catchers, and nearly always they eluded capture because of the ingenuity and daring of the conductors. All was carried on with the utmost secrecy."[1] Gara's work and that of subsequent scholars, however, have made little dent in the Underground Railroad legend in popular history. In a 2007 op-ed piece for the *New York Times*, Fergus M. Bordewich voiced the same complaint nearly half a century later. "Few aspects of the American past," he began, "have inspired more colorful mythology than the Underground Railroad. It's probably fair to say that most Americans view it as a thrilling tapestry of midnight flights, hairsbreadth escapes, mysterious codes, and strange hiding places." If anything, the renewed popularity of the Underground Railroad that began in the 1990s has added to this mythology. The bogus idea that "freedom quilts" provided maps for fugitive slaves is a relatively recent phenomenon.[2]

Thus before delving into the history and operations of the local Underground Railroad, it is important to understand the legends and mythology that have shaped the popular understanding of this fabled institution. Although these legends may be familiar to scholars, they are perceived by much of the public as *the* history of the Underground Railroad. Written down in countless local histories and passed on to casual tourists, they seem to have a life of their own. By analyzing the origins of these legends in Washington County and using the work of other scholars, I hope to dispel at least some of the misconceptions about the Underground Railroad. Only then can a more realistic assessment of the local Liberty Line be achieved. I have also highlighted some of the major differences among scholars to point out ongoing debates in the field.

The popular legend of the Underground Railroad can be broken down into the following elements: 1) The belief that large numbers of fugitive slaves were transported over the Underground Railroad. This study argues that a comparatively small number of slaves made their escape through Washington County and the North as a whole. 2) The belief that the Underground Railroad had extensive operations that reached far into the South. By contrast, this study contends that fugitive slaves were chiefly on their own until they got close to Pennsylvania and even then were sometimes unaware of the existence of the Underground Railroad. Although fugitive slaves may have availed themselves of sporadic assistance and aid from free blacks, slaves, and even the occasional sympathetic white south of the Mason-Dixon Line, they found no *organized* system of help until they got to Pennsylvania. 3) The belief that the Underground Railroad involved the utmost secrecy. This study suggests that this aspect of the Underground Railroad has been vastly overblown. 4) The belief that Underground Railroad agents' primary job was engineering hairbreadth escapes for fugitive slaves from the jaws of bloodhounds and clutches of slave catchers. Although there is evidence for a few harrowing escapes, more often than not local Underground Railroad agents performed more prosaic duties, such as meeting a stagecoach bearing a freed slave. 5) The belief that it was predominantly whites who operated the Underground Railroad for the benefit of an oppressed race. Easily the most transparent of these elements of the legend today, the myth of a "white" Underground Railroad is still embedded in the source material and therefore subtly shapes our perception of the Liberty Line.

The purpose of examining these elements of the Underground Railroad legend is not to suggest that the legend is based entirely on wishful thinking and folklore, but rather that its connection to history is often tenuous. Perhaps Gara put it best when he commented, "There is probably at least a germ of truth in most of the stories concerning the mysterious institution, though the scattered seeds of historical fact which mature into legends have a way of multiplying beyond belief."[3] This study will attempt to explain how the legend came to obscure the history of the local Underground Railroad and to reveal in a few instances how the kernel of truth grew into the legendary Underground Railroad exploit.

TRAFFIC ON THE UNDERGROUND RAILROAD

Earlier writers on the Underground Railroad in Washington County have often suggested that local traffic was quite heavy. A reporter for the *Washington Observer*, for example, claimed in 1904 that western Washington County was the location of "the three most important southern Pennsylvania stations" on the Underground Railroad. Similarly, the eulogist for William Asbury, the former Virginia slave who had settled in Cross Creek and become a conductor, says that Asbury assisted "scores" of fugitive slaves. Although precise numbers are seldom mentioned, most of these accounts give the impression of a steady stream of human traffic through Washington County.

Washington County is very far from an isolated case in this regard. Writers dealing with the Underground Railroad have often given the overwhelming impression that the Liberty Line carried trains full of passengers to the North. Almost invariably they assert that the Underground Railroad did a "big business." Wilbur Siebert estimated that more than forty thousand slaves escaped through Ohio alone in the decades before the Civil War. Attempting to justify Southern secession, the Lost Cause apologist E. W. R. Ewing asserted unequivocally that it was "certain that hundreds of thousands escaped, and that millions of dollars were lost by Southerners." Popular opinion as well perceives heavy traffic on the Underground Railroad. In an informal survey conducted in the 1950s, the average respondent thought 270,000 slaves had successfully escaped in the 1850s alone.[4]

Recent scholarship has challenged the idea that a flood of fugitive slaves inundated the North in the decades leading up to the Civil War. Yet there are still widespread disagreements among historians over how many freedom seekers were successful in their quest to escape from slavery, just as contemporaries in the 1850s disagreed wildly.[5] For example, the *New Orleans Commercial Bulletin* claimed in 1859 that 1,500 slaves had escaped from the South annually during the previous fifty years. The AASS, on the other hand, thought this claim "much exaggerated."[6] There is no single reliable source that can be consulted to adjudicate this dispute; instead, fragmentary sources have to be cobbled together to yield an estimation of Underground Railroad traffic. Pennsylvania has two thousand documented cases of fugitive slave escapes, more than eight hundred of them known because of William Still's records, but whether this constitutes something like 100 percent or 10 percent of slave escapes in the state is unknown.[7] Modern estimates of the number of successful fugitives nationally range from about 30,000 all the way to 150,000.[8]

These discrepancies are important in the debate among scholars about the fundamental nature of the Underground Railroad. Those who believe that our understanding of the Liberty Line has been clouded by myths and legends tend to weigh in on the side of lower estimates. Gara, although he has never committed to an estimate of the number of tickets that the Underground Railroad issued, clearly thinks that estimates of 75,000 passengers are far too high.[9] John Hope Franklin and Loren Schweninger estimate that only between 30,000 and 60,000 fugitives made their escape to the North. Instead, they emphasize that "most runaways remained in the South" and "few were aided by abolitionists or anyone else." The vast majority of fugitive slaves were temporary runaways who hid on the outskirts of their own plantations or with friends and family on neighboring plantations. Such temporary runaways sought to escape a beating, protest mistreatment, or avoid a confrontation with an angry slaveholder or overseer. Although some absconded for several weeks, most runaways returned, tired and hungry, after a few days.[10]

By contrast, those who argue for the effectiveness of the Underground Railroad offer higher estimates. Bordewich believes that between 70,000 and 150,000 slaves may have gained their freedom via the Liberty Line but estimates that "100,000 may be closer to the mark." J. Blaine Hudson contends that 135,000 escaped during the lifetime of the Underground Railroad. Although Stanley Harrold never offers a number, he clearly sides with writers who have offered higher estimates.[11]

Two sources of evidence are helpful when examining the question of how much traffic the Underground Railroad witnessed nationally: the United States censuses from 1850 and 1860, and the population of Canada West (modern-day Ontario), the destination for many fugitive slaves. Both sources pose problems and need to be interpreted cautiously.

The U.S. censuses of 1850 and 1860 seem straightforward. Slave owners were asked to report how many slaves had run away permanently during the previous year. In 1850, they reported 1,011 fugitive slaves out of a total slave population of about 3.2 million, and in 1860, they reported 803 slaves missing out of a slave population of nearly 4 million, or .02 percent of the total. These census statistics should not be considered exact, since they rely on the voluntary reporting of slave owners and reflect imperfections in the census. David Smith argues that voluntary reporting was a major shortcoming of the censuses. He believes that slaveholders may have been reluctant to report fugitives because it reflected on their inability to control their slaves. The counter to Smith is that census takers were the neighbors of those whose slaves had run away and likely would have been familiar with these losses. By contrast, Ewing, in the early twentieth century, blamed a Northern conspiracy for what he regarded as small numbers of fugitive slaves reported in the censuses. "Northern men," he charged, "falsified the census in the two important years of 1850 and 1860, to cover up the facts regarding these depredations." Yet Southerners made no outcry in response to the numbers reported in the 1850 census.[12]

However imperfect they may be, the censuses do give some idea of the relative magnitude of fugitive slave numbers. Contemporaries accepted these figures as being generally accurate, which suggests that there were about one thousand fugitives a year in the entire United States during the peak of Underground Railroad activity in the 1830s, 1840s, and 1850s. The censuses provide the basis for the conservative estimate that perhaps forty thousand fugitives were able to escape successfully from slavery.

The other measure of the success of the Underground Railroad—the African American population of Canada West—is more problematic. Virtually everything written about the Underground Railroad, in both Washington County and a larger context, assumes that the destination of fugitive slaves was this region of Canada. Both contemporaries and later scholars have described substantial black populations in communities such as Windsor, Chatham, and St. Catherines. Benjamin Drew visited many of these communities in the mid-1850s. He estimated that the black population of Canada West was about thirty thousand, nearly all of whom were fugitive slaves.[13] Historian Robin Winks seemingly confirmed the impression that Canada West became the home of many freedom seekers from south of the border before the Civil War. He estimated that the black population of Canada West by 1860 had grown to around forty thousand, of whom three-fourths (or thirty thousand) were fugitive slaves.[14]

Michael Wayne's more recent work on the manuscript census for Canada West, however, has shown these previous estimates of the number of fugitive slaves in Queen Victoria's realm to be off substantially. He concludes that the black population of Canada West did not amount to more than twenty-three thousand people. In short, he contends that historians have vastly overestimated the presence of blacks in Canada West.[15]

Equally significant, Wayne discovered that a substantial part of Canada West's black population did not consist of fugitive slaves. More than 40 percent of those listed in the census were Canadian born. About 30 percent of the American-born blacks had been born in free states and were thus not fugitive slaves. As Keith Griffler has observed, many African Americans left the North because they were "devoured" by prejudice and ostracism of Northern whites.[16] Drew also encountered blacks in Canada West who had purchased their freedom, moved to a free state, and subsequently emigrated to Canada to escape prejudice. J. C. Brown, for example, purchased his freedom from his Kentucky owner and then settled in Cincinnati. When Ohio revived laws requiring African Americans to post a five-hundred-dollar bond so that they would not become "town charges," Brown departed for Canada in the mid-1840s. Aby B. Jones, whose freedom was purchased, never felt truly free in Kentucky and moved to Canada. Of the 70 percent of American-born blacks from the slave states living in Canada West in 1861, Wayne estimates that only about half were fugitive slaves. (Because fugitive slaves were much more likely to be male than female, the presence of a higher-than-expected female population from the slave states would indicate the migration of free married couples from the slave states to Canada.) In total, less than one-third of the American-born blacks living in Canada West were fugitive slaves. Thus Wayne concludes that fewer than five thousand escapees from American slavery were making their homes in Canada when the American Civil War broke out.[17]

The other complicating factor in using the population of Canada West as a proxy for the number of fugitive slaves is that, contrary to popular impression, not all fugitives sought refuge north of the border. Many remained in the free states, particularly Pennsylvania, where there were opportunities for employment. Smith attributes the motivation of slaves who remained in south central Pennsylvania just across the border from where they had escaped from Maryland to their desire to remain in the proximity of relatives.

He believes very few followed the North Star all the way to Canada. Bordewich concurs, estimating that only one-third to one-quarter of fugitive slaves went to Canada. If Wayne is correct that fewer than five thousand fugitive slaves made their way to Canada West, this would indicate a total fugitive slave population of between fifteen and twenty thousand in the United States and Canada. However, Bordewich's estimate is just that—an estimate. There is no reliable way to know what percentage of fugitive slaves remained within the United States.[18]

This study estimates the total number of fugitive slaves in the forty to sixty thousand range, probably toward the lower end of that range. It assumes that the United States and Canadian censuses record relatively accurate estimates of the number of fugitive slaves and offer far better guides than any contemporary, impressionistic guesses. Analyzing traffic on the Underground Railroad is admittedly a tricky business. Censuses before 1850 did not ask slave owners whether any of their bondsmen had run away, so estimates prior to 1850 have to be based on projections. This study assumes that the vast majority of traffic on the Underground Railroad occurred between 1830 and 1860, and that about one thousand slaves annually managed to escape during that period. Perhaps a maximum of ten thousand slaves gained their freedom between the Revolutionary War and 1830 by running away.

The fundamental point to be made here is that the total number of fugitive slaves, whether it be 40,000 or 150,000, was small in comparison to the total slave population of the United States, which in 1860 stood at nearly four million human beings. The escape of fugitive slaves to the North and to Canada constituted a trickle, not a flood.

If the number of fugitive slaves was comparatively small, however, the issue of fugitive slaves was of enormous symbolic importance, particularly politically. "From the beginning," as Matthew Pinsker has commented, "the Underground Railroad was a symbol as much as a physical reality. It was a principal tool in the sectional propaganda war."[19] The origins of the Underground Railroad legend clearly lie in the rhetorical battles between abolitionists and slaveholders fought over the enforcement of fugitive slave laws beginning in the 1840s. Southerners claimed that untold millions of dollars of their property were escaping into the North and Canada with the complicity of Northerners. Their efforts to force stricter compliance with the Fugitive Slave Act of 1793 and ultimately their demands for a new fugitive slave law tended to magnify the actual extent of their losses greatly.

Abolitionists clearly understood this psychology. Commenting on the *New Orleans Commercial Bulletin*'s estimate of slaveholder losses, the AASS's annual report suspected that the paper's motive was "to embitter, as much as possible, the Southern feeling against the North." The effect of Southern propaganda against abolitionists and Underground Railroad agents was to inflate their actual numbers and importance in the North.[20]

Underground Railroad personnel also contributed to the impression that their enterprise handled a large volume of passengers and thereby to the legend. Far from shrouding their operations in secrecy, a number of stationmasters and operatives took out advertisements in newspapers to make their activities known. William Stedman, for example, advertised in the *Cleveland Daily True Democrat* in 1850 that he was the local station-master responsible for getting fugitive slaves to Canada. Alarmed by the extent of Underground Railroad publicity, Frederick Douglass once complained that so many secrets had been revealed that erstwhile friends of fugitive slaves had turned the Liberty Line into the "Upper-Ground Railroad" whose stations were "far better known to the slave-holders than to the slaves." Such advertisements and accounts of actual escapes also fed the legend.[21]

More than anything else, the furor over the Fugitive Slave Act of 1850 helped to shape the legend of the Underground Railroad. Southern demands for a new fugitive slave law grew rapidly after the U.S. Supreme Court issued its decision in the case of *Prigg v. Pennsylvania* in 1842. At stake was the constitutionality of an 1826 Pennsylvania law intended to protect free blacks from being kidnapped and fugitive slaves who had sought refuge in the state from being arrested arbitrarily. Pennsylvania courts found Edward Prigg, a Marylander, guilty of violating this law when he captured a slave named Margaret Morgan and her children and took them back to Maryland in 1837 without any kind of legal hearing. But the Supreme Court reversed Prigg's conviction on appeal, striking down the Pennsylvania law. It held that an owner's rights to recover his property were the same in the free states as in the slave states. Therefore, laws offering suspected fugitives the protection of jury trials, such as Pennsylvania's, were unconstitutional. A number of Northern states responded by passing personal liberty laws that prohibited state officials from participating in the recapture of fugitive slaves. Although these personal liberty laws offered few practical benefits to fugitive slaves, they did distance Northern officials from what had come to be seen as an increasingly distasteful business.[22]

The South's demand for a stiffer fugitive slave law grew immediately out of the passage of these personal liberty laws. It ultimately got such a law in the Compromise of 1850. The new fugitive slave law departed dramatically from the old one by stipulating that the federal commissioners in charge of enforcing the act could force citizens in the free states to assist in the recapture of fugitive slaves. Failure to do so or aiding a fugitive slave could result in imprisonment for up to a year and in a fine of up to a thousand dollars. In the eyes of many Northerners, the new fugitive slave act made them complicit in maintaining the South's peculiar institution. They could no longer cloak themselves under personal liberty laws and claim that recapturing fugitives was none of their responsibility. Now, however, they bore a legal responsibility for upholding slavery, even if the likelihood of being required to assist in recapturing a runaway was quite remote.[23]

Inspired and angered by the new fugitive slave law, Harriet Beecher Stowe dramatized how those remote possibilities could be realized in *Uncle Tom's Cabin*, published in 1852. Confronted with the prospect of her son being sold to a slave trader, Eliza, the novel's heroine, decides to flee her Kentucky home to save her young son. In the novel's most dramatic scene, Eliza takes the desperate measure of carrying Harry across the wintry Ohio River, hopping from one ice floe to the next, to avoid being captured by slave catchers. Eliza and her son find refuge on the Ohio shore with Senator Bird and his family. Bird's humanitarian instincts to help Eliza conflict with his belief in abiding by the law, and Eliza's fate hangs momentarily in the balance before Bird's conscience and sympathy finally get the better of him: "His idea of a fugitive was only an idea of the letters that spell the word,—or at the most, the image of a little newspaper of a man with a stick and a bundle, with 'Ran Away from the Subscriber' under it. The magic of the real presence of distress,—the imploring human eye, the frail, trembling human hand, the despairing appeal of helpless agony,—these he had never tried. He had never thought that a fugitive might be a hapless mother, a defenceless child."[24] Rather than obeying the law, he puts Eliza and her son on the Underground Railroad through Ohio. Stowe's novel, which became the runaway best-selling novel of nineteenth-century America, put the Underground Railroad on the map.

Southerners likewise came to attach a great deal of importance to the new fugitive slave law, if for different reasons. The Fugitive Slave Act of 1850 was the only major concession that the South received under the Compromise of 1850. Meanwhile, the North got the main prize of California, which entered the Union as a free state and upset the sectional balance in the Senate. The North was also successful in eliminating the slave trade from the District of Columbia—one of the demands of the abolitionist petition campaign of the 1830s. Although slavery itself continued in the national capital until 1862, the slave markets that had stood within several blocks of the Capitol ceased to exist. Southerners came to regard Northern compliance with the new fugitive slave act as the real test of the compromise, watching for any hint that the North was willing to brush aside or ignore the new fugitive slave law as a sign of Northern bad faith. Thus, if there is a pronounced bias in the reporting of fugitive slaves in the 1860 census, it is a Southern one. Slaveholders had an incentive to inflate the number of missing slaves in an effort to prove that the North had been ineffectual in enforcing the Fugitive Slave Act of 1850. Yet the actual number of fugitive slaves reported declined from 1850 to 1860, from 1,011 to 803.[25]

Stanley W. Campbell's book *The Slave Catchers* reveals the extent to which sectional blinders and preconceived notions have triumphed over historical fact. Southerners in the 1850s and historians for nearly a century after the Civil War believed that the Fugitive Slave Act of 1850 was a colossal failure, thereby supporting the justification for secession. Campbell's analysis of the enforcement of the law, however, revealed a very different picture: apart from a few spectacular cases, the law was enforced. "In the great majority of cases which came before the federal slave tribunals," Campbell concludes, "slaves were remanded to their owners or were returned to the South at government expense." Yet the North and the South believed otherwise, both at the time and long afterward. Apparently a few notorious cases, such as the rescue of Shadrack from the custody of federal authorities in Boston in 1851 and the 1851 Christiana Riot in Pennsylvania, during which black resistance led to freedom for two slaves and the death of their owner, permanently shaped public perceptions. The issue of fugitive slaves went right to the heart of the quarrel between North and South and laid the roadbed for the legendary Underground Railroad.[26]

If the absolute number of fugitive slaves nationally was quite small, the proportion of fugitive slaves who escaped through western Pennsylvania was even smaller. The salient demographic fact is that there were few slaves in western Maryland and western Virginia (modern-day West Virginia)—the areas from which fugitive slaves were most likely to come. Fugitive slaves were most likely to flee from slave states that shared a border with a free state. In 1850, Maryland reported 279 permanent fugitives out of a slave population of 90,368, while Virginia reported 82 slaves missing out of a slave population of 472,528. Together these states accounted for 36 percent of all the fugitive slaves in 1850, yet they held only 18 percent of the South's slaves. By contrast, South Carolina reported 16 fugitives in 1850 out of a slave population of nearly 385,000. The disparities between Maryland's reported fugitives and Virginia's are also worth noting here. Slaveholders in Maryland, which shared a northern border with Pennsylvania, suffered the largest absolute slave losses and the second-highest relative losses. (Delaware slave owners, who also had to contend with a shared Pennsylvania border, lost more than 1 percent of their tiny slave population of 2,290.) Virginia's 1850 slave population of 472,528, the largest by far of any state, had a more difficult time escaping to freedom than Maryland's slaves. Roughly 95 percent of those slaves lived in the counties east of the Appalachians (current-day Virginia), which meant that they had to cross the Potomac River and through the slave state of Maryland before they could reach the relative safety of Pennsylvania. (Some fugitives could and did board boats bound for Northern ports.) Slaves living in southwestern Virginia had to confront the serious obstacle of the Ohio River if they were to realize their hopes of escaping into the free state of Ohio. The only "easy" escape route open to Virginia slaves was the shared border with the southwestern corner of Pennsylvania. This border ran some sixty miles from east to west, and the panhandle border about seventy miles from the corner north to the Ohio River.[27]

Yet relatively few slaves took advantage of this route. The mountains and valleys of western Virginia were conducive to family farms rather than plantation agriculture. As William W. Freehling has commented, "Mountainous terrain invited a free labor rather than slave labor culture." In all of trans-Allegheny Virginia (the counties that became West Virginia), there were only 20,500 slaves in 1850. They constituted just 4.3 percent of the slave population in Virginia, where one-third of the population was enslaved. The eastern panhandle, settled long before the rest of the counties that became West Virginia, accounted for close to half of all of the slaves in the western counties. Jefferson County alone held more than 4,000 slaves, accounting for more than one-fifth of the total for the western part of the state. In the seven counties contiguous to the Pennsylvania border there were only 527 slaves. They accounted for less than 1 percent of the population of these counties in 1850. Allegany County, Maryland, then the westernmost county in the state and located above the eastern panhandle of Virginia, added 724 people to the total of slaves most likely to seek freedom

Table 2. Fugitive Slaves and Slave Populations, 1850 and 1860[1]

State	1850 Slave Population	1850 Fugitive Slaves (Percent of Loss)	1860 Slave Population	1860 Fugitive Slaves (Percent of Loss)
Alabama	342,844	29 (.01)	435,080	36 (.01)
Arkansas	47,100	21 (.04)	111,115	28 (.03)
Delaware	2,290	26 (1.14)	1,798	12 (.67)
Florida	39,310	18 (.05)	61,745	11 (.02)
Georgia	381,682	89 (.02)	462,198	23 (.01)
Kentucky	210,981	96 (.05)	225,483	119 (.05)
Louisiana	244,809	90 (.04)	331,726	46 (.01)
Maryland	90,368	279 (.31)	87,189	115 (.13)
Mississippi	309,378	40 (.01)	436,631	68 (.02)
Missouri	87,422	60 (.07)	114,931	99 (.09)
North Carolina	288,548	64 (.02)	331,059	61 (.02)
South Carolina	384,984	16 (.004)	402,406	23 (.006)
Tennessee	239,459	70 (.03)	275,719	29 (.01)
Texas	58,161	29 (.05)	182,566	16 (.01)
Virginia	472,528	82 (.02)	490,865	117 (.02)
Total	3,200,364	1,011 (.03)	3,950,511	803 (.02)
Border States	391,061	461 (.12)	429,401	345 (.08)
Rest of South	2,809,303	550 (.02)	3,521,110	458 (.01)

[1] "Fugitive Slaves" represents the number of slaves who were reported fugitives from the state in the preceding year. Siebert, *Underground Railroad*, 378; Ancestry.com, U.S. Federal Census—Slave Schedules, 1850 and 1860. See also https://familysearch.org/wiki/en/United_States_Census_Slave _Schedules. County data for slave populations is available from U.S. Bureau of the Census, Decennial Census of Population and Housing, 1790–1860, https://www.census.gov/programs-surveys /decennial-census/decade.html.

by escaping through western Pennsylvania. The distance from Cumberland, the county seat, to Washington, Pennsylvania, was ninety-nine miles via the National Road.[28]

Analysis of the 1850 and 1860 slave schedules in the census indicates that a modest number of slaves took advantage of their proximity to freedom. The seven Virginia counties contiguous to Pennsylvania reported four fugitive slaves in 1850. Slave owners in Allegany County, Maryland, informed the census taker that six of their slaves had run away in the same year. Virginia slave owners from the border counties reported a significant increase in fugitive slaves in 1860, when thirteen slaves escaped. Those

Table 3. Fugitive Slaves from Virginia and Maryland Counties Contiguous to Southwestern Pennsylvania[1]

County	1850 Slave Population	1850 Fugitive Slaves	1860 Slave Population	1860 Fugitive Slaves
Hancock, Virginia	3	0	2	0
Brooke, Virginia	31	0	18	2
Ohio, Virginia	164	1	100	11
Marshall, Virginia	49	1	29	0
Wetzel, Virginia	17	0	10	0
Monongalia, Virginia	176	2	101	0
Preston, Virginia	87	0	67	0
Allegany, Maryland	724	6	666	4
Total	1,251	10	993	17

[1] Ancestry.com, U.S. Federal Census—Slave Schedules, 1850 and 1860.

slaves represented more than 10 percent of all of the slaves missing from Virginia in 1860. The major reason for the increase was the exodus of all nine of the slaves owned by Isaac and James Kelly from Wheeling. Four slaves were reported missing from Allegany County in 1860. Although slaves in counties contiguous to southwestern Pennsylvania escaped in greater proportion than other slaves in Virginia and Maryland, their numbers were not large. Ten slaves escaped from the bordering Virginia and Maryland counties in 1850, and seventeen in 1860. (See Map 6.)[29]

One other body of evidence has a bearing on the number of fugitive slaves traveling through western Pennsylvania: the fugitive slaves who were reported captured, either by federal tribunals or by the local press. Considerable caution needs to be used in interpreting these data on fugitive captures because federal court records and newspaper reports are incomplete. Undoubtedly many captures of fugitive slaves never appeared in federal records or received much publicity. Campbell found 332 cases involving captured fugitive slaves across the entire United States between 1850 and 1860. Of these, seventy-three (22 percent) occurred in Pennsylvania. The largest number of captured fugitives (thirty-two) was in the central part of the state, in the vicinity of Harrisburg and Carlisle. There were twenty captures in eastern Pennsylvania, mostly in Philadelphia, and only seventeen in western Pennsylvania. These numbers are somewhat deceptive for western

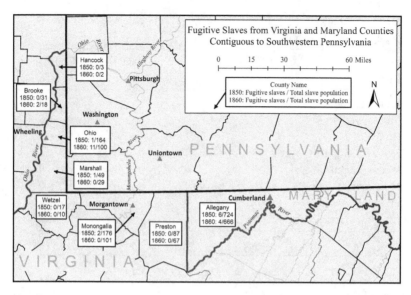

Fugitive Slaves from Virginia and Maryland Counties
Contiguous to Southwestern Pennsylvania

0   15   30   60 Miles

County Name
1850: Fugitive slaves / Total slave population
1860: Fugitive slaves / Total slave population

N

Hancock
1850: 0/3
1860: 0/2

Pittsburgh

Brooke
1850: 0/31
1860: 2/18

Washington

Wheeling

Ohio
1850: 1/164
1860: 11/100

Uniontown

PENNSYLVANIA

Marshall
1850: 1/49
1860: 0/29

Wetzel
1850: 0/17
1860: 0/10

Morgantown

Cumberland

Allegany
1850: 6/724
1860: 4/666

MARYLAND

Monongalia
1850: 2/176
1860: 0/101

Preston
1850: 0/87
1860: 0/67

VIRGINIA

Map 6

Pennsylvania because eight slaves captured as a group near Bedford account for nearly half of the total. There is no record of any slave captures in Washington County. Uniontown in nearby Fayette County witnessed four fugitive slave apprehensions, and Pittsburgh two. If the number of slaves recaptured bears any relation to the volume of Underground Railroad traffic, it would indicate that the western part of the state saw less Underground Railroad activity than the rest of the state.[30]

Thus several considerations suggest that traffic on the Underground Railroad in Washington County was intermittent and comparatively light. The first is that it was quite unusual for a slave to escape bondage, even in counties bordering a free state. Even if *all* of the fugitive slaves who escaped from the border counties of Virginia and Maryland traveled through Washington County, it amounts to a dozen or so fugitives per year. Undoubtedly slaves did escape from Virginia counties that did not share a border with Pennsylvania, but their numbers are not likely to have been large. An examination of the 1860 slave schedules of Virginia counties that did not border Pennsylvania but lay within a one-hundred-mile radius of Washington, Pennsylvania, reveals twelve additional fugitive slaves, two from Harrison County and ten from Taylor County.[31]

Second, neither western Maryland nor western Virginia had large concentrations of slaves who would have constituted a major source of traffic
for the local Underground Railroad. One has to look far afield to find large
slave populations. Virginia's substantial slave population was primarily concentrated east of the Blue Ridge Mountains and secondarily in the Shenandoah Valley. Most counties east of the mountains had slave populations of
over 40 percent; in the tobacco-growing Southside, a number of counties
had a majority of slaves. In the Shenandoah Valley, between the Blue Ridge
and the Alleghenies, slave populations averaged 25 percent. But these areas
were a considerable distance from Washington County. From Martinsburg,
in the upper reaches of the Shenandoah Valley, to Washington, Pennsylvania, was 150 miles as the crow flies, and farther by road.[32]

Distance, however, is merely one consideration. Imposing mountains
lay between the Shenandoah Valley and western Pennsylvania. It was far
easier to follow the roads that ran parallel to the mountains than it was to
cross the mountains. Running in a northeasterly direction from south to
north, the Blue Ridge and Allegheny Mountains funneled fugitives to the
northeast, away from western Pennsylvania. Bordewich concurs that the
southwest-to-northeast orientation of these mountains channeled fugitive
slaves toward the Philadelphia/New York corridor. South central Pennsylvania was a major destination for fugitive slaves not only because of a substantial nearby slave population but also because road networks, which
typically followed valleys, ran in a northeasterly direction.[33]

Clearly the occasional fugitive did find his or her way across the
mountains or followed the National Road westward. Several fugitive slaves
are known to have made their escape from the upper Shenandoah Valley
to Pittsburgh. Dan Lockhart ran away from Winchester and fled to Pittsburgh in 1847. Unfortunately he did not specify the route by which he
made his escape. Although slave catchers momentarily captured him at
the Monongahela House, the noted Pittsburgh hotel where he was working, Lockhart raised such a commotion that friends came to his aid and
freed him. He ultimately made his way to Canada with the assistance of
the Underground Railroad. George Johnson likewise made Pittsburgh his
immediate destination. Born near Harpers Ferry, Virginia, Johnson and
two fellow slaves fled when they learned that a fellow servant was about to
be sold and feared that they might suffer a similar fate. Sleeping by day and
traveling by night, they walked to Pittsburgh by an unspecified route.
Johnson ultimately went to Canada as well. Despite these examples, it still

would seem likely that freedom seekers in the Shenandoah Valley would seek the shortest route to the free states rather than the much longer path that Lockhart and Johnson followed.[34]

To Washington County's southwest, the closest large concentration of slaves was hundreds of miles down the Ohio River in Kentucky. Again, it seems unlikely that many slaves from Kentucky would have followed the Ohio upstream for hundreds of miles when they could cross the river into Ohio. Some fugitives did sneak aboard steamers bound for Pittsburgh, but they would not have traveled through Washington County. Veteran Underground Railroad operatives Thomas and Frances Brown relocated from Cincinnati to Pittsburgh and helped to make the Monongahela House a center of rescues.[35] But there simply was no large concentration of slaves near Washington County to become a potential major source of fugitives.

One of the few pieces of contemporary evidence that bears on this question of the traffic volume on the local Underground Railroad comes from Matthew McKeever, regarded by some as the premier railroad man in Washington County. In a letter written in 1880, McKeever estimated that he had helped about thirty-five to forty runaways during his forty-year career as a conductor. McKeever thus helped an average of one fugitive a year. And since he on one occasion helped a party of eight gain freedom, there were many years when there was no traffic at all on the "railroad" through West Middletown. McKeever was likely to have assisted with a considerable portion of the runaways who passed through the village of West Middletown and western Washington County. The number of fugitive slaves whom he helped is quite consistent with the estimate that the Reverend Arthur B. Bradford, a major figure in neighboring Beaver County's Underground Railroad, sheltered fifty or sixty runaway slaves at his home in Enon.[36]

McKeever's recollections do help to suggest how the legendary Underground Railroad came to dwarf the real history. McKeever emphatically stated that the largest party of slaves he had ever helped escape was eight. Yet many of his contemporaries "remembered" McKeever harboring much larger groups. D. M. Boyd, a longtime justice of the peace in West Middletown, told a reporter in 1884 that he had seen fifteen refugees in McKeever's cellar on one occasion in 1858 or 1859. Others maintained that they had seen similar numbers of fugitives concealed in the woods near the Pleasant Hill Female Seminary run by McKeever and his wife. These observers believed that the seminary had numerous hiding places in its outbuildings where runaways could be concealed. As stories about McKeever's activities were passed down locally, the number of slaves he hid grew, as did the number of secret hiding places. One suspects that it was in the retelling of McKeever's and others' stories long after the Underground Railroad had ceased operation that the embellishments began. It was then that stories of escape tunnels and secret rooms solidified into what might be called the folk history of the Underground Railroad. This folk history, based more on fantasy than fact, assumed written form in the 1880s and 1890s when newspaper reporters and county historians began collecting stories from the aging survivors of the Underground Railroad movement and their neighbors.[37]

Any estimate of the total volume of traffic through Washington County is bound to be a gross approximation. But the available evidence suggests that the number was fairly small. Based on McKeever's recollection and the number of fugitive slaves reported missing from nearby Virginia and Maryland counties, the number of fugitives who made their way to or through Washington County was probably no more than several hundred and certainly less than a thousand. Even if all of the fugitive slaves from nearby counties escaped through Washington County (see Table 3), a maximum of four hundred escaped over a thirty-year period. (This assumes that an annual average of 13.5 escapes—the average of the escapes reported in the 1850 and 1860 censuses—occurred over the thirty-year period when the Liberty Line was operational.) Because Allegany County, Maryland, accounted for more than a third of the reported escapes and because fugitives fleeing from this county would likely have chosen a nearer escape route, the number of fugitive slaves who made their escape through Washington County was far less than four hundred. Even if *all* of the decline in the slave population in these eight counties can be attributed to the Underground Railroad, a maximum of eight hundred slaves would have escaped. (This assumes that the decline of 258 slaves between 1850 and 1860 occurred between 1830 and 1850 as well.) These estimates of fugitive slave traffic through Washington County largely concur with that made by Edward Burns, who argued in 1925 that several hundred slaves had gained their freedom by traveling through western Pennsylvania.[38]

The available evidence suggests that the Underground Railroad in Washington County should be regarded as a branch line over which the Liberty Line operated rather erratically. The main line, by contrast, operated in cities such as Philadelphia, Cincinnati, and Wilmington, Delaware, which were close to or accessible to parts of the South that had large slave populations. The detailed records kept by William Still, chairman of the Vigilant

Committee of Philadelphia, reveal that about one hundred fugitive slaves per year passed through that area in the 1850s. If traffic along the main lines kept the rails shiny and smooth, the irregular traffic in Washington County had difficulty keeping rust from appearing on the rails.[39]

THE LEGEND OF A VAST, WELL-ORGANIZED CONSPIRACY

At the national level, the belief has persisted at least in popular history that the Underground Railroad had a national organization that operated lines extending far into the South. This belief complements the notion that the Liberty Line did a booming business.[40] A reporter for the *Washington Observer* exemplified this belief in 1904 when he described the Underground Railroad as "a perfectly arranged route from the far south to . . . the northern territory" along which were periodic "resting places."[41] The Underground Railroad metaphor lends itself to the misconception that the Liberty Line operated in the same fashion as a real railroad, with a fixed schedule, regular stops, helpful conductors, and executives looking out for the entire operation, which ran deep into the South.

Historians since Gara have rejected the idea that the Underground Railroad was a centrally directed, far-flung operation. Instead, they have emphasized that decentralized, local networks characterized the border North and occasionally reached into the border South. Family and kinship were the main ties that bound together the black and white abolitionists in south central Pennsylvania who helped escaping slaves. The Quaker presence in neighboring Frederick County, Maryland, extended the reach of this network into the Border South. The contested ground among scholars is how far and how extensively into the Border South the Underground Railroad penetrated. Harrold has convincingly demonstrated that the Washington, DC, area featured Underground Railroad stops long before the Metro. But the DC area may be an exception. The scope of the numerous local networks that constituted the Underground Railroad seldom extended beyond border areas that were contiguous to the free states.[42]

For most fugitive slaves the most dangerous part of the journey toward freedom was the escape from slave territory. This was a journey often taken alone, usually without any kind of assistance. Apart from a few areas such as Washington, DC, there simply was no Underground Railroad from the slave South to the North. Even when they crossed the Mason-Dixon Line, many fugitives had little, if any, awareness of how or where to seek assistance from the Underground Railroad network. This is hardly surprising given that less than 10 percent of all slaves could read and write. Particularly in the rural regions of western Virginia, there was little possibility of communication between the few who ran away—typically young males in their teens and twenties—and those left behind. If a runaway did receive assistance, he was apt to receive it from sympathetic fellow slaves or free blacks. To a runaway slave, most whites represented potential threats and were to be avoided if at all possible. Only sheer desperation would lead a fugitive slave to rely on a white person. Until at least 1830, most white Northerners were probably more inclined to help capture runaways, not to help them escape.[43]

By and large, the local historians of Washington County have not succumbed to this illusory notion that the Underground Railroad extended deep into the South. They have assumed that it was operatives on the northern side of the Mason-Dixon Line who helped fleeing slaves board the train and then conducted them to safety. Rather, their major fallacy is in treating the network as a highly organized and efficient business enterprise that operated much like its namesake. They have attributed a degree of organization to the operation that simply did not exist. Perhaps this fallacy can be seen most clearly in accounts of how fugitive slaves got onto the Underground Railroad. These accounts typically portray white abolitionists as the heroes of the Underground Railroad who were ever on the alert to give aid to the oppressed. One reporter described Dr. Samuel McKeehan of West Alexander as follows: "The good old doctor was always on the alert for visitors and made a practice of taking daily solitary rambles throughout the surrounding woods with a view of meeting any fugitives that might be in the neighborhood." Fugitives steered a course for West Alexander because "they had been assured they would find a man who would stand by them, no matter if every slave owner in the south tried to intimidate him." White abolitionists are the heroes of these stories.[44]

Such accounts of the Underground Railroad in the county were typically not very curious about how passengers arrived at the station or "boarded" the train. The notable exception is Howard Wallace's eight-page pamphlet, which is by far the most extensive account written by a local participant in the railroad. Born in 1831, Wallace, an African American, was the son of an Underground Railroad agent who lived in Centerville, in eastern Washington County. Wallace himself served as a conductor. By the

1890s he had discovered that he was "the only one living that aided in helping the slaves through." Wallace's perspective as an African American on the Underground Railroad was quite different from that of white accounts. For one thing, he was interested in how fugitives made it north, and for another, he stressed that the most dangerous part of their journey had been made without the assistance of the Underground Railroad:

> In the first place it was a mystery how they made their way North through the mountains, wilderness and deep ravines, but many of them told me the North Star was their guide. Some by another guide, the moss on the trees always growing on the North side of the trees. They were trying to come North, hearing that the Northern States were free. They encountered great hardships—were weeks on their journey, were greatly fatigued, starved, and sustained bruised feet from walking. They would walk all night and hide under rocks and brambles during the day. It took great courage, and many times they were almost ready to give up and die. In fact, many did. I have conversed with many who made the trip.[45]

Wallace celebrated the heroism of those who were ready to risk all in an attempt to escape from slavery, not that of the Underground Railroad conductors. Wallace's account suggests that the Underground Railroad was a much more haphazard affair than the legend portrays.

Gara goes so far as to assert that the majority of fugitives was unaware even of the existence of the Underground Railroad. Henry Bibb, who lived in Kentucky near the Ohio River, had never even heard of the Underground Railroad until he escaped in 1842. Gara emphasizes that the most difficult part of the journey to freedom was through slave states where there was no assistance available beyond the benevolence and kindheartedness of the occasional stranger, both white and black. (As one aged former slave observed, "They was all kind of white folks, even as they is now.") Even in the free states, however, fugitives were often on their own. They might get something to eat, some spare change, and advice to follow the North Star. Such advice was certainly well-intentioned, but it contrasts sharply with the image of well-protected and pampered passengers that is usually projected onto the Underground Railroad. Many fugitive slave narratives tell of traveling long distances through the free states without any organized assistance from the Underground Railroad.[46]

One of the few accounts offered by a fugitive slave who made his way through Washington County illustrates the secondary role that the Underground Railroad played in escape efforts. Tom Stowe, a slave from a plantation near Vicksburg, Mississippi, had accompanied his owner on trips to the Upper South on a number of occasions. Stowe's owner made an annual pilgrimage to the North to race his horses and gamble. They took the steamboat as far as Wheeling and then traveled overland to Morgantown, Virginia, where Stowe was often left behind to look after the racehorses while his owner went north to Saratoga, New York. Stowe would then rejoin his owner when the latter went on "the sporting tour" home in the fall through the slave cities of Baltimore, Richmond, Charleston, and New Orleans.[47] When a Morgantown grocer whose store Stowe frequented suggested to Stowe that he could escape from slavery, Stowe hesitated, even though he knew that the Pennsylvania border was a scant six miles away. For one thing, though he had known the grocer for several years, he feared betrayal. Even more importantly, he did not want to leave his wife and three-year-old child in Mississippi behind.[48]

Stowe's desire for freedom knew no bounds after he returned home from a horse-buying trip to Texas to find his son sold and to witness his wife die of a broken heart. The next time he made the trip to Morgantown, Stowe slipped his owner's watchful eye and decided to trust the grocer. As the grocer instructed, Stowe dutifully followed the ridges along the west side of the Monongahela River northward through Greene and Washington Counties. His apprehensions about being caught came to a fever pitch after six men tried to capture him just outside of Pittsburgh for the two-thousand-dollar reward that had been posted for him. Stowe fended off his would-be captors with a stout hickory stick and managed to escape. At Pittsburgh, he crossed bridges over the Monongahela and Allegheny Rivers at night and then followed the Allegheny northward. Not until he got to Franklin, Pennsylvania, some eighty-five miles north of Pittsburgh, did an utterly exhausted, hungry, and footsore Stowe appeal for help from a black man he met on the road. Only in Franklin did he stumble onto the Underground Railroad. Stowe traveled at least 160 miles before getting any kind of assistance.[49]

Stowe's avoidance of any human contact for as long as possible reflected the pervasive fear that must have haunted all fugitives. As Frederick Douglass, one of the most famous of those fugitives, put it after he had escaped from Baltimore to New York City in 1838, "I was afraid to speak to any one for fear of speaking to the wrong one, and thereby falling into the hands of money-loving kidnappers, whose business it was to lie in wait for the panting fugitive, as the ferocious beasts of the forest lie in wait for their prey. The motto which I adopted when I started from slavery was this—'Trust no man!' I saw in every white man an enemy, and in almost every colored man cause for distrust."[50] Only the prospect of starvation forced Stowe to let down his guard. What is most striking about Stowe's escape is that his confidant in Morgantown apparently knew nothing about the existence of the Underground Railroad in Pennsylvania. (Stowe's account leaves it unclear as to whether this confidant was black or white.) Yet several stations are known to have existed in southern Greene County just across the Pennsylvania line, as the escape of the Clarksburg Nine (described below) makes clear. Whether these stations were known to escaping slaves is much more problematic. Support for abolitionism was notably less in Greene than in Washington County.[51]

Joseph Taper was another slave who escaped through southwestern Pennsylvania on his own. Writing from his new home in St. Catherines, Ontario, in 1840, he explained to his former master that he had fled Winchester, Virginia, in 1837, "in consequence of bad usage." Taper initially made his way to Somerset, Pennsylvania. He found employment there for two weeks, leaving apparently after he saw a two-hundred-dollar reward posted for his capture. He then spent several years working his way northward through Pennsylvania, making stops in Pittsburgh, Butler County, and Erie. Taper had no difficulty finding employment as a hostler and harvester. He proudly reported that he had been able to make twenty-six dollars a month in Erie. Although it is unclear if his wife and young son escaped with him, they had clearly joined him by the time he had settled in St. Catherines. Taber taunted his former owner by concluding, "My wife and self are sitting by a good comfortable fire happy, knowing that there are none to molest or make afraid. God save Queen Victoria." Taber made no mention in his letter of the Underground Railroad or of any organized assistance; he had won his freedom on his own. As Smith has noted, many fugitives took advantage of employment opportunities in the Keystone State, often remaining there and never moving to Canada.[52]

Larger groups of slaves also fled from bondage in western Virginia without any evident knowledge of the Underground Railroad. The escape of nine slaves from near Clarksburg in Harrison County, Virginia, bears out this contention. It is probably the most famous one in the annals of

Washington County history. Boyd Crumrine refers to it in his history, and although Forrest does not mention the escape specifically in his, it is clear that the route followed by the Clarksburg fugitives is the basis for Forrest's description of Underground Railroad routes in the county. However, little has been written about the Greene County part of their escape or its implications for understanding the extent of the Underground Railroad.

The property of Cyrus "Sipe" Ross, the nine male fugitives—three men and half a dozen boys—made their escape in July 1856.[53] Interviewed by a Detroit reporter nearly four decades after his escape from slavery, Thompson, who was still living in Windsor, Ontario, at the time of the interview, is one of the few fugitives who fled through the county who can be identified by name. (Apparently alerted by the newspaper interview, Wilbur Siebert subsequently recorded Thompson's journey to freedom.)[54] His account of his escape from bondage provides an interesting perspective that contrasts sharply with that offered by local Underground Railroad operatives. For Thompson, the real danger lay in making it to the Pennsylvania state line and fending off his would-be captors. For local conductors and historians, who leave the identity of the nine slaves anonymous, the danger came after Thompson and his eight fellow fugitives had made their way to free soil.

Although Clarksburg is only about thirty miles from the Pennsylvania line, Thompson possessed no concrete knowledge about the Underground Railroad. His escape was a blind and desperate grasp for freedom. Motivated by a beating from his owner a few days earlier, Thompson, who was about thirty years old, obtained the immediate inspiration for his flight from someone he describes as a passing "abolitionist." In exchange for a free drink of whiskey, this stranger offered to tell Thompson how to obtain his freedom. This person provided some shrewd practical advice, suggesting that Thompson steal his owner's horses and that he not divulge the time of his intended break for freedom to his fellow slaves on the Ross farm until the very last minute. His advice to follow the North Star until Thompson reached the Pennsylvania line, however, cannot have been worth the free drink. If this passing stranger truly were an abolitionist and not merely a stranger with a penchant for whiskey, he clearly had no knowledge of the Underground Railroad connections that existed a day's travel on horseback to the north. Nevertheless, one night after Ross "came home as full as he could be," Thompson followed the abolitionist's escape plan and made his way northward on horseback with eight fellow slaves.[55]

The dramatic heart of Thompson's escape story took place when Ross and a party of about twenty whites caught up to the fugitives near Blacksville, Greene County, just across the Pennsylvania border, after the latter had abandoned their horses. Armed only with corn cutters, rocks, and a fierce determination, Thompson and his fellow fugitives used the cover of night to improvise an ambush. When the lead member of Ross's party went down under a fusillade of rocks, the rest fled, allowing the fugitives to escape momentarily. For Thompson, the great danger had passed. He makes no mention in the newspaper interview of his subsequent journey via Underground Railroad safe houses through southwestern Pennsylvania to Cleveland and ultimately to Windsor, Canada.[56]

Although local conductors mention this fight, they portray the rescue of the Clarksburg slaves by an Underground Railroad operative as the real drama of the escape. After the fugitives had beaten back their attackers, Elisha Purr, an African American conductor living near Blacksville, Pennsylvania, came to their rescue. Purr took them into his home and hid them. When Ross soon reappeared and demanded entry into Purr's house, Purr stood in the doorway with a shotgun, defiantly proclaiming that anyone who attempted to enter his home without a warrant would be a dead man. After Ross left, Purr guided the fugitives to Waynesburg. From there the fugitives became passive passengers on the Underground Railroad. They were subsequently led through a series of stations in western Greene and Washington Counties, eventually arriving in Little Washington. They were then sent on to Pittsburgh and Canada. (See Map 7.)[57]

The local narrators of this escape, who included several African American conductors, offer no hints that the Clarksburg fugitives in their frantic escape toward the Pennsylvania border had any knowledge of the Underground Railroad. Of course, the conductors' accounts may merely reflect white conventions of the time, which treated fugitives as rather helpless passengers on the Underground Railroad. Although there is much speculation about the possibility of stations in the northern Virginia counties along the Pennsylvania border, there are no documented stations there that would have provided an Underground Railroad spur into the free states. Connie Park Rice has suggested that Gabriel Holland of Monongalia County may have been a participant in the Underground Railroad but provides no evidence.[58]

Another group of slaves that may have escaped through Washington County similarly demonstrated no knowledge of any Underground Railroad

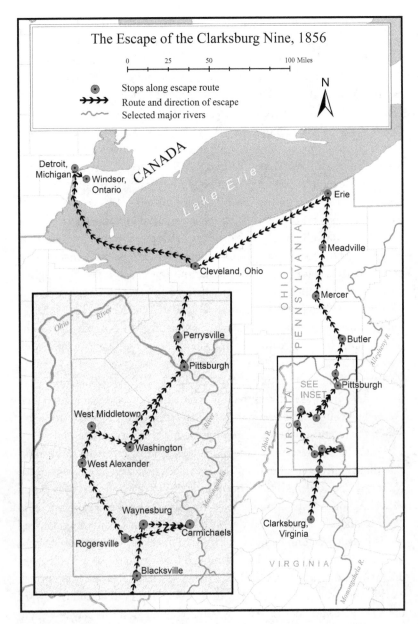

The Escape of the Clarksburg Nine, 1856

0   25   50   100 Miles

Stops along escape route
Route and direction of escape
Selected major rivers

N

CANADA

Lake Erie

Detroit, Michigan
Windsor, Ontario

Erie

Meadville

Cleveland, Ohio

OHIO

PENNSYLVANIA

Mercer

Butler

Ohio River

Perrysville

Pittsburgh

VIRGINIA

SEE INSET

Pittsburgh

Allegheny R.

West Middletown

Washington

West Alexander

Ohio R.

Waynesburg

Rogersville

Carmichaels

Clarksburg, Virginia

Monongahela

Blacksville

VIRGINIA

Monongahela R.

Map 7

connections. In the fall of 1858, ten slaves fled on horseback from Prunty-town in Taylor County, Virginia, located about thirty miles southwest of Morgantown. Their party included five men, three women, and two children. About nine whites and one of their slaves followed the fugitives and caught up with them either in Greene or Fayette County, Pennsylvania. (There are conflicting accounts here. That the fugitives left their horses on the west side of the Monongahela River near Morgantown would suggest that they would have fled through Greene County, which is west of the Monongahela, and subsequently through Washington County.) The attempt to retake the fugitive slaves led to a bloody confrontation in which the slaves prevailed, even though they had just corn cutters, clubs, and makeshift weapons to defend themselves. Newspapers attributed the success of the slaves to the unwillingness of the majority of the pursuing party to engage in what turned out to be a nasty fight. Colonel Armstrong, the owner of some of the fugitives, ended up fighting alone and was nearly killed by a fugitive wielding a corn cutter. Armstrong used his hand to fend off a blow aimed at his head, which left his hand badly mangled and nearly severed his finger. Only Armstrong's appeal to another of his slaves, a man named Dave who had accompanied the search party, saved his life. Dave prevented the fugitives from doing further physical harm to Armstrong. Ironically, Dave appears to have been the father of three of the fugitives. Another member of the search party was badly injured when the runaway slaves made good their escape just before dark. A larger search party the following day was unable to find the fugitives, who were presumed to have escaped to Canada.[59]

Although the escapes of the Clarksburg and Pruntytown slaves indicate that fugitives coming from the South often had no knowledge of the Underground Railroad, the Liberty Line did have a connection between Wheeling and Washington County. This should not be surprising. Ohio County not only shared a border with Washington County but also had residents, such as John Gilmore, living on that border who espoused abolitionist sentiments. Free blacks who resided in Wheeling also served as conductors. "Old" Naylor was the best known of these. According to Forrest, Naylor harbored many fugitive slaves in Wheeling until he could forward them to West Middletown. After the Civil War, the destitute Naylor went to live in West Middletown, where residents donated land and built a house for him so that Naylor could spend the rest of his years in relative comfort.[60]

An undated letter to Dr. Julius LeMoyne also documents the Underground Railroad connection between Wheeling and Washington County:

Altho. unacquainted with you personally, I feel it my duty to acquaint you (confidentially) of a circumstance which transpired here this morning, trusting my information may save a brother man from slavery.

Mr. McClean, former editor of the Argus, of Wheeling, Va., was in my office this (Wednesday) morning, & in conversation enquired who was U.S. Commissioner in Washington, Pa. I did not know—He said, "I suppose if you did you wouldn't tell me, as one of our citizens wants to seize a slave of his there?" He wouldn't tell me who the master was, but I feel it my duty to warn you that, if there is no U.S. Com. there the "master" will soon be there himself, in search—

Please put your colored folks on their guard, especially fugitives from the neighborhood of Wheeling, Va. The bloodhounds are on the scent . . .

Yrs in haste,
J. Heron Foster[61]

The several large-scale escapes that took place in the Wheeling area also bolster the contention that an Underground Railroad station existed there. As noted above, nine slaves owned by Isaac and James Kelly disappeared from Wheeling in 1859. LeMoyne was involved earlier in the successful escape of sixteen slaves from the same vicinity.[62]

Wheeling also contained some residents who were not abolitionists in theory but demonstrated great compassion for runaway slaves in practice. The landlord of the City Hotel was one of these. A slave named Charlie fled westward from Loudoun County, Virginia, after learning that he had been sold. Abandoning his owner's best horse after a fifty-mile gallop, Charlie spent some two weeks traveling the rest of the way to Wheeling on foot. Desperate for food, the fugitive slave entered the City Hotel at daybreak to beg for some bread. The landlord immediately recognized his plight and helped Charlie to cross the Ohio River. Once in Ohio, Charlie again had to find his way northward on his own. Eventually he stumbled onto an Underground Railroad conductor who arranged his passage to Canada through Buffalo.[63]

Although the absolute number of slaves who boarded the Liberty Line in Wheeling bound for destinations in Washington County probably was not large, it was sufficient to alarm slave owners in that city. Wheeling resident Sherrard Clemens in 1847 wrote a letter to Virginia governor William Smith complaining about slaves disappearing from the city. Clemens blamed Washington County abolitionists for enticing local slaves to run away. At least two Washington County Underground Railroad agents—Matthew McKeever and William Asbury—claimed that slaveholders in the neighboring border county had put price tags on their heads. The *Wheeling Intelligencer* also reported on the occasional escape of slaves. Its May 6, 1856, edition noted the disappearance of several slaves. Although the paper speculated that these fugitives had already crossed "the lakes" (meaning the Great Lakes), it urged subscribers to keep a sharp lookout for these missing slaves.[64]

The length and condition of Underground Railroad trackage to the South thus varied considerably depending on location. However light the traffic, lines did operate in the northern panhandle of Virginia between Wheeling and Washington and Wheeling and West Middletown. Connections between Washington County stations and the slaveholding counties to the south, however, were lacking. Slaves hoping to escape northward to freedom had to strike out blindly on their own and hope that fierce determination and good luck would see them through in the absence of reliable information about where to find help. Thus Tom Stowe traveled until he could go no farther before seeking help. Likewise, the fact that the Clarksburg and Pruntytown fugitives had to fight their way to freedom indicates that they had no route map of the Underground Railroad system. The inescapable conclusion is that the Underground Railroad did not extend very far into the slaveholding South from southwestern Pennsylvania. Usually it was only when a fugitive reached the Keystone State that there was there any realistic possibility of systematic aid.

The very metaphor of the Underground Railroad has fostered the illusion that it was a highly organized enterprise whose operations extended deep into the South. Yet it is clear that the Underground Railroad in Washington County had no central leadership. Although individuals such as Matthew McKeever and William Asbury were sometimes referred to as "directors," "engineers," and "presidents," such titles suggest a degree of organization that did not exist. No president directed the operation of this railroad, and no board of directors met quarterly to confer on corporate strategy. LeMoyne's correspondence gives no hint that he ever sought to coordinate the activities of abolitionists and Underground Railroad agents in the county.

The Underground Railroad in Washington County might best be regarded as a very loosely organized network of sympathetic individuals that responded to situations as best it could. Members of the network knew of the stations just above and below their own, but probably did not know much about stations outside of their area. Knowledge of the Liberty Line seems to have been very localized. Conductors in the western part of the county, for example, seem to have been unacquainted with conductors in the eastern part of the county. The memoirs and reminiscences of aging conductors make no reference to Underground Railroad activities on the other side of the county. Matthew McKeever, for example, makes no mention of the network of African American stations that ran through the eastern part of the county. Although the county histories mention by name several black agents who helped white conductors, they display no familiarity with this network. If it were not for Wallace's "A Historical Sketch of the Underground Railroad from Uniontown to Pittsburgh," we would know next to nothing about the role of blacks in eastern Washington County. And if it were not for a few newspaper articles written in the 1880s, we would know nothing about the important network of African American agents who operated in Washington and Canonsburg. Conversely, the African American narrators featured in these articles do not even mention LeMoyne or the McKeevers. A more accurate way of characterizing the local institution would be to say that there were several underground railroads in Washington County whose operations sometimes intersected. Interracial cooperation certainly existed between white and African American agents, but their enterprises were often distinctly different. As Smith has demonstrated in his study of south central Pennsylvania, the lack of African Americans in some townships forced a degree of racial cooperation. As in Washington County, free black communities in Adams County centered in urban areas.[65]

It may be objected that this current lack of knowledge about the organization of the local Underground Railroad is simply a reflection of the utmost secrecy that guarded its operations. There is no evidence whatsoever, however, that a centralized leadership directed traffic on the line. There is also a good deal of evidence that the extent of secrecy involving the Underground Railroad has been vastly overblown.

THE LEGEND OF SECRECY

Part of the fascination with the Underground Railroad undoubtedly stems from the aura of secrecy that supposedly surrounded it. According to the legend, the Underground Railroad operated as a conspiracy of silence. The identity of most agents was carefully guarded to prevent them from being arrested and fined for performing their moral but highly illegal duty. As a reporter observed in the *Washington Observer* paper in 1884, "The severe penalties warranted a degree of secrecy in operations of the Underground Railroad that renders it impossible at this late day to present anything like a complete record, even if it were desirable. Those who were most active kept their counsel so long that they are unable to recall names and dates with certainty."[66] Furthermore, the legend portrays those who were initiated into the mysteries of the organization as being well versed in the techniques of subterfuge. Invariably they employed hidden trapdoors to basements or other secret chambers and tunnels that led to emergency escape routes to foil those who would deny fugitives their freedom.

Modern scholars have offered varied assessments of how secretive the Underground Railroad was. Although they have uniformly questioned whether physical manifestations such as secret tunnels and hidden rooms ever played a major role in its operations, they have been divided about how clandestine its organization and communications were. Gara downplayed the role of secrecy all along the Underground Railroad, noting that many participants bragged openly of their accomplishments and advertised their services. Pinsker likewise believes that most of those who assisted fugitive slaves in Pennsylvania did so publicly and showed little concern for secrecy. Although this may have been true of the state as a whole, border areas such as south central Pennsylvania and Washington County did see a need for secrecy, especially when fugitives had just escaped from slavery. This is hardly surprising. What is surprising is that, at least in Washington County, very casual attitudes about the danger of slave catchers prevailed after the immediate threat of recapture had passed.[67]

Without question, part of the legendary image of the Underground Railroad for secrecy has some basis in local history. Matthew McKeever concealed his role as an Underground Railroad stationmaster from his own family the first time that he harbored runaways on his property. Responding to a Pittsburgh reporter's request in 1880 for stories and information about his Underground Railroad days, McKeever wrote as follows:

> The highest number of slaves I ever shipped at once was eight. They came to our house about daybreak one morning before any of us were up, except a colored man, John Jordan. He took them and hid them in the sheep loft and kept them there four weeks and although we had a

family of eighteen or twenty, not one of them knew they were there, not even my wife.

They were fed all that time out of our spring house and kitchen by John Jordan. There was never anything missed, only the hired girl told Mrs. McKeever somebody was stealing the bread.

That was the first time we ever kept any of them and our reason this time was because we supposed their masters were watching the Canada shore, which happened to be true, but they got tired of waiting.[68]

It would be interesting to know when McKeever finally informed his family about the lodging business he was conducting on the side.

The irony, of course, is that McKeever, LeMoyne, and other individuals in Washington County became notorious or famous for their activities as Underground Railroad agents long before the Freedom Train made its last run. LeMoyne was certainly well known in Wheeling, as the warning note from his informant Foster testifies. Detractors as well as supporters were evidently well aware of LeMoyne's reputation and activities. Following the Christiana Riot of 1851, when fugitive slaves in Lancaster County killed their owner, Edward Gorsuch, in defending their freedom, an anonymous letter writer vilified LeMoyne as the leader of the "aiders & abettors" of treason and murder. His angry correspondent hoped that the Pennsylvania legislature would pass a law to punish those who had advocated resistance to the fugitive slave law, and warned LeMoyne that if such a law passed, "your head will fill a halter yet." The writer went on to discuss an incident in Washington County in which a Virginia slave owner had attempted to arrest his fugitive slave in West Brownsville only to find himself jailed at the behest of local abolitionists. Bloodshed could easily have occurred in Washington County, the writer concluded, if the slave owner had not given up his quarry.[69]

Similarly, the five-hundred-dollar reward placed upon the head of Matthew McKeever and an even heftier price tag on Asbury by Virginia slaveholders indicates that their activities were hardly secretive. Although these men may not have boasted of how many fugitives they had sent along to Canada in the fashion of Wilmington's Thomas Garrett, they took a measured pride in their accomplishments.[70]

McKeever's account reveals one other aspect of how secrecy has been exaggerated in Underground Railroad lore. Although his neighbors later claimed that the McKeever residence had a secret trapdoor leading to a basement hideout, McKeever himself made no mention of this architectural feature in his letter. Instead, he hid fugitive slaves in his sheep loft. At least in rural Washington County, lofts, barns, and other outbuildings provided the typical shelter for fugitives, not secret rooms or chambers. Matthew's brother Thomas hid slaves in his barn. While awaiting transit to Pittsburgh, the nine slaves who escaped from Clarksburg, Virginia, were lodged in barns and sheep sheds during their stay on farms near Canonsburg. Similarly, when Mrs. J. B. Taylor of Monongahela was asked to hide a runaway, she lodged him in the stable that stood at the back of her property along the Monongahela River. Such hiding places reflected the pervasive presence of horses and horse-drawn vehicles in antebellum Washington County. The accounts of primary participants in local Underground Railroad escapes make no mention of secret chambers. The lodgings of fugitive slaves were much more prosaic. Bordewich concurs that "exotic hiding places were rare" throughout the reach of the Underground Railroad.[71]

Despite persistent rumors, secret rooms and tunnels do not appear to have been in the stock-in-trade of urban Underground Railroad agents either. The LeMoyne house is the primary example here. Several architectural studies have concluded that the house has never had tunnels or hidden chambers, as did LeMoyne's biographer, Margaret McCulloch, much to her disappointment. Still, casual visitors still ask about the tunnels, which are rumored to have connected the house to anywhere from the house across the street, owned by LeMoyne's father, all the way to the crematorium at least half a mile away—built by LeMoyne after the Civil War![72]

Rumors of tunnels and secret passageways seem to be a pervasive feature of the Underground Railroad legend. Perhaps some conductor actually incorporated such a feature into his house, but it must have been a very rare conductor. When reputable authorities have investigated claims of tunnels and hidden rooms, they have invariably pronounced that these supposedly clandestine waiting rooms of the Underground Railroad never existed except in heavily romanticized stories. For example, Byron Fruehling, an archaeology student at the University of Akron, concluded after examining seventeen houses associated with the Underground Railroad in Ohio that none of them had secret tunnels or chambers. The Underground Railroad metaphor seems to encourage excessive literalism.[73]

The accommodations that fugitive slaves were offered in the barns, stables, and carriage houses that stood at the back of many town dwellers' lots reflected the social and racial distance that white abolitionists often placed between themselves and the object of their sympathies. As charitable as Matthew McKeever was to fugitive slaves, he was also quite condescending, referring to the people in his charge as "darkies." LeMoyne is one of the few white Underground Railroad figures who apparently housed fugitives in his own dwelling. One piece of evidence here comes from a reminiscence by Curtis Henderson in 1990. Henderson, then eighty-one, recalled his grandmother telling him that his great-grandmother had been born into slavery, escaped in 1853, and was hidden in the LeMoyne house. She subsequently went to live on a farm in Nottingham Township. Usually it was only African American conductors who let fugitives into their own homes.[74]

A good deal of secrecy apparently did surround the transport of passengers aboard the Underground Railroad. When George Walls, a key African American conductor in the Washington network, sought to move the Clarksburg fugitives out of the borough onto farms near Canonsburg, he did so at night and on foot. The Clarksburg Nine eventually rode on wagons the rest of the way to Pittsburgh. Wagons were the preferred mode of transportation if the journey was likely to last into the daylight hours. "The kind of cars we used," Matthew McKeever wrote, "was a good spring wagon, with a chicken coop in each end and the darkies in the middle, with a good cover over them." Joseph A. Gray, a white farmer in northern Greene County, told county historian Earle Forrest that he concealed slaves under grain, hay, or even among pigs when he drove his wagon to the next station in West Alexander. According to Gray, such journeys were made at night to avoid unfriendly eyes. Likewise Asbury hauled runaways in his produce wagon from the Cross Creek area to Pittsburgh.[75]

Fancier transportation was arranged if an element of surprise was desired. Called upon to deliver sixteen fugitives from the Wheeling area to safety, LeMoyne ultimately hired several carriages to accomplish this purpose, thinking that the casual observer would never think to guess that such elegant equipage was carrying their occupants to freedom. Randolph, the slave of James Gillespie, a Southerner who had been educated in Canonsburg, likewise rode to freedom in luxury. Disguised to look nothing like his former self, the fugitive was driven in a barouche directly past his putative owner in Canonsburg.[76]

When fugitive slaves arrived at a station, concerns about safety could be surprisingly lax. Slaves were often hidden in the "Penitentiary Woods" about a mile from West Middletown on the road to Washington. Although the woods appeared solid, they concealed a small cabin and several cleared fields owned by Underground Railroad operatives. Fugitives sometimes spent weeks at this cabin, especially during harvest season. There seems to have been no great urgency to move fugitives along to the next station when work on the harvest was to be done. Such work also enabled fugitives to put some money in their pockets for the journey farther north.[77]

Most of the narrow escapes recorded in the annals of the local Underground Railroad involve fugitives working in the fields, apparently unconcerned about the possibility of being captured. Reynols Parker was hard at work in a field near Centerville when Bob Stump and his gang of slave catchers appeared. Parker ran to the safety of a nearby house and ultimately escaped through the mediation of local abolitionists. Likewise, an unnamed fugitive was caught by his owner while working in one of Matthew McKeever's fields. Fortunately for him, the local justice of the peace was none other than Thomas McKeever, Matthew's brother. McKeever ruled on a technicality that the fugitive was a free man. (For fuller accounts of these incidents, see the next chapter.)[78]

Perhaps the most surprising revelation about secrecy on the Freedom Train comes from the escape of the Clarksburg Nine. Walls led five of the Ross fugitives to James McNary's farm in South Strabane Township. (He had conducted the other four to the farm of William McNary, James's brother, who was much better known for his Underground Railroad activities.) Walls had evidently secured fugitives on the same farm before, because he did not ask James's permission or inform him of his unanticipated guests. Walls hid the runaways in the sheep shed. "I don't think Jim knew they were there," Walls confided in an 1884 interview, "till the boys began to feel lively, and he saw them dance 'Juba' on the top of the shed." (Master Juba was the stage name of William Henry Lane, a free African American who was widely acclaimed as the champion dancer of his time and inventor of the tap dance.) Walls subsequently promised McNary that he would forward the fugitives to Pittsburgh as soon as possible. It is evident, however, that the Clarksburg fugitives had little fear of capture after they had made it to McNary's farm.[79]

The secretive aspects of the local Underground Railroad have been greatly overdone. The publicity given to prominent operatives, the lack of tunnels or hidden rooms, and the lengthy stays of fugitives at harvesttime all suggest that this supposed attribute of the Underground Railroad owes more to legend than to history. Only if one considers the fundamental nature of the Underground Railroad as melodrama, however, does the reason for "secrecy" become apparent.

THE LEGEND OF HAIRBREADTH ESCAPES

It is easy to make the Underground Railroad into a melodrama pitting good against evil. The contrast between good abolitionists and evil slave catchers has been a staple of the Underground Railroad probably since its inception. These stock characters assumed a recognizable identity in the pages of *Uncle Tom's Cabin*. Ranged on one side are the pure-hearted, white abolitionists (usually Quakers, such as Stowe's characters Simeon and Rachel Halliday, who help Eliza and her husband escape) and fugitive slaves with a hunger for freedom. On the other are foulmouthed, whiskey-swilling slave catchers (or the owner himself) with their bloodhounds eager to snatch their victims back into the hell of slavery. One character in *Uncle Tom's Cabin* describes Tom Loker and his gang of slave catchers as being "hot with brandy, swearing and foaming like so many wolves."[80] Whereas Stowe's Quaker abolitionists are the height of sobriety, industriousness, and Christianity, her villains are lazy ne'er-do-wells who take the Lord's name in vain. The hairbreadth escape epitomizes the confrontation between these forces of good and evil and is the central narrative thread of almost all Underground Railroad stories.

In keeping with this legend, Underground Railroad agents typically used their wits instead of violence or force to defeat their adversaries when the freedom of others was at stake. The story of Madelaine LeMoyne's ruse to send the soldier away without his quarry is a perfect illustration of how abolitionists outfoxed and ultimately defeated would-be captors. This is not to suggest that all of the stories told about dramatic escapes are fabrications or inventions. What I suggest instead is that the structure of Underground Railroad narratives inevitably leads to such a confrontation and colors the entire way in which we perceive the Underground Railroad historically.

The story of how Thomas McKeever thwarted the designs of the owner of a fugitive slave from Wellsburg, Virginia, illustrates this narrative thrust. The fugitive had been recaptured near West Middletown on a farm owned by Matthew McKeever. The owner was prepared to follow legal procedure in re-claiming his lost property. Along with the handcuffed slave, he brought a Wellsburg attorney named DeCamp, witnesses, and a writ from a Virginia magistrate into Judge Thomas McKeever's office in West Middletown. According to one observer, the Reverend John Clark, the Methodist minister in West Middletown from 1841 to 1842, slave owners in the Virginia panhandle would have liked nothing better than to see an antislavery judge being forced to remand a fugitive slave back into his owner's custody. McKeever was determined to see a different outcome. He began the hearing by demanding that the handcuffs on the alleged slave be removed, proclaiming, "Our laws do not permit the trial of a man in irons." Because the manacles had been fastened so tightly, a blacksmith had to be summoned to take them off. McKeever took advantage of this lull in the proceedings to whisper to the slave, "Deny everything they attempt to prove and claim you are a free man."[81]

When the trial began, the fugitive followed McKeever's advice and claimed that he was in fact a free black from Carlisle, Pennsylvania. (Another source says Somerset, Pennsylvania.)[82] A witness to the event, D. M. Boyd, recalled in 1884 that the fugitive rattled off the names of acquaintances and friends in that Pennsylvania town in a compelling fashion. Asked to prove his assertions, the runaway requested a ten-day delay in the proceedings so that he could bring in witnesses who would support his claims. McKeever demanded a one-thousand-dollar bond to vouchsafe his appearance. Much to the owner's surprise, Colonel W. W. McNulty of West Middletown agreed to post bail for the fugitive. To the owner's chagrin, McKeever also demanded a five-hundred-dollar bond of him. The owner promptly put down the requisite amount in cash. McKeever refused to accept the money, declaring it "forfeit, not bail." He then ruled that the alleged fugitive was a free man. Cowed by the gathering sympathetic crowd and a group of some forty menacing black men led by William Asbury, the owner could only mutter in frustration as his former slave was escorted from West Middletown as a free man. Asbury forwarded the fugitive to Canada.[83]

Whether grounded in fact or in fiction, stories such as those involving Madelaine LeMoyne and Thomas McKeever create the impression that Underground Railroad personnel were constantly involved in hairbreadth escapes. The relatively small numbers of fugitive slaves escaping through Washington County should help dispel this impression. The record of Julius LeMoyne's activities as an Underground Railroad agent should further underline the point that dramatic escapes were quite exceptional.

LeMoyne's activities on behalf of slaves were a good deal more prosaic than stereotypes of Underground Railroad stationmasters would suggest. (Ironically, the only story of a narrow escape from slave catchers involving the LeMoyne House features his wife, not LeMoyne himself.) LeMoyne often served merely as a sympathetic listener, friend, and adviser to African Americans with pressing problems, as the case of Nelson Gant illustrates. Emancipated in Loudoun County, Virginia, in 1846, Gant was forced to leave the state of Virginia without being able to secure the freedom of his wife, Maria. (Significantly, LeMoyne's biographer turned Gant into an escaped slave.)[84] Gant went to Pennsylvania and apparently sought LeMoyne's help and advice in rescuing his wife from slavery. LeMoyne hosted Gant and put him in touch with Martin R. Delany, the Pittsburgh Underground Railroad agent. Both Gant and his wife landed in jail when the plan to steal Maria out of slavery was betrayed by a fellow black in Washington, DC. A Loudoun County court found the Gants innocent of the charges brought against them, primarily because she refused to testify against him, even in the face of a threat "to be sold to the far south." Gant and his wife were released, although she was released into the custody of her owner. Gant concluded his letter to LeMoyne by relating that it would cost $775 to buy his wife out of slavery. Gant somehow raised this money and settled in Zanesville, Ohio, with his wife later in 1847. There he became financially successful, and according to local tradition in Zanesville, an Underground Railroad operator in his own right.[85]

LeMoyne also performed the humble task of meeting stages bearing ex-slaves who had been emancipated by their owners and helping them on their way. In 1847, for example, Thomas Lee of Cadiz, Ohio, asked LeMoyne to meet a stage bearing a black woman who had recently been freed after Lee somehow managed to convince her owner that slavery was morally wrong. He asked LeMoyne to put the woman on a stage to Cadiz to join her husband, who had run away the year before from a different owner.[86]

Although modern-day visitors are told the story of the six fugitive slaves hiding under Mrs. LeMoyne's bed, historically the most dramatic incident related about LeMoyne's activities involved a far larger number. As LeMoyne's biographer wrote, "The older children long remembered the day when twenty-five slaves at one time were concealed in their mother's big room in the second story."[87]

At first glance, an 1844 letter to LeMoyne seems to support the memory of LeMoyne's children. Writing from Washington, DC., William H. Brisbane requested LeMoyne's assistance in finding lodging in Little Washington for twenty-seven slaves from the Carolinas. The casual reader might suppose that Brisbane's letter was that of a fellow Underground Railroad agent who had rescued these slaves from a life of bondage, and that it was these slaves whom the LeMoyne children remembered being hidden in the house. The small discrepancy in number can be easily understood. Other sources shed a very different light on this story. The March 16, 1844, edition of the *Washington Reporter* announced that twenty-seven emancipated slaves had recently passed through Little Washington under the care of their former owner, the Reverend W. H. Brisbane. Brisbane, a wealthy planter and Baptist minister from South Carolina's Sea Islands, had faced increasing doubts about the morality of slavery after coming into contact with abolitionist literature in 1833. Jailed twice for voicing his misgivings about slavery and subjected to many threats, Brisbane sold his slaves to his brother-in-law in 1835 and moved to Cincinnati. There he came under the influence of James Birney and became thoroughly convinced of the evils of slavery. Brisbane subsequently entered into lengthy negotiations to buy back his former slaves for the purpose of freeing them, an offer that was ultimately accepted. Thus Brisbane was personally supervising the transportation of his freedmen to Ohio when he passed through Washington in 1844. Although the newspaper article does not specify that Brisbane stayed at the LeMoyne house, it seems very likely, given Brisbane's request to LeMoyne for lodging. It also seems likely that the LeMoyne children "remembered" the incident as one involving fugitive slaves and not one in which the former owner was actually leading freed blacks to a new home on free soil. Madeleine LeMoyne, who told of this event decades later, was one year old at the time.[88]

The Brisbane episode suggests that many of the memories and stories that have been told about LeMoyne have been distorted or exaggerated by his reputation as a preeminent Underground Railroad agent. LeMoyne did do something extraordinary by opening up his home to a large group of former slaves, but he is remembered for having done something very different. His abolitionist image has even turned people who have no well-documented affiliations with the Underground Railroad into stationmasters. The campus tour of Washington & Jefferson College touts Davis Hall, about a block away from LeMoyne's East Maiden Street home, as an Underground Railway stop. The claim has no firm foundation. The builder and occupant of the house, Colin M. Reed Sr. (1804–1888), was a banker who has only tenuous connections to the abolitionist cause. Reed does not appear on any list of local abolitionists and is not mentioned in any account as an Underground Railroad agent. Reed's signature on the 1838 petition against the gag rule is his only known affiliation with abolitionism. The probable reason why Reed's house is claimed as a stop is that his nephew, George W. Reed, married LeMoyne's daughter Madeleine. The marriage, however, did not take place until 1907, long after Colin M. Reed and LeMoyne were both dead.[89]

LeMoyne did perform some of the tasks usually associated with Underground Railroad agents. For example, he safeguarded fugitives who were being hidden elsewhere in Washington. LeMoyne's help was solicited when a group of sixteen slaves fled from Wheeling for fear that they would be sold farther south. This fear had arisen when their owners (Crumrine identifies them as people named Wilson and Mitchell) vowed to sell them after the owners discovered their slaves were attending a church school to learn how to read and write. The slaves bolted for freedom and found their way to the home of a Mrs. Houston near Washington. It took LeMoyne two days to arrange for carriages to take the runaways across the Ohio River. LeMoyne slept in Houston's barn for two nights to protect the widow and the fugitives from any harm.[90]

If we discount the apocryphal story of the six slaves hiding under the bed, however, there is not much high drama or romance in LeMoyne's Underground Railroad activities. Vicious bloodhounds and foulmouthed, hard-drinking slave catchers simply do not figure in LeMoyne's assistance to runaways. Nor do secret rooms and hidden tunnels in the basement of LeMoyne's house. The legend of the Underground Railroad has obscured his real role as an abolitionist and as an agent.

If LeMoyne helps us to separate fact from fantasy about the Underground Railroad, he also serves to illustrate the problems of evidence that confront any historian dealing with this popular institution. More is known about LeMoyne than any other Underground Railroad operative in Washington County. In many instances the only evidence linking an individual to the Underground Railroad is a mention in a county history. In LeMoyne's case, we have primary documents in the form of letters to him and a full-scale biography. Yet even with LeMoyne the evidence regarding his Underground Railroad activities is scant, consisting of no more than half a dozen sources. (So far as is known, LeMoyne himself never offered any autobiographical observations about his days as an operative.) These sources clearly establish LeMoyne's involvement in the Underground Railroad (witness his help to the Wheeling fugitives), but they do not offer any conclusive proof that fugitive slaves stayed in his home. The preponderance of the evidence only allows that it is very likely that LeMoyne harbored fugitive slaves in his residence. As the authors of the LeMoyne House's nomination as a place of national historical significance concluded, "It is reasonable to assume that Julius LeMoyne was occasionally called upon to aid fugitive slaves, among his many other antislavery activities and his other social concerns. His home at 49 East Maiden Street was clearly a center of antislavery activity in many forms and it is quite likely that he and his family gave aid to fugitives in one form or another."[91] Secretary of the Interior Bruce Babbitt, on September 25, 1997, designated the LeMoyne House as a National Historic Landmark.

LeMoyne's varied antislavery efforts as speaker, correspondent, antislavery agent, friend to African Americans, and occasional Underground Railroad conductor may seem very mundane and unexciting compared to the dramatic stories of narrow escapes and desperate battles with slave catchers that are the staple of the Underground Railroad legend. That there were confrontations locally between the defenders of fugitive slaves and those chasing them is undeniable, as the case of the fugitive slave brought before Thomas McKeever illustrates. Similarly, the Clarksburg and Pruntytown fugitives fought desperately so that they could continue their quest for freedom. The point to be made here is that hairbreadth escapes were extraordinarily rare, just as the escape of fugitive slaves was a comparatively rare event. Such escapes have become so central to the Underground Railroad legend that they have overshadowed the real accomplishments and sacrifices of abolitionists and distorted our understanding of the Underground Railroad.

THE LEGEND OF WHITE ABOLITIONISTS

The final element of the Underground Railroad legend is that it was predominantly a white operation. One of Gara's major criticisms in 1961 of the existing scholarship on the Underground Railroad is that it focused almost exclusively on white agents and largely ignored African Americans. Gara's criticism is twofold. First, previous writers on the Underground Railroad put whites in charge of its operation and acknowledged the participation of blacks only in the equivalent role of porters. Second, these writers failed to recognize that escaping slaves themselves bore most of the burden. Their accounts typically portray the fugitives as hapless, passive passengers, while the white engineers emerge as the heroes.[92]

The scholarship of the last four decades has unearthed the major contributions African Americans made to the Liberty Line. In Pennsylvania, Charles L. Blockson's *The Underground Railroad in Pennsylvania* (1981) and William J. Switala's *Underground Railroad in Pennsylvania* (2001) have added greatly to our knowledge of biracial participation in the Keystone State. Fergus M. Bordewich's *Bound for Canaan* (2005) and Keith Griffler's *Front Line of Freedom* (2004) have likewise emphasized the critical role that

African Americans played in the Underground Railroad. Meanwhile, the republication in 2005 of William Still's *The Underground Rail Road*, which originally appeared in 1872, has made available the most complete contemporary record kept by any stationmaster, white or black. Still's detailed notes on the hundreds of slaves who escaped through Philadelphia make the contributions of African Americans, as both Underground Railroad agents and engineers of their own escapes, abundantly clear. Renewed interest in the Underground Railroad at the local level since the 1990s has also emphasized the African Americans' active participation in the road to freedom.[93]

This element of the Underground Railroad legend has been so thoroughly critiqued and exposed that it might seemingly not warrant inclusion here. Yet it is important to recognize that the overwhelming amount of evidence available today to the student of the Underground Railroad has been shaped by the white abolitionist legend. It was whites who wrote the county histories that began to appear in the 1880s, and it was whites who paid the subscriptions that would have their names appear in the commemorative biographies published in the 1890s. It was white newspaper reporters who interviewed the surviving abolitionists and stationmasters in the closing decades of the nineteenth century and in the early twentieth century. Although they occasionally spoke to black informants, these reporters and historians wrote from a decidedly white perspective. Only Howard Wallace's brief pamphlet, published in 1903, has survived to tell the story of the Underground Railroad in Washington County from a black perspective, and it is not mentioned in any of the local histories. In short, the source materials for any history of the Underground Railroad reflect an almost thoroughly white perspective. They reflect the assumption that white abolitionists were the true heroes of the Underground Railroad.

Washington County is quite fortunate in that the county historians and newspaper reporters who recorded anecdotes about the Underground Railroad did not totally neglect African Americans. Forrest, for example, acknowledged that Tar Adams had been working as an Underground Railroad conductor long before any white person locally enlisted in the abolitionist cause. Were it not for Forrest, we might not be aware of Old Naylor, the free black in Wheeling who directed slaves to safe houses across the Pennsylvania border. Without Crumrine, we might not know about Samuel W. Dorsey, the black barber in Washington who helped to forward fugitive slaves to Canada. In fact, Crumrine in his very brief account of the local institution was much more forthcoming about black participants in the Underground

Railroad than whites. As he wrote in 1882, "It is too soon to make known the names of persons who assumed the responsibility of caring for and aiding those fugitives on their way." He cloaked the identity of white Underground Railroad personnel because there were those in the local community who still believed that a law was a law and ought to be observed. He applied this stricture to whites only, observing that "no one would impute much wrong to the colored man who became the conductor of his brethren from slavery to freedom."[94] And were it not for an enterprising newspaper reporter who interviewed Walls and other retired black conductors for a series of articles on the local Underground Railroad in the 1880s, the surviving materials for a history of the institution would be a good deal poorer.

Even when these local histories and newspaper articles include black agents, they typically do so in a condescending manner. Forrest portrays Tar Adams as a sort of court jester who deceives slave catchers by playing lame. One would never know from his account that Adams was a skilled gunsmith. Osborne Mitchell, in a 1908 newspaper article, likewise portrayed Old Naylor as a deceiver who took in audiences with his performance: "To all appearances he was drunk three-fourths of the time; nobody remembered when he had not been so." Although Naylor's inebriated behavior misled nearly everyone about his furtive role as an Underground Railroad agent, some were not so easily fooled. But when they attempted to interrogate Naylor about his activities, he was always too intoxicated to answer their questions. African American conductors function primarily in these accounts by feigning ineptitude, and never by playing it straight.[95]

Significantly, Forrest ignores or overlooks several accounts of the local Underground Railroad that portray blacks as full-fledged participants in the operation. Forrest made no mention of Wallace's pamphlet detailing Underground Railroad operation in the eastern part of the county. Wallace's account suggests that African Americans were the head engineers in that section of the county—a possibility that the local histories never even contemplate. Forrest also neglected to mention Walls's major role in running Underground Railroad operations in Washington County. One knowledgeable observer in 1884 regarded Walls as the preeminent figure in the local Liberty Line, but his name has not appeared in any of the local histories that discuss the Underground Railroad.[96] An examination of the Underground Railroad routes that traversed Washington County makes it abundantly clear that African Americans played a crucial role locally in the running of the Liberty Line.

CHAPTER FOUR

The Underground Railroad Network
in Washington County

The Underground Railroad has typically been described in terms of the "routes" that it operated for slaves escaping to freedom. For many reasons, however, the terminology of routes and the Underground Railroad metaphor associated with it can be extremely misleading. For starters, this terminology suggests that fugitive slaves were passive passengers aboard the Freedom Train and ignores the reality that many fugitives escaped on their own with minimal organized assistance. As David Smith has observed, "routes" also suggests that escapes from slavery were "too regularized."[1] The "stations," "conductors," and "baggage" of the Underground Railroad metaphor lend themselves all too easily to the idea that the Underground Railroad adhered to a strict timetable with scheduled stops along the line. The metaphor suggests as well that there was a heavy volume of trains carrying fugitive slaves north. As I argued in the previous chapter, Washington County did not constitute a main line of the Underground Railroad. Instead, it was a seldom-used branch line that saw only occasional traffic. For all of these reasons, the Underground Railroad might better be conceived as a network of safe houses—"the network to freedom," as the National Park Service designates it—rather than as a map of railroad routes.[2]

This network in Washington County was largely decentralized. Just as in south central Pennsylvania, those fleeing slavery dictated this decentralization. Many were unaware of the availability of help and hesitated to ask for it because of the threat of betrayal. Accordingly, fugitives surfaced in unpredictable places and "boarded" the Underground Railroad in a haphazard fashion.[3] The Underground Railroad locally did not operate according to any timetable or fixed schedule. Only in cases where a free black was able to initiate assistance for escaping slaves, as Old Naylor did in Wheeling, does there seem to have been anything like a regular "route."

Another reason for regarding the local Underground Railroad as a network instead of a linear route is that potential dangers often dictated that fugitive slaves be sent in a different direction. A fugitive might well be conducted in a circuitous, zigzag path. Even though local historians took pains to point out that conductors might take fugitives in roundabout ways to avoid pursuers, they continued to describe the Underground Railroad in terms of routes.

Another problem is that the routes described with such seeming authority by earlier local historians are sometimes based on rumor, hearsay, and flimsy evidence. Once in print, however, these routes have acquired a life of their own and reappear whenever a subsequent writer discusses the operations of the local Underground Railroad. Earle Forrest, for example, claimed in his county history that one route began at Crowe's Mills in western Greene County and then proceeded through a series of stations into western Washington County. Without citing Forrest, Margaret McCulloch, in her biography of Julius LeMoyne, likewise described a route originating at Crowe's Mills that led to stations up the line. Although William Switala, in his 2001 study of the Underground Railroad in Pennsylvania, acknowledges Forrest as the source of his information, he too describes a route that entered the Keystone State at Crowe's Mills. The difficulty is that Forrest provided no evidence for the existence of a station at Crowe's Mills. No prior source mentions Crowe's Mills either. Perhaps Forrest had some unknown informant who told him about this site, but we have no way of knowing this. The repetitive description of Underground Railroad routes makes it seem as if they are based on authoritative sources and hard evidence even when this may not be the case. As noted in chapter 3, many Underground Railroad stations have been manufactured out of thin air. Repetition makes it true.[4]

Finally, historians of the local Underground Railroad have often constructed a route on the basis of a single escape. Boyd Crumrine, in his 1882 history, described how the Clarksburg Nine were conducted to freedom by means of a series of "stations" in Greene and Washington Counties. Crumrine's portrayal of this escape appears to have become the basis for the route supposedly followed by numerous fugitives escaping through Washington County. Most of the stops that Forrest mentions in the western part of the county show up initially in Crumrine's account. Howard Wallace's description of the paths followed by fugitives through eastern Washington County, which was based upon personal observations and experience, stands as a notable exception to these accounts, which reconstructed routes long after the Underground Railroad ceased operations. Wallace's account, which names specific individuals, has a much more solid foundation of evidence than others.

The relatively small number of fugitives involved, the lack of hard evidence for some of the routes, and the tendency of authors to repeat previously described pathways to freedom are all problematic. Considerable caution should thus be used in reading the description of so-called routes in Washington County that follows.

A final cautionary note is in order before proceeding, and that is that the facts about the Liberty Line have often been blended so thoroughly with the legends that it is difficult to disentangle them. The only source we have for much of the information about the local Underground Railroad comes from stories recorded by local historians, who tended to have a highly romanticized view of the Liberty Line. As Cheryl LaRoche has observed, the difficulty lies in detecting parts of the story that are "false and misremembered" from the core truth that they may contain.[5]

The geographical situation of Washington County meant that fugitive slaves arrived from three directions instead of just from the south. (See Map 8.) To the west lay the northern panhandle of Virginia, the tier of four counties between the Pennsylvania border and the Ohio River. Hancock, Brooke, Ohio, and Marshall counties all shared a border with Washington County. The panhandle was slaveholding country, although barely so. It resembled Washington County before the passage of Pennsylvania's gradual abolition law. Brooke County's inhabitants included 237 slaves out of a total population of 7,040 in 1830, or 3.3 percent. Ohio County, Brooke County's southern neighbor, had 365 slaves out of 15,590 inhabitants in that same year, or 2.3 percent. By 1860 Brooke County's slave population had fallen to 18 and Ohio's to 100. Some of these slaves made their way a short distance east and found their way to the Underground Railroad in Washington County.[6]

Fugitive slaves also arrived in Washington County from the south. To the immediate south of Washington County lay Greene County and then, crossing the Mason-Dixon Line, Monongalia County, Virginia. Monongalia contained roughly the same concentration of slaveholders as the

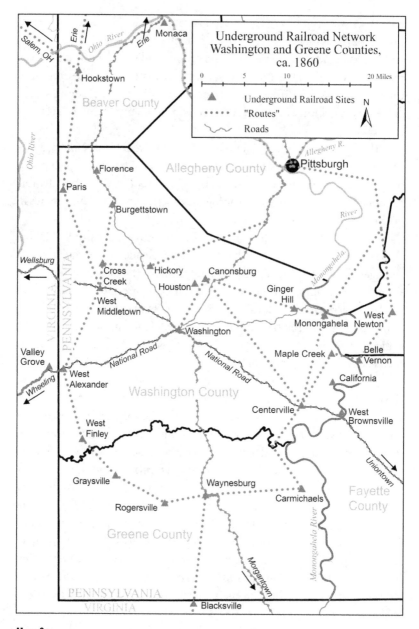

Map 8

panhandle counties; the county in 1830 contained 362 slaves, or 2.6 percent of its population. By 1860 the slave population had fallen to 101. There is no consensus on the role played by the Underground Railroad in Monongalia County. Some have suggested that the Monongahela River, which flowed north from Morgantown in Monongalia County to Pittsburgh along the eastern boundaries of Greene and Washington Counties, provided a natural highway to freedom. Crumrine, however, dismisses this notion on grounds that slave owners expected fugitives to boat down the Monongahela River. Consequently, freedom seekers avoided the river. The story of Tom Stowe, particularly the advice he received to follow the river northward, suggests that the river did provide guidance for escaping slaves. Connie Park Rice has suggested that Gabriel Holland of Morgantown may have been a participant in the Underground Railroad, but there is little concrete evidence about Monongalia County.[7]

The Monongahela River did figure in at least one escape plan. At the outset of the Civil War in 1861, still another group of slaves from Clarksburg, Virginia, made a bid for freedom. Armed with improvised weapons made out of farm implements, this group stole horses from their owners and made their way to Morgantown. Although their owners caught up with them there and took back the horses, they allowed this small but defiant army of slaves to head north. The slaves apparently boated down the Monongahela to Pittsburgh, where they settled.[8]

Some fugitive slaves who arrived from the east also escaped through Washington County. The immediate source of these fugitives was Uniontown in neighboring Fayette County, a major hub on the Underground Railroad operated by African Americans. Although the more distant sources of the runaways who made it to Uniontown are obscure, the National Road, running out of Maryland in a northwesterly direction toward Uniontown, likely played an important role. The unnamed fugitive slave who killed one of his would-be capturers near Mt. Washington Tavern in 1845 was certainly using the National Road to escape. It is highly likely that Dan Lockhart and George Johnson followed the National Road in their journey to freedom in Pittsburgh from the upper Shenandoah Valley. The black teamsters who plied their trade along the National Pike offered the most obvious means by which escaping slaves could have found their way into western Pennsylvania. One of the few known incidents featuring the National Pike as an escape route, however, involved a stagecoach. When Robert Davis, a sympathetic passenger from New England, came across a sixteen-year-old runaway named Sam, he offered to pay Sam's fare to freedom.[9] As elsewhere, free blacks seem to have been the primary agents in assisting fugitive slaves escaping via the National Road. Wallace mentions two agents in Uniontown by name: Curry and Payne. The Underground Railroad diverged in a number of directions from Uniontown: to the northeast, toward Blairsville; to the northwest, toward Pittsburgh; and to the west, toward Washington County.[10]

The direction from which a fugitive arrived in Washington County greatly influenced which network he traveled through the county. Although these routes had no fixed roadbeds and allowed for improvisation in case of emergencies, a fugitive coming from Uniontown was likely to be put on the eastern network of the Underground Railroad through the county. Those coming from the direction of Wheeling were apt to travel the western network. Those arriving from the south could end up traveling on any of these networks.

Virtually all of the existing Underground Railroad narratives assume that the destination of fugitives was Canada. However, Michael Wayne's work on the 1861 Canadian census indicates that far fewer slaves found refuge in Queen Victoria's realm than was once thought. The local narratives overlook the fugitives who stayed in Washington County or other parts of the free states. Curtis Henderson's great-grandmother provides one example of a fugitive who took up residence in Nottingham Township in eastern Washington County. Another is Alfred Crockett (1820–1900), who escaped from Frederick, Maryland, in 1855 and made his way to Pittsburgh. After working in Pittsburgh for several years, he settled in the borough of Washington with his family in the early 1860s.[11] More than a quarter of the borough's black population of 217 people in 1850 had been born south of the Mason-Dixon Line, but how many of these were fugitives is impossible to know. Wallace's account suggests that considerably more fugitives who had passed through the county made Pittsburgh their home until the passage of the Fugitive Slave Act of 1850 put the safety of former runaways living there in jeopardy. "It was very strict," Wallace observed, "and the slaves were compelled to flee for a place of safety." According to one estimate, more than two hundred Pittsburgh blacks, including fugitives and free blacks, fled the city for Canada within two weeks of the passage of this law.[12]

Information about the networks followed by fugitives fleeing to Canada out of the county is sketchy at best. Most accounts mention simply that Canada was the destination of these runaway slaves. Pittsburgh crops up most frequently as an intermediate place of refuge. From there, fugitive slaves were sent to Cleveland or directed to follow the Allegheny River and the tributaries of the Ohio north. The main destinations, in addition to Cleveland, were Erie and Buffalo. Presumably boats ferried fugitives on the last leg of their journey across Lake Erie or the bridge over the Niagara River. Tom Stowe made his way to Buffalo before crossing over this bridge into Canada.[13] In the one case where the itinerary followed by passengers from Washington County is known, the path to Canada was a good deal more indirect. In 1856, the group of nine fugitives from Clarksburg was directed to Pittsburgh and Cleveland. They were then sent to Detroit and finally across the Detroit River to Windsor, Canada.[14]

Not all of the Underground Railroad traffic out of Washington County went to Pittsburgh. A secondary network led out of the county along its western border into Beaver County. The northernmost sites that have been identified on this network are Paris and Burgettstown. According to a Beaver County historian, the Underground Railroad followed Raccoon Creek north out of Washington County into Beaver County, where it emptied into the Ohio River several miles west of Monaca. After crossing the river, fugitives were then taken to Black Hawk. Here the Washington County network probably joined those out of Pittsburgh that led to adjacent Columbiana County, Ohio. Julius LeMoyne probably directed the carriages that he had hired to transport the group of sixteen fugitives to this western network.[15]

THE WESTERN NETWORK

Fugitive slaves came into western Washington County from the south and from the west. Thus several pathways to freedom converged in the western part of the county. One came from the Virginia counties due south of Pennsylvania; one came from the panhandle counties to the southwest; and one originated in Ohio and Brooke counties that were due west.

Traditional accounts hold that the southwestern path connected a network in Greene County that began at Crowe's Mills on the western Pennsylvania line. (See Map 9.) These sites would have aided fugitive slaves fleeing from Marshall and Wetzel Counties in Virginia. Other Greene County stations along this pathway included Isaac Teagarden's on Wheeling Creek and the farm of Joseph Gray near Graysville. The Gray family often hid fugitives in a dense thicket about a half mile from their farmhouse. From Graysville

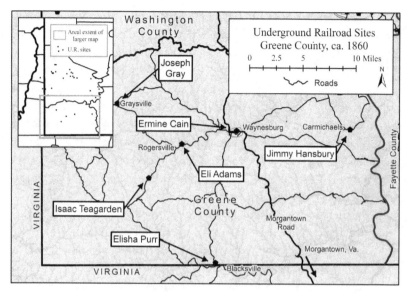

Map 9

fugitives were apparently taken to safe houses in western Washington County or to Waynesburg, the Greene County seat, where Ermine Cain, a free black who worked as a barber, directed fugitives to the next "stop." Cain often directed fugitives to a network in western Washington County.[16]

Several pathways have been identified that led from Virginia across the southern border of Pennsylvania into Greene County, none of them well documented. The first entered Pennsylvania near Mount Morris, approximately where I-79 enters the state today. Slaves fleeing from Morgantown could have followed this route into Pennsylvania. This route had three separate branches that left Mount Morris. The main one led to Bob Maple's mill in Mapletown and then crossed the Monongahela River near Grays Landing; it led to Uniontown. The second branch headed due north to Waynesburg, while the third branch ran northwest to Graysville.[17]

The escape of the Clarksburg Nine through Greene County is the only one for which substantial evidence exists. It illustrates another path by which fugitives made their way from the Mason-Dixon Line through Waynesburg to western Washington County. According to Cain, it was Elisha Purr who put the fugitive slaves from Clarksburg on the Underground Railway and conducted them from the border village of Blacksville to Waynesburg. Cain hid the fugitives there until he thought it safe to move them elsewhere. Cain's reputation as an Underground Railroad agent was apparently well known, because "Sipe" Ross, the owner of these slaves, offered Cain three hundred dollars a head if he would reveal their whereabouts. Cain refused, saying, "No sir; if I knowed where your slaves are, all the money in the South wouldn't git me to tell." David Thompson and his fellow runaways subsequently followed a zigzag path across Greene and then Washington counties. Cain directed them first to the home of Jimmy Hansbury, a free black living in Carmichaels. Cain then routed the runaways to Eli Adams, near Rogersville, about seven miles west of Waynesburg. Thompson also says that he stayed with Joseph McCurdy, who is listed as a mixed-race individual living near Rogersville, in his flight through Greene County. The Clarksburg Nine were then taken to West Alexander and West Middletown, stations in western Washington County. The fugitives from Ross found refuge in Little Washington before being transported to Pittsburgh and ultimately Canada.[18]

The path followed by these fugitives through Greene and Washington Counties illustrates the Underground Railroad's lack of a fixed itinerary. The most direct way from Waynesburg to Washington was almost due north. The runaways, however, were sent east to Carmichaels, then west, then north, and finally southeast to Washington. They must have traveled more than three times the twenty-five miles between Waynesburg and Washington.

Fugitive slaves traveling from the west also found refuge at a network of safe houses along the western border of Washington County. (See Map 10.) Considerable evidence exists that there was Underground Railroad activity in Wheeling, Virginia, located in Ohio County. One indication is the letter written by a Wheeling newspaper editor to LeMoyne, noted in chapter 3, warning him of the arrival of slave catchers. Another is the story of Old Naylor or "Free" Naylor, so called because he was a free black. According to Forrest, Naylor "devoted his life to helping slaves on their way to freedom" and had many places to secure runaways in Wheeling until they could be forwarded to West Middletown. Although Naylor was from time to time suspected of helping runaways, he played drunk convincingly enough when the occasion demanded that his questioners left feeling that "such a drunken fool could have had no hand in abducting their slaves."[19]

Naylor and other free blacks in Wheeling directed escaping slaves to western Washington County. Wheeling probably provided most of the

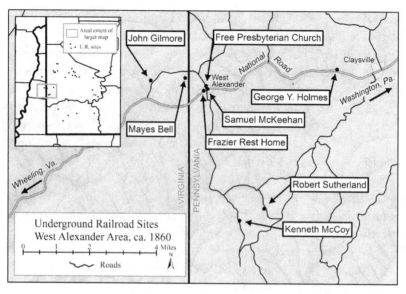

Map 10

fugitives seeking refuge in these border stations, although Wellsburg, just up the Ohio, provided some. LeMoyne assisted a group of sixteen fugitives from Wheeling on one occasion, and the 1860 census provides evidence of another group of nine slaves who escaped from Wheeling. Farmers who lived in the panhandle counties that shared a border with Pennsylvania also saw their slaves disappear. James W. Rice, who lived just across the border from West Alexander, Pennsylvania, claimed that his father lost twenty slaves in this fashion. Unlike many slave owners, his father did not pursue his former bondsmen. The censuses between 1830 and 1860, however, raise some perplexing questions about Rice's claims. They reveal that William Rice did not own any slaves during that time period. He lived in Donegal Township in Washington County until moving with his growing family to Ohio County, Virginia, at some point in the 1830s. Nor do any free blacks appear to have lived on his farm.[20]

Three major safe houses can be identified in western Washington County. A reporter for the *Washington Observer* in 1904 characterized them (with some exaggeration) as "the three most important southern Pennsylvania stations" of the Underground Railroad to which "all slaves coming up through Virginia were directed." The southernmost one was the farm of

Kenneth McCoy, some five miles south of West Alexander. McCoy had become the leader of abolitionist forces in West Finley Township in the 1840s and one of the founders of the Free Presbyterian Church in West Alexander. On one occasion he is reported to have sheltered eleven runaways in his barn. Another account says that as many as seventeen escaping slaves found temporary safety in the basement of McCoy's house. Neither of these accounts can be independently verified. In an interview, Harold Hutchison remembered being shown when he was a young teenager in the early 1930s the basement room where fugitive slaves were hidden. Although the original stone farmhouse is no longer standing, Hutchison easily pointed out where it was located. Mrs. McCoy, then in her "high eighties," he recalled, showed him the room at the back of the basement and then told a family anecdote passed down from pre-Civil War times. If a group of slave catchers was hotly pursuing a fugitive, her father-in-law would insist that they stay for a meal. To make sure that the fugitive got a good head start, Kenneth McCoy would read Psalm 119, a particularly long psalm, before the meal. Kenneth's son John also became involved in the Underground Railroad.[21]

According to Forrest, the farm of S. Mayes Bell was used as a hiding place if the McCoy farm was being closely watched. Bell lived just across the Virginia line to the northwest of West Alexander. Bell was among the abolitionist leaders of eastern Ohio County until he moved to West Alexander in 1856. Robert Sutherland's farm on Walnut Valley Road, on the opposite side of the ridge from the McCoy farm, may also have been used as an emergency hiding place. Sutherland was one of the founding members of the antislavery society that began meeting at McCoy's house in the mid-1840s. His obituary states that he "frequently aided hound-hunted slaves to escape to free territory by the 'underground railway system.'" Another place of refuge in West Finley Township was the farm of Michael Hackaress, an African American who lived in the southern part of the township.[22]

The second of these "stops" along the western border was the village of West Alexander. West Alexander stood at the crossroads of two networks, one coming up from Greene County and the other from Wheeling and the west along the National Road. The most notable Underground Railroad activist in West Alexander was Dr. Samuel McKeehan, whose house still stands at the corner of the Old National Road and Liberty Street. A reporter for the *Washington Observer* offered the following highly romanticized account of McKeehan's activities shortly after the turn of the twentieth century: "Sometimes they would rush to this haven of safety with the bay of

4. Grave marker of Kenneth McCoy, West Alexander, PA

hounds ringing in their ears, and not infrequently the sturdy old doctor was hard put to keep his house free from the eager search of the men who looked on the dark skinned man and women as so many chattels." Dr. Mc-Keehan supposedly scoured the woods around his house to search for fugitive slaves who might be lurking there. In 1865, at the age of ninety, McKeehan stood on the outskirts of West Alexander to welcome home returning Union veterans. Now that the Union had been restored and slavery was dead, he proclaimed, he was ready to die. He died the following year.[23]

Another West Alexander area resident who became an unlikely participant in the Underground Railroad activities was the previously mentioned James W. Rice. Although Rice claimed that West Alexander abolitionists had caused his father, who lived three miles west of West Alexander in Virginia, the loss of numerous slaves, Rice himself sympathized with fugitive slaves. (Rice offered no explanation as to why he himself sided with runaway slaves rather than with their owners.) In 1904 he recollected that he had encountered posses demanding to know where a gang of sixteen slaves had escaped. When Rice later caught sight of these runaways, he directed them to a hiding place in the woods and subsequently to Dr. McKeehan.

5. Home of Samuel McKeehan, West Alexander, PA. Photo courtesy of Deborah Mainwaring.

Rice also recalled seeing a slave driver by the name of Sam Madden taking coffles of slaves numbering from ten to twenty-five through West Alexander to Wheeling.[24]

Other West Alexander area residents identified as being involved in the Underground Railroad include John Gilmore, John Atkinson and his son Samuel, and the three Witham brothers, Peregrine, George, and William. Most of them lived just across the Virginia line. Gilmore lived on a farm little more than a mile from West Alexander. As noted previously, his barn hosted the first antislavery meeting in this area. Reportedly the barn also later sheltered a number of fugitive slaves. Samuel Atkinson, described in his obituary in 1926 as "probably the last of the group of underground railroad conductors" in the area, lived as a youth on his father's farm on Castleman Run in Brooke County, Virginia. He escorted a number of escaping slaves to Thomas McKeever's station in West Middletown, Pennsylvania. In a letter printed in the *Claysville Recorder* in 1916, Atkinson recounted how abolitionists sometimes aroused the ire of their neighbors. One neighbor who owned four slaves had his bondsmen attempt to set fire to the Atkinsons' gristmill on three separate occasions. "The man was too cowardly to fire my father's buildings himself," Atkinson noted, "but sent the colored people to do it." Only the fact that his brothers were sleeping in the gristmill saved the structure. After being caught, the slaves assumed responsibility for the attempted arson, but the Atkinsons apparently had other ideas about who was responsible. The slaves' owner subsequently left the region for the west. Samuel Atkinson also helped to deliver in September 1860 what he called the "last consignment of slaves on the Underground Railroad." A slave family consisting of a man, woman, and child took shelter in his father's house that fall. After eluding a search party, Atkinson and his brother were able to deliver the family safely to West Middletown.[25]

Underground Railroad conductors in the West Alexander area evidently directed traffic along three different networks toward freedom. The preferred route involved sending fugitives to West Middletown, some twelve miles to the north, and was the one followed by the Clarksburg fugitives. Escaping slaves were also sometimes sent directly from West Alexander east along the National Road to Washington. A third pathway apparently led off toward the northwest to the Ohio River, but little is known about it. Samuel Atkinson mentions that his uncle, George Trimble, operated a station near Salem, Ohio, in Columbiana County. According to Atkinson, this was heavily traveled in the three years before the Civil War. He reported that as many as twenty-six fugitives stayed in his uncle's barn at one time.[26]

West Middletown was often regarded as the center of Underground Railroad activity in the county. (See Map 11.) It served as a haven for fugitive slaves coming from West Alexander, Wheeling, and Wellsburg, on the Ohio River. According to legend, nearly every house in West Middletown at one time harbored a fugitive. The actual history is not so simple. As noted previously, the pastor of West Middletown's Presbyterian Church, Samuel Taggart, held such strong antislavery views that he ended up splitting the congregation. Some thirty members left the church in 1844 to form the Patterson's Mill Associated Presbyterian Church and hired a pastor from the South.[27]

The leading family in the local Underground Railroad was undoubtedly the McKeevers. Three prominent abolitionists came from the family: William and his two sons, Matthew and Thomas.[28] William has been described as one of the first abolitionists in Washington County. As noted in chapter 2, his outrage at seeing a chained coffle of slaves being driven through the village of West Middletown prompted his becoming an abolitionist. Although

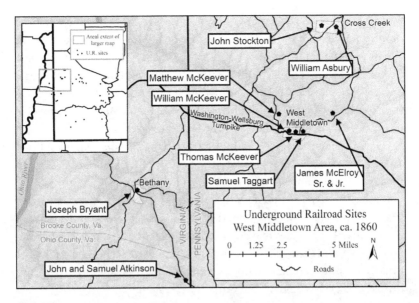

Map 11

some rumors link William McKeever, who died in 1838, with the Underground Railroad, there is no concrete evidence of his involvement.[29]

It was the brothers Matthew and Thomas McKeever who became famous locally as Underground Railroad conductors. Matthew figures prominently in virtually every story told about the Underground Railroad in West Middletown. Although Thomas is sometimes mentioned as a participant, he does not appear in many of the stories. It is Matthew, for example, who is the principal character in the anecdotes told by Captain James McElroy. Abolitionism ran in the McElroy family. His father was an abolitionist who operated a mill not far from West Middletown. McElroy relates that, when he was about fifteen, McKeever sent two slaves to his father with instructions to pass them along to Paris, the next station, in the northwestern corner of Washington County. The younger McElroy was assigned the task of driving the family carriage at night to Paris. McElroy later learned that the two slaves had arrived safely in Canada.[30]

The other anecdote is a good deal more colorful. Several different versions of it exist, but McElroy's is by far the most interesting. According to McElroy, an escaping slave stumbled into West Middletown, barely two steps ahead of his owner and the owner's bloodhound. The slave was quickly taken to the McKeever station and concealed in a barn. The bloodhound, however, sniffed out the fugitive. The slave owner was prepared to take his runaway with him when McKeever insisted that he appear before the justice of the peace, Thomas Odenbaugh, and prove that he was the legal owner of the slave. McKeever meanwhile notified his friends of what was transpiring, including the McElroys. By the time the McElroys arrived at the justice's office, a considerable crowd had gathered.[31]

Before the proceedings before the justice began, the senior McElroy asked if the slave owner was indeed the owner of the bloodhound lying on the floor. The slave owner affirmed that he was. McElroy then proposed, "I move that this bloodhound does not leave this town alive." According to his son's account, all of the men from the village present seconded the motion: "In less than ten minutes that dog was hanging to the limb of a tree in front of the office, and the master was on his way out of town, believing it wasn't healthy for him to remain a minute longer than necessary. In three days thereafter that slave man was in Canada a free man."[32]

Matthew McKeever never ran into difficulties with the law, probably because his West Middletown neighbors were generally supportive of his activities. The same was not true of his brother-in-law Joseph Bryant, a fellow abolitionist who lived across the line in Brooke County, Virginia. On one occasion Bryant sent a number of fugitives to McKeever, who in turn forwarded them to Pittsburgh. Bryant was turned in by an informer, accused of assisting runaway slaves, and hauled off to Wheeling to await trial. A five-hundred-dollar reward was subsequently offered to anyone who could bring McKeever into Wheeling, "dead or alive." He decided not to "venture down there about that time." The judge let Bryant off because he believed that Bryant as the accomplice should not be punished "while the principal was at large"—obviously a reference to McKeever.[33]

Thomas McKeever plays an important part in only one of these stories told about the McKeever family. That story, related in chapter 3, told how Thomas, as justice of the peace, had outwitted a Virginia slave owner when he ruled that the Virginian's bond was "forfeit, not bail," thereby allowing a captured fugitive slave to leave his office as a free man. Although William Asbury lived in the nearby village of Cross Creek, his involvement in the rescue of the fugitive slave involved in this case bears mention here.[34]

John Brown's role in the Underground Railroad in West Middletown is ambiguous. Contemporary testimony clearly establishes that Brown railed against slavery in his visits as a wool buyer in the early 1840s to area aboli-

6. Home of Thomas McKeever, West Middletown, PA. Photo courtesy of Deborah Mainwaring.

tionists, but whether Brown was inciting slaves to run away and helping them remains unclear. The claim that Brown laid the tracks of the Underground Railroad into the area is decidedly not true. Even if one includes only white operatives, Matthew McKeever would have precedence by some twenty years. McKeever, Asbury, Adams, and unknown others had been engaged in this for some time before Brown ever appeared in the county.[35]

One scholar contends, however, that Brown's purchases of sheep and wool may have been a subterfuge to hide his real business—that of bringing slaves to freedom. According to Richard O. Boyer, there is good reason to believe that Brown used his business as a cover to steal slaves out of northern Virginia. Boyer speculates that Brown's periodic visits during the 1840s to the McElroys and McKeevers in West Middletown did involve slaves he had rescued. If Boyer is correct, John Brown's first actions to realize his commitment to end the scourge of slavery in the United States may have occurred in Washington County.[36]

According to James W. Murdock (1863–1954), a man simply known as "Sly" was another West Middletown resident active in the Underground

Railroad. Sly occasionally borrowed horses to aid escaping slaves. On one occasion he went to Wellsburg to rescue a slave couple who were to be sold to the South. Sly eluded the men who pursued him and the couple and subsequently moved the couple to a station near Burgettstown, where they departed for Canada. Murdock learned of Sly's Underground Railroad activities from David Brownlee, a friend whose father had loaned Sly the horses.[37]

Several known escape networks led out of West Middletown. One—that followed by young James McElroy—went north to Paris in the upper northwestern corner of the county. Nothing more is known about this site. A second took fugitive slaves northeast to the station near Burgettstown mentioned by Murdock. The first and second networks led northward into Beaver County and across the Ohio River.[38] A third network, favored by Asbury, led through Hickory to Pittsburgh. The Clarksburg Nine followed yet another path to the east to the county seat of Washington.

THE CENTRAL NETWORK

The most direct way from the Virginia counties lying directly south of Washington County would have been through Waynesburg in central Greene County to the town of Washington in central Washington County. An old Delaware Indian trail, the Catfish Path, entered Pennsylvania at Brant Summit in Greene County and wended its way north through Waynesburg and Washington before eventually reaching the Ohio River near Pittsburgh. Early settlers turned the trail into a road that is still largely followed by Route 19 today. However, there is little documentation for any Underground Railroad stations between Waynesburg and Washington along this road. In the one specific case that is well known, the slaves who escaped from Clarksburg in 1856 and made it to Waynesburg were directed to stations in the western part of Greene and Washington Counties. Only then were they taken to stations in Washington. Switala speculates that there must have been a stop somewhere along the Waynesburg–Washington Road, since the distance between the two county seats was twenty-seven miles—a long way to travel in one night.[39]

Ermine Cain, who helped engineer the escape of the Clarksburg slaves from Waynesburg, provides an indication that fugitive slaves were forwarded directly from Waynesburg to Washington on occasion. Discussing the circuitous path to Washington taken by these slaves, Cain observed, "You see, it wouldn't do to run them in one direction. We never did that unless things looked pretty risky; then I've known instances where they were shot right on till they got to Pittsburg."[40] Cain, however, does not mention any specific stations between Waynesburg and Washington.

The only plausible station agent in southern Washington County is the Reverend James H. Henderson, pastor of the Cumberland Presbyterian Church in Morris Township. At first, Henderson would appear to be a very unlikely candidate. He bears the distinction of having registered the last slave in Washington County in 1845. However, in 1851 he wrote to the *National Era*, an antislavery newspaper in Washington, DC, appealing for money on behalf of Thomas Rubey, a slave who was soliciting money in Washington County to purchase his freedom. Henderson specified that money should be sent to himself, F. Julius LeMoyne, or Samuel McFarland, some of the stalwarts of the local abolitionism. Either Henderson had a change of heart about slavery, or registering the slave may have had a very different motive than would appear to be the case. Conceivably, Henderson might have been registering a slave from out of state (nine-year-old Harriet had been born in Kentucky) in order to procure her freedom after having lived for six months in Pennsylvania. In any case, by 1851 he had joined the abolitionist cause.[41]

The town of Washington was the principal station in central Washington County. (See Map 12.) Runaways were directed there from West Middletown, West Alexander, Waynesburg, and from the direction of the Monongahela River. Free blacks such as Tar Adams played a prominent role in the history of the Underground Railroad in Washington and in all likelihood began helping fugitives long before local whites joined. The presence of a substantial free black community as well as that of influential whites probably made it the hub of Underground Railroad operations in the county.

By far and away the most famous name associated with the Underground Railroad in Little Washington was that of F. Julius LeMoyne, who achieved a prominence in national abolition circles that no one else in the county matched. He is only one of two Underground Railroad operatives whom Wilbur Siebert lists for the county in his pioneering study. (Matthew McKeever is the other.) But LeMoyne's prominence should not overshadow the contributions of other individuals to the cause of freedom. Also, LeMoyne's active involvement in the Underground Railroad probably lasted for less than a decade. As his biographer notes, by 1846 "the most strenuous and heroic days of abolition were over for the Doctor." The lingering effects of cholera, rheumatism, and added girth increasingly limited his activities.

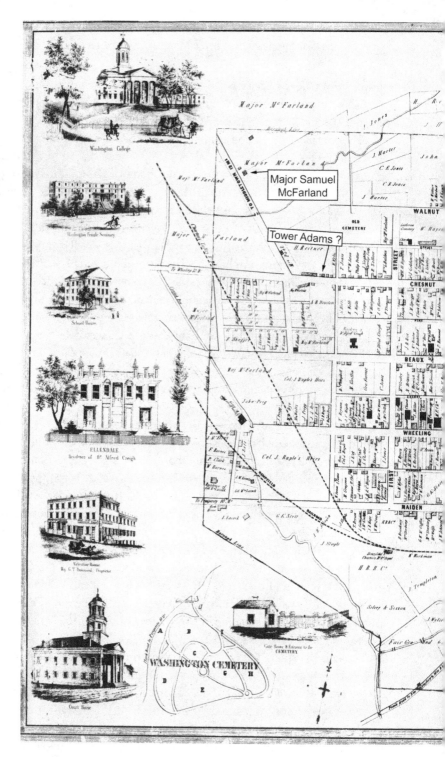

Major Samuel
McFarland

Tower Adams ?

Map 12

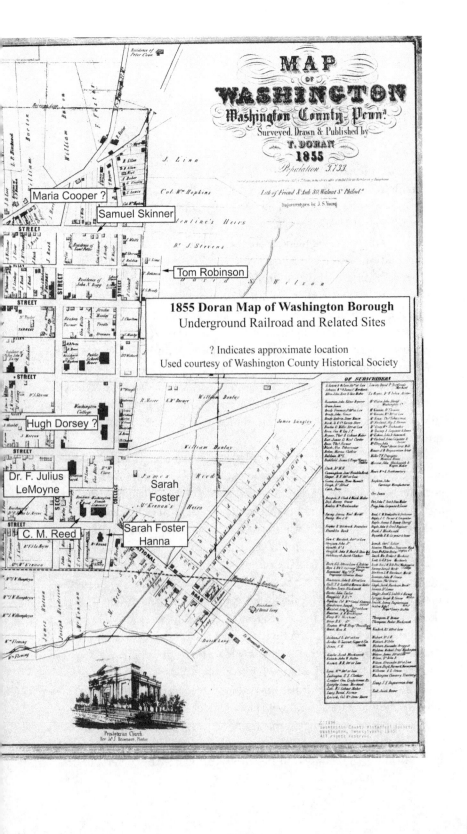

MAP OF WASHINGTON

Washington County, Penn*

Surveyed, Drawn & Published by

T. DORAN

1855

Population 3,733

Lith of Friend & Aub 80. Walnut S* Philad*

Daguerreotypes by J. S. Young.

Maria Cooper ?

Samuel Skinner

Tom Robinson

1855 Doran Map of Washington Borough
Underground Railroad and Related Sites

? Indicates approximate location
Used courtesy of Washington County Historical Society

Hugh Dorsey ?

Dr. F. Julius
LeMoyne

Sarah
Foster

C. M. Reed

Sarah Foster
Hanna

Presbyterian Church
Rev J* J. Brownson, Pastor

LeMoyne did take an active role in helping to organize a national antislavery convention in Pittsburgh in 1852, but this was one of his last public efforts in behalf of the cause. Incapacitated by pain, LeMoyne by the mid-1850s had all but given up his medical practice and retired from public affairs.[42]

Major Samuel McFarland (1795–1868) seems to have taken over the leadership role in white Underground Railroad circles in Washington as LeMoyne's health deteriorated. It was McFarland who had defended Kit Sharp, the captured fugitive slave accused of murdering his owner. He became one of the founding members of the Washington Anti-Slavery Society in 1834 and later ran for local office on the Liberty Party ticket. Also like LeMoyne, he became the vice-presidential nominee of a short-lived anti-slavery party in 1856. Unhappy with the conservative stance on slavery of the First Presbyterian Church, McFarland and his wife Mary joined the Free Presbyterian church some twenty miles away in West Alexander. McFarland's large sheep farm just west of the borough limits, on what is now Jefferson Avenue, apparently hosted fugitive slaves numerous times. He reportedly sheltered eighteen fugitives on one occasion. Osborne Mitchell commented in a 1908 newspaper article on the Underground Railroad that "It was by no means unusual for this gentleman to give shelter to six or eight runaways at a time."[43]

McFarland's Underground Railroad connections may in fact be better documented than LeMoyne's. Although the numbers of fugitive slaves reportedly housed by McFarland may have been vastly inflated, we do have one eyewitness account of his role in the escape of the Clarksburg Nine. George Walls, an African American conductor then living on a farm in South Strabane Township, told a reporter in 1884 that it was McFarland who had arranged for the Clarksburg Nine to be brought from West Middletown to Washington. "I got word from Major McFarland to be on the lookout for them," Walls recalled, adding that "a man named Adams" (very likely Tar Adams, who lived on West Chestnut Street near McFarland) helped to bring them in. The fugitives may have stayed at Noah Clouse's blacksmith shop in Canton Township before being delivered into McFarland's hands. McFarland split the fugitives up in Washington, leaving five at the home of Samuel Skinner on Walnut Street and four at Tom Robinson's on Chestnut Street. Both were black conductors.[44]

Walls played a significant role in the successful escape of the Clarksburg slaves and in the local Underground Railroad. Although he does not appear in any of the county histories, he was recognized by contemporaries as one of the major forces in the movement. John C. McNary, a Canonsburg attorney, described Walls in 1884 as "the general agent of the line in this county." McNary had occasion to know. In 1856, when McNary was an adolescent, Walls had delivered some of the Clarksburg fugitives at night to the farm of William H. McNary (John's father) in Chartiers Township, several miles west of Canonsburg. It is evident from the son's account that Walls had made frequent runs with fugitive slaves to William H. McNary's farm. Walls escorted the other contingent of Clarksburg runaways to the farm of James S. McNary, William's brother, in South Strabane Township.[45]

Walls is one of the few Underground Railroad agents whose own testimony we have. Interviewed in 1884, a year before his death, he related his role in several escapes. The most notable of these involved Randolph, the slave of a Carolinian named Gillespie who had returned to visit Canonsburg, where he had been educated, in the 1840s. Seeing an opportune moment when Randolph was alone, Walls asked him if he wanted to be a free man. Walls whisked him away when Randolph expressed a desire for freedom. He first hid Randolph with William Wassler, who was a black tenant on Major J. H. Ewing's Meadowlands farm several miles south of Canonsburg. Later, with the assistance of his white abolitionist neighbor, Joseph Lee, Walls had Randolph moved to a more secure location at Michael Hackaress's station some thirty miles southwest in southern West Finley Township. Eventually Walls engineered Randolph's escape to Canada via Canonsburg. According to Walls, Lee drove the cleverly disguised Randolph right past his former owner in Canonsburg without the owner being any the wiser.[46]

Walls apparently stood at the center of a network of white and black Underground Railroad agents and sympathizers. Although no connection has come to light between him and LeMoyne, Walls did have contact with many of the names prominently featured in local accounts of the Underground Railroad, including Samuel McFarland and Tar Adams. He also had many contacts within the black community of Washington and vicinity whose names have not been recorded anywhere except in several 1884 newspaper articles.

The majority of those names (such as Skinner and Robinson) surface in the East Chestnut/East Walnut section of Washington that historically has been the center of the black community. This neighborhood, which later came to be known as "The Hill," extended between those streets for several blocks north of what was then Washington College and between Second Street (College Street today) and College Street (Lincoln Street today).

7. Home of James McNary, North Strabane Township

8. Home of William McNary, Chartiers Township

A cabin built by former slaves of William Hoge, who donated land to them, still stands in this neighborhood.[47] The neighborhood was also home to the Wright AME Church. Another name connected to the Underground Railroad from this neighborhood was Joseph Brooks, a black teamster who was hired to transport the Clarksburg fugitives from the McNary farms to Pittsburgh. Although Walls does not mention him, Henry Bolden, a black barber who lived on North Lincoln Street in this neighborhood, was also involved in the Underground Railroad in an unspecified capacity. Maria Cooper, who had moved her family to Washington after gaining her freedom in Virginia, likewise made her home in this area.[48]

This neighborhood was the center of African American resistance in Washington. It housed most of the identifiable black Underground Railroad agents and an AME church. Beyond aiding fugitive slaves, residents sought to enforce racial solidarity in matters that were crucial to this community. In August 1856, the *Liberator* (Boston, MA) reported that unnamed blacks in Washington had tarred and feathered a fellow black "in consequence of it being clearly proved that he was employed by slaveholders, in hunting up fugitives." The paper did not name the object of this treatment or offer further details.[49] However, the *Pittsburg Chronicle*'s account of August 16, 1856, makes it highly likely that African Americans in Washington had taken reprisal against this individual because he was suspected of having assisted the slave catchers pursuing the Clarksburg Nine, who escaped in July of that year. The paper reported that the black community "rose en masse" against this defector. African American Underground Railroad activists in Pittsburgh had treated a suspected traitor to their cause with similar harshness several years earlier, when they beat severely a free black accused of betraying fugitives.[50]

Another free black associated with the Underground Railroad in Washington was the barber Samuel Dorsey, whom Crumrine mentions as a participant in the Clarksburg escape. (Some accounts say "Hugh" Dorsey, who also had ties to the Underground Railroad.) Dorsey figures in another story in which a slave owner had stopped at an inn in Rankin Town (part of present-day Washington) with four slaves. The fifteen-year-old daughter of innkeeper Agnes Rankin was outraged when the slave owner threw some food to the slaves "as if they were dogs." The daughter translated her outrage into action. At some point during the night three of the four slaves disappeared, the fourth staying behind only because he was too old. Reputedly it was Dorsey who guided the slaves on the beginning leg of their journey to freedom.[51]

As late as 1910, there was reluctance on the part of some whites to be publicly identified with slave rescues and the Underground Railroad. Local historian Joseph McFarland reported in his book published that year that the Rankin daughter, by then an "aged lady," had refrained from telling about this incident previously because of threats made by the slave owner. Crumrine's 1882 history likewise declined to identify white participants whose involvement was not widely known.[52]

Another Underground Railroad agent in Washington was the attorney J. W. F. White, who later became a judge. About 1847, a slaveholder in Harrisonburg, Virginia, had freed three of his slaves, who took his name, Mc-Causland. The freed slaves, consisting of an elderly man, his wife, and a younger woman, came to Washington and bought a farm about six miles outside the town. In 1849 another black man named Charles Brown arrived, married the younger woman, Matilda, and bought a thirty-acre farm in South Strabane Township. Things appeared to be going well for both couples when a white stranger arrived in 1850 and inquired about Brown. Brown turned out to be a fugitive slave, and the stranger wanted to employ White's services to recapture him. White refused the offer but managed to keep the slave owner in his office long enough to warn Brown by a note that he was a hunted man. Brown fled immediately to Erie County, New York, where he waited until his wife could sell their Washington County farm. With some financial assistance from White and the proceeds from the sale of their farm, the Browns moved to Stamford, Ontario (now a part of Niagara Falls). The Browns and their two young children appear in the 1851 Canadian Census.[53]

Sarah Foster Hanna, the longtime principal of the Washington Female Seminary on East Maiden Street, was another white who may not have been ideologically committed to assisting fugitives but was moved by their plight. Hanna does not appear on any list of local abolitionists or Underground Railroad agents, but Walls revealed that Hanna had forwarded two fugitives who had escaped from Morgantown to him. "They had walked their shoes off—were in a terrible fix," he commented. He did not say how Hanna had come to know about the two runaways or how she had known to contact him, only that they made it as far as Pittsburgh. This incident is Hanna's only known involvement in the Underground Railroad.[54]

The flight of the Clarksburg fugitives reveals one network by which escaping slaves made their way from Washington to Canada. As noted above, Walls first escorted David Thompson and his fellow escapees to farms near Canonsburg. (See Map 13.) He then arranged for Joe Brooks to drive them to

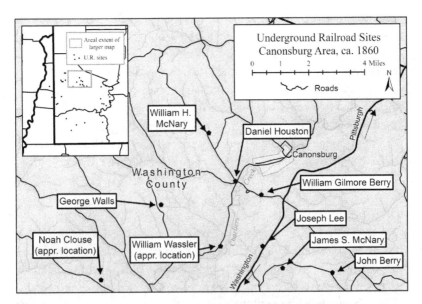

Map 13

Pittsburgh from a rendezvous point at Jarrett's Tavern, which was located in South Fayette Township just across the Allegheny County line. Two black conductors from Pittsburgh, John Peck and Samuel Bruce, met the party at Saw Mill Run and then conducted it to Pittsburgh. Austin Bryant, an African American who was then working at the famous Monongahela House hotel, also helped the Clarksburg slaves on their road to freedom. He escorted them from Pittsburgh across the Hand Street Bridge (currently the Ninth Street Bridge) to what was then Allegheny City on the north side of the Allegheny River. There Thompson says that he stayed at the home of George Dimmey, a black wagoner who lived near the North Common. The Clarksburg fugitives also stayed at Bruce's house in Allegheny City according to Bryant's account. The fugitives were then transferred to safe houses in the Butler Valley on their journey north. They made stops in Butler, Mercer, and Meadville before reaching Erie. They were finally directed to Cleveland and then Detroit, where they crossed over into Windsor, Canada.[55]

The Clarksburg escape is one of the very few through Washington County in which the networks north of the county and the final destination are known. It is very difficult to assess whether other fugitives followed the same pathway north. The overwhelming impression given by local accounts, however, is that Pittsburgh was the intermediate destination for most of the fugitives who passed through the borough of Washington. The only evidence that would indicate a different path from Washington comes from a case involving LeMoyne, who apparently directed escaping slaves to contacts in Beaver County. Crumrine notes that when LeMoyne hired stagecoaches to take sixteen fugitives from Mrs. Houston's barn, they conveyed them across the Ohio—downriver from Pittsburgh. If LeMoyne had been sending fugitives to Pittsburgh, it seems likely that Crumrine would have mentioned crossing the Monongahela and Allegheny Rivers.[56]

THE EASTERN NETWORK

Two escape networks converged in eastern Washington County near West Brownsville along the Monongahela River. One route, of lesser importance, supposedly led from Morgantown and the south along the Monongahela River. Little is known about it. This was the path Tom Stowe followed, although it should be pointed out that Stowe had no assistance during his journey until he had gone well beyond Pittsburgh. The other network in eastern Washington County linked Uniontown, in Fayette County, to Pittsburgh. Slaves fleeing from western Maryland or the eastern panhandle of Virginia could follow the National Road westward from the Pennsylvania border in Somerset County to Uniontown, which was home to a substantial black community. Agents there directed some fugitives along routes that led directly north or to Pittsburgh but sent others westward along the National Road to Washington County.

Most of what is known about the network from Uniontown through eastern Washington County comes from Howard Wallace. His historical sketch of the Liberty Line, written in 1903, is by far the most extensive written by any local agent and the only source of information about most of the agents in the eastern part of the county. This network appears to have operated independently from those in the rest of the county. None of the county histories even mentions this black Underground Railroad.[57]

According to Wallace, most of the fugitive slaves who traveled through eastern Washington County began their journey on the Underground Railroad in Uniontown. The journey from Uniontown to Brownsville was quite dangerous because the small community of Hopwood near Uniontown was proslavery. Many of its inhabitants, he claimed, would betray slaves for small amounts of money. At least four fugitive slaves were captured in the

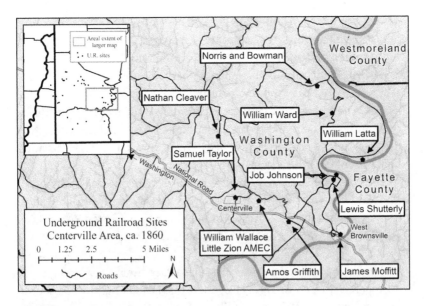

Map 14

Uniontown area and returned to their owners between 1850 and 1861.[58] Thus considerable caution had to be used in moving fugitives from Uniontown to Brownsville on the eastern bank of the Monongahela. Wallace identified free blacks including Lloyd Demas, Simeon Artis, and Thomas Cain as the conductors who received fugitives from Uniontown. The route then crossed the river into Washington County at West Brownsville, the first destination west of the river. (See Map 14.) There James Moffitt, one of the few white operatives in this network, sheltered fugitives at his house on the corner of Bridge and Main Streets. Unfortunately it is no longer standing.[59]

Fugitive slaves were then guided through the heavily wooded Denbo area before they emerged on the National Road near Malden. They were subsequently taken to the home of Wallace's father in Centerville. From Centerville fugitives would be guided to either Ginger Hill or Maple Creek, the latter being the main destination. Wallace mentions George Norris as one of the agents in the Maple Creek area. Norris appears in the 1850 census as a thirty-eight-year-old farmer. He was married and had four children and owned property worth $735. Wallace also mentions a Bowman family in the Maple Creek area. Two black families with this name were living in Fallowfield Township in 1850, both neighbors of Norris. Lydia Bowman, age forty-six, had four children living with her and owned $300 in property. Samuel Bowman, thirty-one, appears as a propertyless laborer who lived with his wife and four children, as well as an adult male who may have been his brother. Railroad construction in the early twentieth century has substantially altered the topography of the area along a small tributary of Maple Creek where these families once lived. No trace of the small black community can be found today. Other names mentioned in connection with the Maple Creek area include Peter Cleaver and John Frye, both whites about whom very little is known.[60]

From the Maple Creek area, fugitive slaves were directed to the site of what was to be Donora, where they were rowed across the Monongahela River to a small black settlement near Belle Vernon, where the Ross, Basier, and Minney families provided aid. The next destination was Robtown (West Newton), followed by Pittsburgh.[61]

The alternative route from Centerville to Pittsburgh was via Ginger Hill and apparently Canonsburg. Wallace says that he took fugitives on several occasions to Ginger Hill, where Milton Maxwell took care of the fugitives. Maxwell in 1850 was a thirty-year-old, mixed-race tenant farmer living with his wife, two children, and a woman who may have been his mother. By 1860 he had acquired his own farm; by 1870 he had moved his family to Iowa. Maxwell may have directed fugitives to Canonsburg or directly to Pittsburgh. Wallace does mention that a fugitive slave named Renols [as Wallace spelled his name] Parker sought safety in Canonsburg before heading for Pittsburgh and then Canada. Regrettably, Wallace does not name the agents in Canonsburg who aided Parker. Those most likely to have assisted fugitives in Canonsburg would be the trio of African Americans who wrote to Julius LeMoyne asking him to address a countywide black political meeting: Daniel Arnet, James Brown, and F. L. Chambers.[62]

The core of the Underground Railroad network identified by Wallace in eastern Washington County was clearly black. Apart from Moffitt in West Brownsville, whites' role was to supply material aid to the network. Wallace lauded "white friends who had sympathy for the slave" and who contributed "clothing and other means to help them along." Sometimes that aid was quite generous. Wallace was effusive in his praise of the Quakers and other farmers in his neighborhood who were ready to lend a hand when needed. "I do not think I ever had one to refuse me," Wallace commented. Even after his two prized horses Suze and Bill had spent a hard day in the field, Wallace's neighbor Samuel Taylor was willing to lend them to transport a few runaways to safety. "Their contributions were always liberal," Wallace said of his Quaker neighbors. "I shall always have a warm place in my heart for the Friends. They have done many things for our downtrodden race."[63]

Wallace witnessed one dramatic episode during his days as an Underground Railroad conductor. Shortly after the passage of the Fugitive Slave Act of 1850, eight "rough" Virginians led by Bob Stump caught up with the fugitive Parker in Centerville, and surrounded him while he was at work in Nathan Cleaver's field. (Cleaver's farm may well have been a stop on the Underground Railroad.)[64] Rather than letting himself be captured, Parker bolted for a nearby house, despite the shots being fired at him. He went up an extremely narrow stairway to the second story and then threatened to bash in the head of the first person who stuck his head in the stairway. A standoff resulted between Parker and his pursuers, who were extremely reluctant to venture up the stairway. Finally, at dusk, two Centerville residents, a black named Henry Smith and a white named Isaac Vaile, told the leader of the Virginians that they would bring Parker to him at Brownsville the next morning.

Their ruse worked. As soon as the Virginians had left, Parker came down the stairs and was on his way to Canonsburg, where he waited until the rest of his family could meet him. Wallace urged Parker to go "to Canada for permanent safety," a piece of advice that Parker followed. Wallace credits Moffitt with encouraging Stump and his slave catchers to leave without further pursuit of their quarry. According to Wallace, Moffitt warned Stump that Brownsville was full of a "rough set of niggers and that it was dangerous to stay there." Fortunately for Smith and Vaile, the Virginians did not press charges against them. They could have been heavily fined under the provisions of the 1850 fugitive slave law. So far as can be determined, no one was ever prosecuted in Washington County for violations of the act.[65]

Wallace himself later went to Canada, although apparently in search of good wages rather than for fear of slave catchers. Several considerations suggest this conclusion. First, Wallace left Centerville in 1854, while most blacks who were concerned about the snares laid by the new fugitive slave law departed from the United States shortly after the law's passage. Second, Wallace says that he spent some time in Windsor, Ontario, "employed at railroad repairs." And finally, he returned to Centerville after a "few" years in Canada. If he had fled to Canada in fear for his safety, his security would not have been enhanced if he returned after just a few years. Wallace

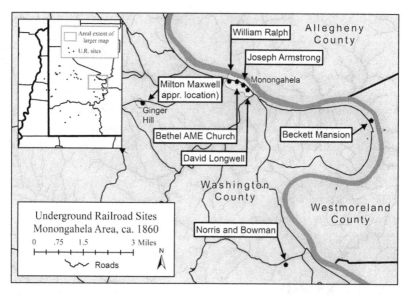

Map 15

reported although he met many former slaves in Canada, he did not encounter "many that went through here."[66]

Although there were clearly other Underground Railroad safe houses in eastern Washington County apart from the ones mentioned by Wallace, it is not clear how they fit into the local network of stations. We have anecdotes and sketchy information about sites in California and Monongahela but lack a larger perspective on them. (See Map 15.)

California, Pennsylvania, was almost certainly a stop after its founding in 1849. There the leading figure was Job Johnson, whose involvement in the abolitionist cause was of long standing. Johnson advertised in Le-Moyne's antislavery paper, the *Washington Patriot*. Johnson's Hotel, which once stood at the corner of Wood and First Streets, operated as a safe house for fugitive slaves. Writing in 1949, Nan Hornbake, the author of a book on California's history, claims that she personally was shown a small closet on the second floor of the hotel where fugitives were hidden. She adds that fugitives found their way to the hotel from the wharf on the Monongahela River. Presumably these fugitives had stowed away on steamers coming downriver from Morgantown. According to the same author, Johnson forwarded fugitives to Washington, Pennsylvania. Another site identified in

California is Lewis Shutterly's house at 800 Park Avenue. The Shutterly house, which is still standing, was apparently used when the Johnson Hotel was being closely watched. Other names that surface in connection with California include David Veatch, W. M. Stone, and Samuel Rothwell. Rothwell, in an 1893 interview, acknowledged the role that he and Job Johnson had played in the California Underground Railroad network. The Latta Stone House in Roscoe also reportedly served as a safe haven, although information on it is very sketchy.[67]

Monongahela was another river town that offered refuge to fleeing slaves. William Ralph (ca. 1813–1897), an African American, was the mainstay of the Underground Railroad there. Starting out as a stage boy, Ralph eventually owned his wagon and coal business and served as a minister in the AME Church. As a coal dealer, he met a staunch white abolitionist named Mary Taylor, the wife of Joseph B. Taylor. Her nephew, Joseph Armstrong, recalled years later how he as a ten- or eleven-year-old boy had helped Ralph to hide fugitive slaves in the hayloft of his aunt's barn. Armstrong on several different occasions rowed fugitives who had stayed in his aunt's barn across the Monongahela River. A man who helped the fugitives to the next stop in Pittsburgh met Armstrong on the other side of the river. Armstrong believed that Ralph feared to house fugitives in his own stable because too many people came by it on errands for it to be secure. Armstrong in 1908 remembered Ralph as "the representative colored man of the town for fifty years, a man of gigantic frame and great strength with a character above reproach."[68]

Although the mists of time and legend shroud the operations of the Liberty Line in Washington County, several conclusions stand out. The first is that a modest number of fugitive slaves did escape through the county, sometimes on their own and sometimes with assistance. Although that number will never be known with any exactitude, Edward Burns's estimate that perhaps several hundred fugitive slaves escaped through western Pennsylvania seems quite reasonable. The nearby or contiguous areas of Virginia from which the vast majority of fugitives were likely to come simply did not have a large slave population. The seven Virginia counties that shared a border with western Pennsylvania held only 527 people in bondage in 1850, a number that had fallen to 327 by 1860. What proportion of that decline can be attributed to flight via the Underground Railroad cannot be known. No William Still or David Ruggles, both of whom kept detailed records of the people whom they helped, has emerged in western Pennsylvania. The 1860 census, which reported that thirteen people had fled from these counties the previous year, can only serve as a crude guide.[69]

In comparison to south central Pennsylvania or southern Ohio, Washington County emerges as a branch line of the Underground Railroad. These other areas could draw upon a much greater slave population for potential fugitives than Washington County. They could also draw upon a black population that was much more urbanized and literate—both major factors in who was likely to flee from slavery—than the Appalachian region from which most of the fugitives traveling through Washington County had fled. All of the evidence points to much heavier traffic through these areas than through southwestern Pennsylvania.[70]

A second conclusion is that African Americans in Washington County and southwestern Pennsylvania were at "the front line of freedom," in Keith Griffler's phrase. They were the primary points of contact with fugitive slaves and often undertook the most dangerous operations of the Underground Railroad that entailed either moving freedom seekers from slave territory or helping them to escape pursuit. Again it is important to emphasize that those who attempted to leave their shackles behind bore the biggest risks. The risks were greatest for those who fled northward through Monongalia County, Virginia, and Greene County, Pennsylvania, where organized support either did not exist or was confined to a small number of African Americans. The available evidence, which is slender, indicates that fugitive slaves passing through these areas were unaware of any specific source of help. (By contrast, those seeking to flee from the Wheeling area could seek out the counsel of Old Naylor.) Slaves south of the Pennsylvania border in what was then Virginia may have heard about the Underground Railroad, but they had no concrete knowledge of where to turn for assistance. For example, Tom Stowe, the Mississippi slave who fled from Morgantown, made his way down the Monongahela to Pittsburgh on his own. David Thompson, the leader of the Clarksburg Nine and the only other source of direct testimony on this question, likewise displayed no awareness of Underground Railroad agents.[71] Yet help was available in southern Greene County. Elisha Purr, the African American agent living near Blacksville, offered a temporary haven for the Clarksburg Nine and made arrangements for moving them to safety along the network of predominantly black operatives in Greene County.

The aid rendered to the Clarksburg fugitives illustrates the crucial but largely supportive role that whites played in their escape. Only after the immediate danger of recapture had passed did the McKeevers and other whites become involved in helping to get these fugitives first to Pittsburgh and ultimately to Canada. White abolitionists typically played a much more prominent role in the Underground Railroad after the initial escape had been made and the fugitives had reached the relative safety of free territory.[72]

Numerous other examples demonstrate the primary role of African Americans in putting fugitives in contact with the network of agents that we know as the Underground Railroad. Naylor in Wheeling was central in providing assistance to fugitives and slaves in that city. The network of black agents in eastern Washington County provided the core assistance for fugitive slaves coming from the south or the east. Matthew McKeever's hired hand, John Jordan, was the person the group of escaping slaves turned to for assistance in West Middletown. It is also important to remember that the local blacks had been assisting fugitive slaves for several decades before white abolitionists in Washington County began organizing networks to aid escaping slaves in the late 1830s.

This is not to suggest that the white abolitionists who began helping fugitive slaves at this time played a minor role. To the contrary, they were essential in helping to form a network of assistance that spread out across most of the county, not just Washington and other places where small black communities had been established. LeMoyne's career illustrates the numerous ways in which white abolitionists contributed to the cause, not just by assisting fugitive slaves to escape but also by providing leadership and financial assistance to a much broader movement. Meeting a stagecoach bearing an emancipated slave and helping that person on the next leg of the journey to Ohio is not the stuff of high drama, but LeMoyne engaged in numerous acts that aided African Americans.[73] Few, if any, of the African Americans then living in the county could have afforded to hire carriages to carry fugitive slaves to freedom. Although some whites, such as the McKeevers, became the primary points of contact for fugitive slaves, the most significant help from whites came after fugitive slaves had already found their way onto the Underground Railroad.

The interracial character of the Underground Railroad appears to have varied considerably depending on the county's geography. In eastern Washington County, the network of agents described by Wallace was overwhelmingly black, whereas whites played a much more prominent role in the western part of the county, which had a much smaller black population. The lack of references to Wallace's network by white abolitionists and its neglect by later county historians almost suggest that two separate Underground Railroads operated in Washington County. So does the celebration of Julius LeMoyne's role in the Underground Railroad and the absence of George Walls in local accounts. But the escape of the Clarksburg Nine clearly illustrates that, at least in the western parts of the county and in Little Washington, the Underground Railroad involved interracial cooperation and was frequently a joint operation. To employ the old metaphor, the local Underground Railroad might be imagined as two separate lines that shared many points of interchange but often ran independently. It was a joint, cooperative venture.

Fragmentary evidence suggests that the racial background of local Underground Railroad agents influenced the next destination of fugitives beyond Washington County. Based upon a limited number of accounts, black agents typically guided fugitives to Pittsburgh, whereas white agents bypassed Pittsburgh in guiding fugitive slaves toward Lake Erie. Black operatives selected Pittsburgh as a destination for two reasons. First, a well-established network of whites and blacks provided a secure way of sending fugitive slaves from Washington to Pittsburgh, as is illustrated by the path the Clarksburg Nine traveled to Pittsburgh. Second, Pittsburgh featured a large free black population whose leaders, such as John Vashon and John Peck, had organized an effective vigilance system by the 1830s. The Philanthropic Society, an organization formed in the 1830s by free blacks in Pittsburgh, initially offered protection against kidnapping but extended its assistance to runaway slaves. By the 1850s travelers brought their slaves through Pittsburgh at their peril. The black staff of the Monongahela House, Pittsburgh's most noted hotel of the era, assisted in the escape of several slaves. Although Pittsburgh's abolitionists sometimes had to purchase the freedom of captured slaves, R. J. M. Blackett emphasizes that no fugitive who made it to Pittsburgh was ever returned to slavery permanently. He believes that the absence of rescue cases in Pittsburgh after 1855 reflects the hard-won knowledge of slave owners that Pittsburgh's black community, provided crucial assistance by whites such as Charles Avery, was so well organized that they stood little chance of reclaiming their runaways. Black abolitionists in Washington County routinely turned to this effective network to assist fugitive slaves who had made it to their county.[74]

By contrast, white agents such as LeMoyne appear largely to have bypassed Pittsburgh and directed fugitive slaves through the northwestern part of the county to white collaborators in Beaver County, Pennsylvania, and eastern Ohio. The most likely destination in eastern Ohio would have been the Quaker community at Salem, where many Quakers had relocated from Washington County. The Quaker community in New Brighton and the home of Arthur B. Bradford (the founder of the Free Presbyterian Church) in Enon in Beaver County were alternative destinations.[75] However, apart from LeMoyne's hiring of the stagecoach to convey the fugitives from Wheeling north to the Ohio River and Lake Erie, and the mention of Paris in northern Washington County, very little is known about these routes. Still, there are clear exceptions to the generalization that white Underground Railroad operatives directed the people in their care through northwestern Washington County, as Matthew McKeever sent the Clarksburg Nine through Washington en route to Pittsburgh.[76]

The final conclusion to be drawn here is that the network of African American and white Underground Railroad agents proved quite effective in offering assistance to fugitive slaves who either settled in the county or fled farther north. The last recorded slave capture in Washington County involved Christian Sharp, who was convicted in 1828 of murdering his owner and captor. As in south central Pennsylvania, successful slave renditions ceased in Washington County after the rise of radical abolitionism among whites.[77] However, Fayette County, Washington County's neighbor to the east, which had never been friendly to abolitionism, witnessed four successful captures of fugitive slaves in the 1850s.[78] By contrast, Washington County witnessed at least four recorded rescues from would-be slave catchers between 1840 and 1860. The rescue of Renols Parker in Centerville is a classic example. In another incident in nearby West Brownsville, local officials threw a Virginia slave owner into prison in 1851 when his intentions to recapture his slave became known.[79] The two other known instances in which local abolitionists thwarted slave owners occurred in West Middletown. In one case, Thomas McKeever in his capacity as justice of the peace, supported by a substantial crowd sympathetic to the captured fugitive, ruled against the slave owner and freed the accused. In the other, James McElroy hung the owner's bloodhound and persuaded the owner that his life was in danger if he persisted in his claim. In three of these escapes, local law officials supported or sanctioned the actions of Underground Railroad operatives. As in Pittsburgh, slave owners encountered staunch opposition in abolitionist centers such as West Middletown and West Brownsville.[80]

The Fugitive Slave Act of 1850 provides further indirect evidence of the effectiveness of Washington County's Underground Railroad network.

This draconian law caused African Americans—both fugitive slaves and free blacks—to flee to safety in Canada. The lack of legal safeguards in the new law meant that no black person was safe from potential capture and rendition. The effect on Pittsburgh was immediate. By the end of September 1850, at least one hundred blacks had departed the city, and another forty had abandoned Allegheny City (today's North Shore) for Canada West. The Monongahela House lost all of its black staff. The effect of the new fugitive slave law in Pittsburgh and Allegheny City lingered as well: these communities saw a sharp decline in their black populations during the 1850s. The 1860 census revealed that 800 blacks had left Pittsburgh during the 1850s, and 706 had left Allegheny City.[81]

The new fugitive slave act certainly made its presence felt in Washington County. Charles Brown barely escaped the snares of the new act thanks to a timely warning from a local attorney. Yet the law did not have the same severe impact that it did in neighboring Allegheny County. The black population of Washington County actually increased during the 1850s, growing from 1,559 in 1850 to 1,726 in 1860. The Fugitive Slave Act of 1850 did not prompt the same exodus that occurred in Pittsburgh. The most plausible explanation would be that the free blacks and fugitive slaves harbored in the county felt relatively safe. Cooperation between the black community and sympathetic whites had created a climate in which reasonable expectations for personal security prevailed. Fugitive slaves such as Alfred Crockett and Curtis Henderson's great-grandmother stayed. So did emancipated slaves such as Maria Cooper.

They stayed despite the hostility sometimes vented by Washington's Democratic newspaper, the *Examiner,* which probably spoke for a majority of Democratic-leaning Washington County. (The Democratic Party swept the fall 1850 state elections in the county.) The paper called for strict adherence to the 1850 fugitive slave law and harsh punishments for those who aided and abetted fugitive slaves. Without mentioning local names, the *Examiner* castigated those who threatened to nullify the act in the name of a higher law. "To prevent the execution of one of the regularly and constitutionally enacted laws of the land," one *Examiner* writer warned, "the whole body of northern *niggerdom*, embracing the colored and their white advisors and accomplices, have banded together and established a precedent, which, if sanctioned and observed, would eventuate in the destruction of all law and the drenching of the whole land in blood."[82]

The racism unleashed after the passage of the new fugitive slave law and deteriorating conditions generally caused some local African Americans to reassess their futures. Martin Delany, the one-time student at Jefferson College and of Julius LeMoyne, entered a new phase in his career and became a black nationalist. He despaired of integration and began to advocate an exodus of African Americans from the United States. Washington County residents such as Franklin Chambers and Peaching Herring likewise despaired of the future and departed for Liberia later in the decade. But they represented a tiny minority of African Americans in the county. Despite the lack of employment opportunities and the harsh rhetoric of the *Examiner*, the vast majority of African Americans stayed put in Washington County.[83]

The overall effectiveness of the Underground Railroad in Washington County may well offer a clue as to why legends about the local line have persisted for so long. Although the stories exaggerate the number of fugitive slaves helped, romanticize its secrecy and hiding spots, and magnify the dangers involved, they do contain a core of truth that an Underground Railroad once ran through Washington County and enabled an unknown number of freedom seekers to find help and safety.

The End of the Line

The story of the Underground Railroad is one of the defining stories in American history. The story of Harriet Tubman first liberating herself and then leading scores of other slaves to freedom is as American as George Washington chopping down his father's cherry tree. Tubman's story, like countless others told about the Underground Railroad, is a tale of personal courage, bravery, and resourcefulness. It is also about danger, secrecy, and evil. But above all else, it is a powerful story about human freedom and the desperate measures some Americans took to gain that freedom. And unlike the story about Washington and the cherry tree, which Parson Weems seems to have manufactured out of thin air, the stories told about Tubman and the Underground Railroad have a real basis in history.

The rub, of course, is that myths and legends have grown up around the real history of the Underground Railroad in the same fashion as they did around George Washington. In Washington County and elsewhere, popular legends have vastly magnified the numbers of conductors and fugitives on the Underground Railroad, veiled its operations in a cloak of utter secrecy, and magnified the danger of slave catchers. While Weems's commercial and patriotic motives in making young George into the quintessential national hero are transparent today, the motives for embellishing the real history of the Underground Railroad are not nearly so clear and probably far less conscious.

Nevertheless, legends about the Underground Railroad have their own history and, more speculatively, their own motives. As Larry Gara has pointed out, the legend of the Underground Railroad took shape in the decades before the Civil War, concurrent with the establishment of safe

179

houses for escaping slaves. Abolitionists deliberately used the Underground Railroad as a propaganda tool to point out that black people who attempted to escape slavery, despite grave risks, belied the rosy, paternalistic views Southerners painted of its peculiar institution.

The second period in which the Underground Railroad legend took shape and became fixed, roughly between 1880 and World War I, is of far greater significance. This is the period during which newspaper reporters, local historians, and Wilbur Siebert, the first professional historian of the Underground Railroad, asked aging conductors and agents for their recollections of the great romantic adventure in which they had participated. Siebert published his monumental work in 1898. Locally in this period, Boyd Crumrine published his history of Washington County in 1882; the *Washington Observer* ran a lengthy series on the exploits of local abolitionists in 1884; and Howard Wallace wrote his pamphlet around the turn of the twentieth century. Earle Forrest's county history, published in 1927, offers the only substantial account of the local Underground Railroad written after World War I. Apart from Gara's book, which appeared in 1961, there was very little interest in the Underground Railroad either nationally or locally until the 1980s.

The most obvious motive for recording abolitionist stories in this second period is that the generation that served on the Underground Railroad was dying off. Another likely motive was that writing about the Underground Railroad enabled the younger generation to become vicarious participants in the heroic actions of grizzled abolitionists. Their tales gave these young writers a sense of connection with stirring and profound events that were noticeably absent in their own lives. They enshrined the stories that they heard as "history." As Gara has noted, neither Siebert nor the hundreds of local historians north of the Mason-Dixon Line raised probing questions about the accuracy of the memories they mined. The dominant motif of this "history" in Washington County was that a staunch and courageous minority of local white abolitionists, assisted occasionally by free blacks, had rescued countless numbers of hapless fugitive slaves and put them safely on the road to freedom. As chapter 3 pointed out, the "history" of the Underground Railroad in Washington County tended toward exaggeration and selectivity. It vastly inflated the number of fugitive slaves who made their way through the county and largely treated the passengers on the local route as anonymous pieces of baggage.

It is probably no accident that the legend of the Underground Railroad took shape during the absolute nadir of race relations in post-Civil War America.[1] The end of Reconstruction in 1877 meant the end of federal protection for the political and civil rights of the freedmen in the South; the 1890s brought about legalized segregation in state after state in the form of Jim Crow laws. The Supreme Court's decision in *Plessy v. Ferguson* in 1896 lent the sanction of the federal government to these laws, which segregated blacks and whites from cradle to grave. The wave of lynchings that began in the 1880s added the threat of death to those blacks who refused to accommodate the increasingly virulent racism of the white South. Discriminatory racial attitudes were not confined to south of the Mason-Dixon Line, as the occasional racial slurs used in local Underground Railroad accounts illustrate. Although Pennsylvania never passed laws to establish legal segregation, de facto segregation was very much a fact of life in Washington, Pennsylvania, until the 1960s. Local blacks were expected to sit in the balcony of movie theaters, forced to attend a segregated elementary school, and not welcome in the department stores or restaurants that then lined Main Street.[2]

The creation of the Underground Railroad legend in Washington County between 1880 and 1915 may have served as a way of deflecting white residents' awareness from the grim realities of race relations at the time. It was comforting to think that one's ancestors had done their part to combat the evils of the day. The pervasive assumptions in these memoirs and anecdotes from Washington County are that the Underground Railroad brought thousands of slaves to freedom and that the Civil War brought universal freedom to the nation's black population. In short, the Underground Railroad and the Union Army had solved America's problem with race. Samuel Atkinson epitomized this attitude when he concluded his account of how he and his brother had successfully transported a slave family to West Middletown on the eve of the Civil War: "Next the Civil War and the end of slavery forever."[3] Reminiscing about venerable abolitionists may have been a way of reassuring white Northerners that America's race problem had been solved and that they need have no pangs of conscience about the present. As David Blight observes, "By converting the realities of the Underground Railroad into romantic adventure stories—about themselves—people could turn reminiscence into a welcome alternative to the complicated and conflicted race relations plaguing the United States at the turn of the twentieth century."[4] The collective legend created at this time about the Underground

Railroad was clearly not just about the past; it also reflected contemporary thinking about race. Significantly, not a single Underground Railroad account from Washington County discusses then-current racial issues.

The third phase of the Underground Railroad legend encompasses the late twentieth and early twenty-first centuries. After more than a half century of general indifference, popular interest in the venerable Liberty Line has surged locally and nationally since the 1980s. A major factor of this resurgence was undoubtedly the publication and broadcast of Alex Haley's *Roots* (1976/1977), which stimulated a great interest in black genealogy. Charles L. Blockson's extensive research into the Underground Railroad was one expression of this renewed fascination with the means by which slaves became free people. One can also point to Faith Ringgold's *Aunt Harriet's Underground Railroad in the Sky* (1992) as heralding an explosion of children's literature on this subject. The establishment of the National Park Service's Network to Freedom in 1998 and the National Underground Railroad Freedom Center in Cincinnati, which opened in 2004, reflects the growing prominence of the subject. Meanwhile, local historical societies in hundreds of localities, Washington County included, have devised educational and outreach programs featuring the Underground Railroad. This book owes its existence, at least indirectly, to the Washington County Historical Society's decision to feature the Underground Railroad in its educational program.

This renewed interest in the Underground Railroad has resulted in a significant modification of the legend, one that in large measure is consistent with the "real" history of the institution. This modification has placed black Americans at the center of the Underground Railroad. It has rescued fugitives from playing the role of passive passengers and insisted that they were among the true heroes of the saga of the Underground Railroad. It has also asserted the rightful place of black conductors, agents, and stationmasters in that history. Both of these corrections are long overdue.

The "new" Underground Railroad, however, has many of the same flaws as the old one. In many respects, it has simply built upon the same roadbed—the same old legend—without substantially questioning or modifying it. The Underground Railroad is still envisioned as a network extending far into the South that did a landmark business in transporting fugitive slaves to freedom. It still has its secret tunnels and hidden codes. It still features harrowing escapes from evil slave catchers. The Underground Railroad still has its adventure, romance, and melodrama. As this book has sought to demonstrate, this legend, while it may have a slender basis in history, is for the most part a wishful distortion of what can be documented about the Underground Railroad.

The motives behind the new legend of the Underground Railroad are in fact quite laudable. The new Underground Railroad is a feel-good story about the reconciliation of the racial chasm that has separated Americans for most of their history. If the past has for brief moments demonstrated the possibility of racial cooperation, then surely the future has even better possibilities. The efforts of Dr. F. Julius LeMoyne certainly indicate that those moments happened historically. Even though the twenty-five slaves who were supposedly hidden in his attic were free people, LeMoyne's willingness to host a large contingent of blacks headed for Ohio speaks much about his capacity for racial tolerance. And certainly one can understand the desire of black Americans to see recognized that their ancestors were no mere passive victims of slavery, but bold spirits who shook off the shackles of slavery in a risky bid for freedom. Examples of this endeavor, such as Tom Stowe and David Thompson, likewise exist, but the vast majority of American slaves remained in bondage due to the huge imbalance of power and the practical obstacles to escape from slavery.

This most recent phase of the Underground Railroad legend's development has seen a sharp divergence between popular and scholarly understandings of the Underground Railroad. Historians are well aware of Gara's debunking of the myths and legends surrounding the Liberty Line and have for the most part moved beyond his revisionism. They have concerned themselves with documenting the pivotal role played by African Americans in numerous locales in enabling fugitive slaves to escape, and highlighting the importance of AME churches as safe havens.[5] Eric Foner's 2015 book, for example, unearthed previously unknown documents that reveal the operations of the vigilance committee in New York City headed by David Ruggles.[6] That popular views of the Underground Railroad still feature many legends and hoary stereotypes about the institution is old news to historians.

However, subtle tensions still exist among historians with regard to the fundamental nature of the Underground Railroad and the role that legends play in shaping our understanding of it. Skeptics such as David Blight have followed Gara in calling attention to the continual magnetic pull of the legendary Underground Railroad. Other scholars such as Stanley Harrold, while acknowledging this critique, have insisted that the Underground Railroad was much more robust and important than the skeptics would allow. Harrold regards the issue of fugitive slaves and the Underground

Railroad as a battleground that led to the Civil War and the violent clashes over fugitives that occurred along the border between North and South as a harbinger to that conflict. Gara, by contrast, dismisses the idea that the Underground Railroad was a central cause of the Civil War out of hand.[7]

This study of the legends and realities of the Underground Railroad in Washington County may not resolve these tensions among historians, but it does argue that these tensions need to be kept in the foreground of analyses of the Underground Railroad. It also contributes to an understanding of the extent, effectiveness, and nature of the Underground Railroad in one region that has been little studied. To summarize the argument, Washington County (and more broadly southwestern Pennsylvania) emerges as a region in which an effective network of friends of fugitives assisted a fairly small number of freedom seekers to find temporary or permanent havens. Despite local claims that Washington County operated some of the most important stations in the Keystone State, it is more accurate to state that these stations were on a branch line of the Underground Railroad. Washington County differed substantially from south central and eastern Pennsylvania in the number of fugitive slaves who made it their pathway to freedom. Unlike these other border areas, which attracted fugitive slaves from a much broader geographic area, Washington County's escapees originated fairly close to the county. The network of Underground Railroad agents clearly extended to Wheeling but did not extend beyond the Mason-Dixon Line to the South. The county bears striking similarities to the other border regions in Pennsylvania and along the Ohio River in that the core support for the Underground Railroad came from the black community, especially when it came to providing initial assistance to fugitive slaves. Even so, as in many other communities, white abolitionists have typically gotten top billing.

Washington County also departs from other northern localities in the composition of white abolitionists who began contributing to the Underground Railroad in the late 1830s. The county's substantial Presbyterian presence (shared with Allegheny County) distinguished it from other nearby counties, such as Fayette County and Greene County, where white abolitionism was a dead letter. The county also differs from border areas of Pennsylvania in which Quakers were the primary religious denomination aiding fugitives. Although the Presbyterian Church as a whole was not strongly antislavery, the Free Presbyterians and dissenting Presbyterian sects locally gave the county's white antislavery activity a unique flavor. To judge by the extensive antislavery petition drives of the 1830s, they created a well-organized network sympathetic to the cause of the slave. Washington County thus presents a paradox in comparison to south central Pennsylvania. Abolitionists there were unable to create long-lasting abolitionist societies but operated highly traveled Underground Railroad routes; abolitionists in Washington County created viable abolitionist societies but operated only a branch line of the Underground Railroad.

The persistence of Underground Railroad legends in Washington County may well reflect this abolitionist heritage. Memories of the arrival of radical abolitionism and the organizing of communities to combat the evil of slavery naturally nurtured the belief that Washington County was the hub of Underground Railroad activity in the Commonwealth of Pennsylvania. Although many localities claim an Underground Railroad heritage, Washington County may have more justification than most.

In any case, the legends persist, like the hydra of Greek mythology, which grew a new head every time Heracles cut off one of its heads. I recently attended a local Underground Railroad workshop whose principal speaker displayed the Underground Railroad quilt that she had made based upon the photographs in Tobin and Dobard's *Hidden in Plain View*. The quilt, she explained, contained a secret code involving the Underground Railroad. I bit my tongue. I was attending the workshop as a casual observer, not an invited participant, so I vowed to state the historical case against Underground Railroad quilts in another forum. In light of the minimal effect Gara's critique and that of others have had on the Underground Railroad legend, it is probably a sanguine hope to think that this one will kill the hydra. The legend of the Underground Railroad is deeply engrained in the popular culture of Americans. Nevertheless, this study of one county in southwestern Pennsylvania may serve as a guide to those who want to examine the operation of the Underground Railroad and understand the legends built upon it. They may think twice the next time they hear about the secret but lost tunnels of an alleged Underground Railroad stop.

Underground Railroad Sites
in Washington County

The following analysis examines some sixty abolitionist and Underground Railroad sites or people in Washington County. The sites range from those that are extremely well documented to those that are probably bogus. The analysis of each site includes information about the site, where that information came from, and an indication of how reliable that information is. The appendix is an attempt at a comprehensive list of sites in Washington County, but undoubtedly a few have fallen through the cracks.

Some of the information appearing in this analysis of individual sites also appears in the text. With a few exceptions, more information is given here. The notable exception is Dr. F. Julius LeMoyne, about whom much has been written. I have been more concerned here with developing biographical portraits of individuals about whom very little or nothing is known.

For this analysis, I have divided the sites into six categories. I have awarded each site a number of stars based upon the amount and quality of information about that site. In keeping with the Underground Railroad motif, I have designated these "North Stars," after the name of Frederick Douglass's newspaper.

Rating these sites is admittedly an inexact science. The sites do not fall neatly into categories, and I have often wavered as to whether a site belonged to one category or another. In particular, I have had a difficult time deciding whether a site should be classified as a two- or three-star site and even wondered sometimes whether to retain both of these categories. In the end I decided to keep both of them because they made a useful and significant distinction.

Some examples may help to clarify this distinction. John Stockton, the pastor of the Cross Creek Presbyterian Church, serves as good illustration of a two-star site. Stockton has clear credentials as an abolitionist, so it makes sense that he might have a connection to the Underground Railroad. However, the only link between him and the Underground Railroad is a claim made by a historian of the Cross Creek Presbyterian Church that the church aided many fugitives. The historian provided no details or examples to back up this claim. Thus my evaluation is that while it is plausible that Stockton was involved in the Underground Railroad, there is no concrete evidence to support this contention.

George Y. Holmes serves as an example of three-star site. Holmes, a Baptist preacher who lived in Coon Island in the western part of the county, likewise has abolitionist credentials. However, a specific story of Holmes's involvement in the Underground Railroad has survived. Furthermore, two sources point to Holmes's activities as an Underground Railroad agent. Specific details and evidence are available in Holmes's case, in contrast to Stockton's case.

There is one further complication in this rating system: a few individuals have been included who played a peripheral role in the Underground Railroad and for whom the evidence is quite clear. A good example would be Samuel Taylor of Centerville. Taylor was not strictly a part of the Underground Railroad; he never apparently hosted any fugitive slaves. He was, however, willing to lend his horses to the Wallaces when they needed to move escaping slaves to the next station. That Taylor's house is still standing— with the name "Taylor" embedded in the side of the house—made his inclusion hard to resist. I have not attempted to rate sites such as Taylor's.

5 North Stars = Convincing proof from several independent sources that the site was an Underground Railroad station. Written contemporary evidence and primary sources are available.

4 North Stars = Site was almost certainly a stop, but is only mentioned in one primary source.

3 North Stars = Preponderance of evidence suggests that the site was a stop. Some details or stories exist about the site, but the evidence is secondhand.

2 North Stars = The site may have been a stop, but few or no details are available. Evidence is fragmentary or incomplete, and may come from only one source.

1 North Star = Probability of site being a stop is low. Evidence is very slim and not very good. Local oral traditions may be the only source.

0 stars = No evidence or a spurious site. Evidence contradicts claims made for the site.

The sites are listed by geographical regions and, within a region, alphabetically. The geographical regions are as follows: the West Alexander area, the West Middletown area, the Washington area, the Canonsburg/Meadowlands area, the Monongahela area, and the Centerville area. These areas correspond to the maps found in chapter 4.

In listing the sources for these sites, I have used the following shorthand when referring to a number of commonly used sources:

Barker Map	J. Barker, "Barker's Map of Washington County, Pennsylvania" (North Hector, NY: William J. Barker, 1856)
Beers	J. H. Beers, *Commemorative Biographical Record of Washington County, Pennsylvania* (Chicago: J. H. Beers, 1893)
Caldwell	J. A. Caldwell, *Caldwell's Illustrated Historical Centennial Atlas of Washington County* (Condil, Ohio: J. A. Caldwell, 1876)
Crumrine, Notes	Boyd R. Crumrine, "Underground Railway" xjv-j-380 in Historical Collection, Miller Library, Washington & Jefferson College, Washington, PA. These are the handwritten notes that Crumrine prepared for his history of Washington County. They are much more specific and revealing than his printed account of the Underground Railroad.

Crumrine, *History*   Boyd R. Crumrine, *History of Washington County, Pennsylvania, with Biographical Sketches . . .* (Philadelphia: L. H. Everts, 1882)

Forrest   Earle R. Forrest, *History of Washington County, Pennsylvania* (Chicago: S. J. Clarke, 1926)

McFarland   Joseph McFarland, *Twentieth Century History of Washington County* (Chicago: Richmond-Arnold, 1910)

Wallace   Howard Wallace, "Historical Sketch of the Underground Railroad from Uniontown to Pittsburgh" (Uniontown, PA: privately printed, 1903)

THE WEST ALEXANDER AREA

This area encompasses the village of West Alexander, West Finley Township, Donegal Township, and neighboring parts of Brooke and Ohio Counties in what is now West Virginia.

John and Samuel Atkinson
Four stars

Location: John Atkinson's farm was located on Castleman Run in Brooke County, Virginia. The farm was probably about five or six miles from West Alexander. (The Atkinson farm appears on the West Middletown area map.)

Site analysis: According to John's son Samuel (1840–1926), the Atkinson farm served as an Underground Railroad station. Samuel Atkinson, in a letter to the *Claysville Recorder,* recounted that he had personally delivered a family of fugitive slaves to Thomas McKeever's station in West Middletown, some ten miles to the northeast. In this letter, Atkinson claimed that he had delivered the "last consignment of slaves on the Underground Railroad." A man, woman, and child were brought to his father's house late on a Saturday night in the fall of 1860. The Atkinsons kept the family for the entire next day. When the pursuers who had been watching the house left to get supper, Atkinson and his brother left with the fugitive slaves for West Middletown. He had not gotten very far, however, before the woman spotted the pursuers on horseback. Samuel instructed her to keep going while he met the party. The pursuers apparently did not recognize him as John's son, because they accused his father of being a "Black Abolitionist" and revealed that they intended to nab the fugitive slaves and his father that evening. As the pursuers rode in the direction of his house, Samuel rendezvoused with his brother and the family of fugitive slaves and then hastily went to West Middletown.

The Atkinsons were threatened with reprisals on several occasions by their slave-owning neighbors. According to Samuel, a neighbor sent his slaves to burn the Atkinsons' gristmill. "The man was too cowardly to fire my father's buildings himself," Atkinson recalled, "but sent the colored people to do it." The slaves attempted to burn the gristmill down on three separate occasions. It was saved only because Atkinson's sons were sleeping there as a preventative measure. After the slaves were caught in this last attempt, the slave-owning neighbor moved to the west.

Samuel Atkinson's uncle, George Trimble, who lived near Salem, Ohio, was likewise involved in the Underground Railroad. Samuel reported seeing twenty-six slaves in Trimble's barn at one time, noting that traffic on this route picked up considerably in the three years before the Civil War.

Sources:
Claysville (PA) Recorder, July 24, 1926
1850 U.S. Census

Mayes Bell
Five stars

Location: Sources are contradictory about the location of Samuel Mayes Bell's farm. (Usually he is referred to as Mayes Bell.) According to the January 5, 1904, *Washington Observer*, Bell's farm stood about a mile and a half south of the village of West Alexander, thus placing it at the southern end of Donegal Township in Washington County, Pennsylvania. The *Observer* account further states that the original owner of the barn on this property, John Gilmore, sold it to Mayes Bell.

It is almost certain, however, that the Bell farm referred to in Underground Railroad accounts was on the Virginia/Pennsylvania line in Ohio County, Virginia. A property map indicates that his 149-acre farm was located on the Virginia side of the border, just northwest of the village of West Alexander.

Several other sources call the location mentioned in the *Observer* account into question. First, both the 1840 and 1850 censuses show Bell and his wife, M. A., living in Ohio County, Virginia (West Virginia as of 1863). Furthermore, all of their children were born in Virginia, according to the 1860 census. Thus Bell spent most of his adult, married life before the Civil War in Ohio County, Virginia.

Second, although Bell and his family did move to Donegal Township in 1856, township tax records indicate that he did not own real estate in that township. (Bell was born in Donegal Township in 1814.) The Bells apparently moved to West Alexander after the death of his mother in 1856, perhaps to be closer to his seventy-one-year-old father, Moses. Donegal Township tax records indicate that Mayes Bell was assessed in the late 1850s for the ownership of a horse and a carriage, but not for real estate. In addition, there is no record in the Washington County Recorder of Deeds office of a real estate transaction between John Gilmore and Mayes Bell. Thus it seems clear that the Bell farm mentioned in Underground Railroad accounts was across the border in Virginia.

Site analysis: Samuel Mayes Bell is mentioned several times in accounts of the Underground Railroad in the vicinity of West Alexander. The Bell farm was used as an Underground Railroad stop when it was deemed too dangerous to take fugitive slaves to Kenneth McCoy's farm some five miles to the south of West Alexander in West Finley Township, Washington County.

Bell, John Bell (possibly his brother), Dr. Samuel McKeehan, and John Gilmore (1796–1863), another Virginian who lived near West Alexander, spearheaded abolitionist efforts in the West Alexander area. The first antislavery meeting in the area was held at Gilmore's barn, probably in the 1840s. Gilmore's farm was located about a mile and a half northwest of West Alexander in Ohio County. The site is on Atkinson Crossing Road, about one-half mile north of the National Road (modern-day Route 40).

The organizers of this meeting saw their mission at least initially as an educational one. They distributed pamphlets to nearby farmers and subsequently held a number of antislavery meetings in the barn. Their handbills ultimately laid out the reasons why "every honorable man should assist slaves every way to gain their freedom."

Bell and his wife moved to Washington, Pennsylvania, at some point in the 1860s, because they appear living in that town in the 1870 census. There he is listed as a wool buyer. By 1880 they had moved to Pittsburgh, where he continued his career as a wool buyer. Mayes Bell and his wife disappear from the historical record after 1880.

Sources:
Washington (PA) Observer, January 5, 1904
Claysville (PA) Recorder, November 30, 1928
1840, 1850, 1860, 1870, 1880 U.S. Census
Forrest, 424
Caldwell, 196
Map of Ohio County, West Virginia (Wheeling, WV: Koller and Conrad, 1918)

The Frazier Rest Home
One star

Location: The Frazier Rest Home, still standing, is located on the Old National Pike in West Alexander.

Site analysis: Family tradition has it that this rest home, probably built by Andrew B. Frazier (1752–1838), may have been an Underground Railroad stop. Even descendants of the Frazier family do not press this claim strongly. Peter J. Topoly notes that the Fraziers' farm would have been a good stopping place "if the Fraziers were a part of the railroad." The strongest claim to this being a station is that the Fraziers emigrated from Scotland and subsequently to western Pennsylvania along with families who do have documented ties to the Underground Railroad, such as the McCoys and Sutherlands. However, the Fraziers remained part of the Three Ridges Presbyterian Church in West Alexander when the McCoys and Sutherlands left to join the abolitionist Free Presbyterian Church in 1849. Moreover, no available evidence connects the Fraziers to the Underground Railroad. Although this possibility cannot be ruled out, it seems unlikely that the Fraziers were involved.

Source:
Peter J. Topoly to Joan Ruzika, May 8, 1991, Box B58, Folder 1, Washington County Historical Society

John Gilmore
Five stars

Location: John Gilmore's farm was located just across the Pennsylvania line in Ohio County, West Virginia. His farm was located on Atkinson Crossing Road, about half a mile north of the National Pike, and thus about a mile and a half from the village of West Alexander, an antislavery hub in Washington County, Pennsylvania. Gilmore's farm passed into the hands of Andrew J. Varner, whose property can clearly be identified on a 1918 farm map of Ohio County. Gilmore's barn, where the first antislavery meeting in this border area was held, was razed in 1928.

Note: Although an account in the January 5, 1904, *Washington Observer* states that Gilmore's barn was located southwest of the village of West Alexander in Washington County, Pennsylvania, this account is clearly in error. The census indicates that Gilmore lived his entire adult life in Ohio County, Virginia.

Site analysis: Born in Derry, Ireland, John Gilmore (1796–1863) accompanied his parents when they migrated to the Upper Ohio Valley. His father William first appears in the 1810 census in Elizabeth Township, Ohio County, Virginia.

The first inklings of John Gilmore's abolitionist sympathies appeared in 1839, when he drafted a petition to Congress requesting that slavery be abolished in the District of Columbia and that the expansion of slavery be halted. At least ten of his neighbors signed this petition, including George and Peregrine Whitham. When their local congressman refused to support this petition, Gilmore and his neighbors solicited former president John Quincy Adams, then a congressman from Massachusetts, to present their petition. The petition incensed many in Ohio County and led to a demand for Gilmore's resignation as justice of the peace. Gilmore refused to resign, declaring that abandoning the office "would be a dangerous precedent, establishing the principle that a difference of opinion amongst the members of a court on a political or moral question is a sufficient cause to justify the majority to require the minority to resign."

Two years later, in 1841, Gilmore held the first antislavery meeting in the border county area. At least twenty-five individuals signed the statement of principles arrived at during the meeting. Gilmore's barn became the meeting place of panhandle abolitionists because it was one of the few venues open to them. It was also used as a safe haven when Kenneth McCoy's station five miles south of West Alexander was being watched.

Sources:
Forrest, 424
Washington (PA) Observer, January 5, 1904
Map of Ohio County, West Virginia
Claysville (PA) Recorder, May 28, 1915; March 12, 1915; August 20, 1915
1810, 1820, 1830, 1840, 1850, 1860 U.S. Census

George Y. Holmes
Three stars

Location: George Holmes's farm was located in Coon Island, about one mile west of Claysville in Donegal Township along the National Road. His farm appears on the 1856 Barker Map of Washington County. There is no house or building on the site today; all that remains is an open field.

Site analysis: George Holmes (1820–1903) emigrated with his family from Scotland in 1830. Holmes inherited the farm his father had purchased in 1832 when his father died in 1847.

Beers describes Holmes as the last survivor of the fifteen abolitionists of Donegal Township who voted for the Free Soil ticket. These abolitionists, all of whom lived in or near West Alexander, certainly would have included Dr. Samuel McKeehan, Kenneth McCoy, and David Howell. Unlike the others, who were Presbyterians, Holmes was a Baptist. Although he was not ordained as a minister, he frequently preached in Baptist churches in North Wheeling, Washington, and Claysville.

The one anecdote to survive about Holmes's Underground Railroad activities touches upon his role as a preacher. Holmes was harboring two escaped slaves at his house when two proslavery neighbors who were suspicious of his activities came to his residence. Holmes was engaged in the family worship when these neighbors came to call. Observing the arrival of these unwelcome visitors, Holmes extended the worship far beyond its usual length so that his neighbors would leave. Eventually they did. Holmes had them followed to make sure that they had gone home. Only then did he steer the fugitive slaves to West Middletown.

Sources:
Beers, 369
Claysville (PA) Recorder, February 25, 1916

David Howell
Three stars

Location: Unknown, although probably in Donegal Township in western Washington County

Site analysis: David Howell (1827–1917) shows up in several Underground Railroad accounts. Born in West Finley Township, Howell took up the trade of a harness maker in Washington, Pennsylvania, with his brother George. After his marriage in 1851, he took his new bride to live in Limestone, in Marshall County, Virginia. Howell and his growing family moved several times in the subsequent decade. The 1880 census shows that the Howells' first child, Charles, was born in Virginia in 1853, but that the next two were born in Pennsylvania in 1855 and 1858. Minnie, born in 1862, was born in Virginia. (David does not appear in the 1860 census, so his location then cannot be specified.) All of the four youngest children, born after Howell's return from fighting in the Civil War, were born in Pennsylvania. Howell apparently spent most of his post-Civil War years in West Alexander.

According to his obituary in the *Claysville Recorder,* Howell worked with many of the notable figures in the Washington County Underground Railroad, such as Dr. F. Julius LeMoyne, Thomas McKeever, Dr. Samuel McKeehan, and Mayes Bell. (In fact, Howell's role as an Underground Railroad conductor is the first of his activities mentioned in his obituary.) Howell's primary role was to conduct slaves from Greene County to West Middletown. He also helped to guide slaves from the border counties of Virginia to safety. Another account says that Howell went as far as Waynesburg in Greene County to secure the freedom of fugitive slaves.

Sources:
Claysville (PA) Recorder, February 25, 1916; June 8, 1917
1880 U.S. Census

Kenneth McCoy
Five stars

Location: The McCoy farm is located on the Old Brick Road in West Finley Township, about five miles south of West Alexander. An 1880s farmhouse is still standing, although it has fallen into disrepair. The original farmhouse, which was built in the 1820s or 1830s, was torn down long ago. According to a newspaper account in the *Claysville Recorder*, runaway slaves were hidden in a small room in the basement of the original farmhouse. Harold Hutchison confirmed that a room at the back of the basement served this purpose. Mrs. McCoy (probably the wife of Kenneth's son John) showed Hutchison this room when he was an adolescent in about 1930.

Site analysis: Kenneth McCoy's involvement in the Underground Railroad is well documented. In about 1845, McCoy (1791–1873) organized an antislavery society at his home that became the nucleus of an underground railroad in the West Alexander area. Others who joined this antislavery society were John Henderson, James and Alexander Sprowls, Robert and Isaac Sutherland, and Kenneth's son John McCoy (1836–1909). Kenneth McCoy joined the West Alexander Free Presbyterian Church when it was founded in 1849.

McCoy's was one of the major stations in western Washington County. On one occasion, he harbored eleven fugitives in his barn. One account states that seventeen runaways were once hidden in the back cellar room of the farmhouse. When it became known that the McCoy farm was a station and therefore dangerous for fugitives, McCoy began sending runaways to the nearby farms of John and Mayes Bell.

McCoy's son John was also involved in the Underground Railroad. According to an account in the *Claysville Recorder*, John McCoy told about an occasion when he came across a footsore, weary, and hungry female slave who was resting on a stump by the side of the road. He instructed her on where to hide until he could return with food for her. After procuring food in West Alexander, McCoy returned and led her along the ridge that led in the direction of the next station, West Middletown. It is fortunate that McCoy left the road, because not long afterward a party of men went through West Alexander asking for the female slave. A West Alexander resident reportedly responded, "No, but John McCoy was here awhile ago and if he sees her you never will." McCoy later saw these same slave hunters taking the valley road from his perspective far above them.

Kenneth McCoy and his wife, Jane Brownlee McCoy, are buried in the Old Cemetery in West Alexander.

Sources:
Beers, 1021
Forrest, 424
Washington (PA) Observer, January 5, 1904

Washington (PA) Reporter, October 2, 1909

Wheeling (WV) Intelligencer, August 1, 1910

Claysville (PA) Recorder, February 25, 1916

Crumrine, *History*, 981

Harold Hutchison to author, October 24, 2006

Samuel McKeehan
Five stars

Location: Corner of Old National Pike and Liberty Road, West Alexander. The house is still standing.

Site analysis: This two-story house was the home of Dr. Samuel McKeehan (ca. 1775–1866). A veteran of the War of 1812, McKeehan resided in West Alexander from 1826 until his death in 1866. He took a prominent part in abolitionist and Underground Railroad activities in this small village in western Washington County. Along with John Gilmore and Mayes Bell, he organized one of the earliest antislavery societies in western Washington County and neighboring Ohio County, Virginia. McKeehan became one of the founding members of the Free Presbyterian Church in West Alexander when it was organized in 1849.

This physician also opened his home to fugitive slaves who were fleeing from nearby Virginia farms. James W. Rice recalled directing sixteen slaves who were being pursued by mounted slave catchers to McKeehan's residence. According to one account, slaves were forwarded to McKeehan's from Kenneth McCoy's farm some five miles south of West Alexander and then on to Matthew McKeever's station in West Middletown, about twelve miles to the north.

McKeehan reportedly scoured the woods on his daily rambles in an effort to find any fugitives who might be hiding. If he did come across any runaways, he instructed them on where to hide until nightfall, when he led them to his house.

At the conclusion of the Civil War, McKeehan at age ninety welcomed home returning soldiers. Now that slavery was dead and the Union restored, he remarked, he was ready to depart this life. He is buried in the Old Cemetery in West Alexander. McKeehan's grave marker has been toppled over, however, and is difficult to find.

Sources:
Washington (PA) Observer, January 5, 1904
Washington (PA) Reporter, October 17, 1866
Crumrine, *History*, 747
Wheeling (WV) Intelligencer, August 1, 1910

Robert Sutherland
Three stars

Location: Sutherland's farm was on Walnut Valley Road in West Finley Township. He was an immediate neighbor of Kenneth McCoy's. Sutherland's farm was on the eastern side of the ridge from McCoy's farm.

Site analysis: Robert Sutherland (1815–1903) was one of the original seven members of the antislavery society that organized at Kenneth McCoy's house in 1844–1845. He was also among the founding members of the Free Presbyterian Church in West Alexander. Little is known specifically about Sutherland's Underground Railroad activities. His obituary does state that Sutherland "frequently aided hound-hunted slaves to escape to free territory by the 'underground railway system.'"

Sources:
Washington (PA) Daily Reporter, March 7, 1903
Claysville (PA) Recorder, August 20, 1915
"Session Book of the Free Presbyterian Church of West Alexander"

Free Presbyterian Church, West Alexander
Five stars

Location: This church is no longer standing. The site is north of the Old National Pike (Main Street) on Liberty Street in West Alexander.

Site analysis: The "free" Presbyterian movement grew out of the dissatisfaction of abolitionist Presbyterians in the late 1840s with the stance of national Presbyterian bodies on the issue of slavery. The Free Presbyterian Church in West Alexander was the only one of its kind in Washington County.

The Reverend Joseph Gordon organized the Free Presbyterian Church in West Alexander in 1849. The Free Church attracted members of local abolitionist and Underground Railroad circles such as Kenneth McCoy, John and Mayes Bell, and Dr. Samuel McKeehan. A number of abolitionists and Underground Railroad agents who lived in neighboring Ohio and Brooke counties in Virginia attended this church. Among them were the Atkinson family from Castleman's Run in Brooke County and the Witham families from Ohio County. The Free Presbyterian church also gained adherents from as far away as "Little Washington" who were unhappy with the conservative stance of the Presbyterian churches there on slavery. Samuel McFarland and his wife, Mary, joined the Free Church in West Alexander. All told, the church had 163 members.

The Free Presbyterian Church in West Alexander closed its doors in 1867 after the cause for which is had been established ceased to exist.

Sources:

Session Minutes, 1849–1867, Free Presbyterian Church of West Alexander, West Alexander Presbyterian Church archives

One Hundred Seventy-Fifth Anniversary of Presbyterianism at West Alexander, PA (West Alexander, PA: United Presbyterian Church, 1965), 14

Jason Haley, "Washington County Presbyterians: Abolitionism in a Divided Congregation" (Honors thesis, Washington & Jefferson College, 2002)

Claysville (PA) Recorder, December 20, 1912

THE WEST MIDDLETOWN AREA AND CROSS CREEK

William Asbury

Five stars

Location: Cross Creek. Exact location unknown.

Site analysis: William Asbury (d. 1846) was one of the first African Americans involved in the Underground Railroad in Washington County. According to the historian of the Cross Creek Cemetery, Asbury was "head engineer on the 'Underground Railroad' from his residence to Pittsburgh" from 1837 until his death in 1846. Asbury used the pretext of hauling produce to the Pittsburgh market to conceal fugitives he was taking to the next station. Asbury became so infamous that a reward of one thousand dollars was reportedly put on his head in Wheeling, Virginia.

Asbury also conducted fugitive slaves to safety by an alternative route through Washington. According to D. M. Boyd of West Middletown, who was interviewed for an 1884 newspaper article, Asbury conducted fugitives first to Washington and "well on to Jarrett's tavern"—a station in southern Allegheny County on the route to Pittsburgh.

Asbury was born a slave in Virginia. According to family legend, he grew to be so unruly that his owner ultimately freed him. Asbury and his wife, Lettitia, ultimately settled in Cross Creek around 1830.

Apparently Asbury worked closely with Underground Railroad operatives in West Middletown, some six miles to the south. On one occasion, he led a group of about forty blacks armed with clubs to West Middletown after a fugitive slave had been captured and led before the justice of the peace in West Middletown. After Thomas McKeever, the justice of the peace, ruled against the slave owner, the latter was about to protest until Asbury arrived on the scene. Asbury and his followers quickly formed a cordon around the fugitive and ushered him out of West Middletown as quickly as possible. The fugitive made good on his escape.

A black man named John Brown assisted Asbury in many of his Underground Railroad ventures. According at an 1884 newspaper article, Asbury and Brown "conducted scores of refugees to places of safety."

Asbury is buried in the Cross Creek Cemetery.

Sources:

Washington (PA) Observer, November 20, 1884

Dave Molter, "Tracking Underground Railroad Not Easy," *Washington (PA) Observer-Reporter*, May 6, 1990

John Asbury, "Asbury Family History," Washington County Historical Society

James Simpson and James K. Reed, *History of the Cross Creek Graveyard and the Cross Creek Cemetery*

Forrest, 426–27

Joseph Bryant

Four stars

Location: Bethany, Brooke County, West Virginia. The exact location is unknown.

Site analysis: According to Matthew McKeever, his brother-in-law Joseph Bryant operated an Underground Railroad station in the village of Bethany.

Bryant transferred fugitives from Wheeling to his in-law's station at West Middletown, just across the border.

Bryant is the only stationmaster known to have spent time in jail for his activities. One of the men who helped bring a shipment of fugitives to Bryant's station later turned state's evidence and revealed Bryant's participation in the escape of these slaves. The slaves' owner had Bryant arrested and lodged in the Wheeling jail. Bryant refused to post bond and spent fifteen days in jail. The judge who heard this case believed that Matthew McKeever was the principal culprit and let Bryant go.

Source:
Forrest, 427

Noah Clouse
Three stars

Location: Noah Clouse owned a blacksmith shop in West Middletown, a borough some twelve miles west of Washington, Pennsylvania, according to the 1860 census. However, narratives that mention Clouse's involvement in the Underground Railroad locate his blacksmith shop in Canton Township, the township just west of Washington. Clouse may have been working in his father's blacksmith shop in Canton Township at the time the incident involving him occurred. The 1850 census lists Christopher Clouse, a seventy-three-year-old blacksmith, living in the township in 1850. Noah Clouse was forty years old in 1860. The locations of the Clouse sites are unknown.

Site analysis: Noah Clouse played a role in the escape of nine slaves from Clarksburg, Virginia, in 1856. According to Crumrine, Clouse harbored the fugitives in his blacksmith shop after they had been hidden on Matthew McKeever's farm in West Middletown. The Clarksburg fugitives were then taken to Tom Robinson's and Samuel Skinner's houses in Washington.

Sources:
Crumrine, Notes
1850, 1860 U.S. Census

James McElroy Sr. and James McElroy Jr.
Five stars

Location: James McElroy Sr. appears in the 1840 census as a forty- to fifty-year-old man living in Cross Creek Township, near the village of West Middletown. According to his son, James Jr., the McElroys lived a mile and a quarter east of the village on the Pittsburgh Road. The deed to the property that the senior McElroy bought in 1836 indicates that his land straddled Cross Creek, lying partly in Cross Creek Township and partly in Hopewell Township. (McElroy owned four other farms in the vicinity.) McElroy Sr. built a large steam mill on this property. Originally known as McElroy's Mills, the property later became known as Wilson's Mills after the death of James McElroy Sr. It is likely that these mills were the property of Robert Wilson, whose name appears on the 1856 Barker Map. The Caldwell Map of 1876 in fact shows a mill on Wilson's property. By 1910 these mills had burned. Their exact location is unknown, although they are probably under what is now Cross Creek Lake.

Site analysis: James McElroy Sr. was a flour miller who died in 1848, leaving behind his wife and nine children. He had many ties to the McKeever family in West Middletown, to abolitionism, and to the Underground Railroad.

Beginning about 1830, McElroy and his family began attending a Disciples of Christ Church that met originally at Matthew McKeever's home near West Middletown. McElroy's association with this noted abolitionist extended beyond church matters. His son, James McElroy Jr., provides most of what is known about his Underground Railroad activities.

McElroy Sr. became an acquaintance of John Brown in the early 1840s when Brown was traveling through western Pennsylvania buying wool. Brown stayed frequently at the McKeever and McElroy homes. As James Jr. noted many years later in his "Recollections," "I well remember that Brown would come over to our house in the evening after riding all day in the neighborhood buying wool. Our men neighbors would gather in, mostly to listen to talk between Brown and my father on the abolition of slavery. Brown was desperately in earnest and very bitter in his denunciation of slavery and the apologizer for it."

James McElroy Jr. (1825–1913) also became a participant in the Underground Railroad. He recalled long after the Civil War an occasion when

Matthew McKeever directed several slaves to his father's house. McKeever asked McElroy's father to deliver the slaves to Paris in northwestern Washington County. McElroy Sr. asked his fifteen-year-old son to prepare the family carriage and take the fugitives to this destination. The young McElroy drove all through the night to accomplish this errand. They later learned that the slaves successfully made their way to Canada.

McElroy Jr. also offers one of many versions of a story involving his father and a recaptured fugitive slave. The fugitive had found refuge at Matthew McKeever's station just outside of the village, but the owner and his bloodhound tracked him down. Gathering some men who were working in a nearby field, McKeever insisted that the slave owner take the slave to West Middletown so that the justice of the peace could determine whether the slave was actually his property. The slave owner reluctantly agreed.

Meanwhile, a messenger had arrived at the McElroy farm, where the McElroys were cutting wood. James Sr. hastily mounted a horse and galloped off to West Middletown, where he found a large crowd gathered in Justice Thomas Odenbaugh's office. There McElroy learned the details of what had happened.

Before the justice could rule on the matter, McElroy asked the slave owner whether the dog lying at his feet was his. When the owner affirmed that it was, McElroy said, "I move that this bloodhound does not leave this town alive." The assembly immediately seconded this motion and proceeded to hang the dog from a tree in front of the office. The frightened slave owner decided to leave West Middletown without his property. The fugitive arrived in Canada three days later.

McElroy Jr. makes no further mention of Underground Railroad activities on his part after his father's death in 1848, although he continued to live in the area. After his father's estate was settled, he moved to the family's homestead in neighboring Mount Pleasant Township and built a frame house. McElroy served as captain of the militia company from West Middletown that marched off to war in 1861.

Sources:
James McElroy, "Recollections," 2, 10–12, 14
1840, 1850, 1860 U.S. Census
Crumrine, *History*, 811–24
Barker Map
Caldwell
"Death of Capt. J. McElroy," *Jamestown (ND) Weekly Alert*, September 25, 1913

Matthew McKeever
Five stars

Location: 122 Seminary Road, near West Middletown

Site analysis: Matthew McKeever's house is probably the best-known Underground Railroad site in western Washington County. It is one of two Washington County sites that Wilbur Siebert listed in his 1898 groundbreaking study of the Underground Railroad.

Matthew McKeever (1797–1884) was raised in an abolitionist family. His father, William (1758–1838), was one of the first abolitionists in Washington County.

McKeever is one of the few operatives who left testimony about his involvement in the Underground Railroad. In a letter written in 1880, he said that he had been involved in the Underground Railroad for some forty years, during which time he helped some thirty-five to forty individuals escape the bonds of slavery. The largest group of slaves that he helped at one time was eight. McKeever's account makes it clear that assisting fugitives was a very sporadic activity.

Fugitive slaves came to McKeever's station outside of West Middletown from the south and from the west. From the south, runaways were forwarded from Kenneth McCoy's station south of West Alexander and from Dr. Samuel McKeehan's in that village. McKeever also received fugitives from the direction of Wheeling and Wellsburg.

McKeever forwarded fugitive slaves to a number of other stations. Accounts indicate that he sent fugitives to Washington, the county seat, as well as to Pittsburgh. Slaves directed to Little Washington were ultimately routed through Pittsburgh. James McElroy Jr. recalled that McKeever once delivered fugitive slaves to his father's mill on Cross Creek. McElroy Sr. then asked his fifteen-year-old son to deliver the fugitive slaves to Paris, in northern Washington County. McElroy's account indicates that a second route ran northward from the county to Canada.

Part of McKeever's fame stems from his acquaintance with John Brown. McKeever initially met Brown when the latter was buying sheep in western Pennsylvania in 1842. But as Brown became more deeply involved in abolitionism, the two men began spending long evenings talking about the evils of slavery. Although there is no hard evidence, there is some speculation that Brown used his sheep business as a cover for helping slaves in western Virginia to make a bid for freedom and McKeever's station was part of this route.

In addition to his cellar, McKeever made use of a large, densely wooded area known as Penitentiary Hill near West Middletown as a hiding place for runaway slaves. Although this woods appeared to be solid, there was a cleared field at the center of it that McKeever used for growing grain. Fugitives often labored there to "work out their board" until arrangements could be made to send them to Canada.

Sources:
Forrest, 424, 427
McElroy, "Recollections," 10
Washington (PA) Observer, November 20, 1884
Boyer, *Legend of John Brown*, 347–53
Osborne Mitchell, "Abolitionists and Anti-Slavery Days," *Washington (PA) Reporter*, August 15, 1908

Thomas McKeever
Five stars

Location: 56 E. Main Street, West Middletown, and Patton Lane, near the Grove United Presbyterian Church, West Middletown. McKeever sold his house in the village of West Middletown in 1854 and bought a farm on the outskirts of the village, where he lived until his death in 1865. Both houses are still standing.

Site analysis: Thomas McKeever was part of an abolitionist family. His father, William, was one of the early exponents of abolitionism in Washington County, and his brother Matthew became one of the best-known Underground Railroad conductors locally. Thomas McKeever took an active role in the abolition societies that were organized in the mid-1830s. In the 1840s, he ran for the Pennsylvania legislature on the Liberty Party ticket.

Numerous sources link McKeever to the Underground Railroad. McKeever hid slaves in the cellar of his house in town and later in the barn on his farm property. As Matthew McKeever wrote in 1880 in response to a reporter's inquiry that was later published in the *Pittsburg Dispatch*, "My brother Tommy shipped a good many."

The most famous story involving Thomas McKeever's activities as an abolitionist, however, involves a fugitive slave from Wellsburg who had been caught by his Virginia owner while working in Matthew McKeever's cornfield. (Several versions of this story exist. One version says the slave was from Wheeling.) The owner and his attorney brought the slave in handcuffs, along with a warrant, to a judge of the county's circuit court, Thomas McKeever.

According to the Reverend John Clark, who served from 1841 to 1842 as a Methodist minister in West Middletown, McKeever had become "the object of unstinted hatred and bitter maledictions across the border" because of his Underground Railroad activities. These supporters of slavery would have liked nothing more than to force McKeever to order the return to slavery of a fugitive from that institution. They came armed with witnesses, two lawyers from Wellsburg, and a writ from a Virginia magistrate.

Thomas McKeever determined otherwise. He began the court session, conducted in his office in West Middletown, by demanding that the manacles be struck from the fugitive, stating, "Our laws do not permit the trial of a man in irons, before he is condemned as guilty." The manacles had been fastened so tightly that a smith had to be called to get them off. According to Clark's account, while waiting for the smith to appear, McKeever whispered to the fugitive slave, "Deny everything they attempt to prove and claim you are a free man."

When the trial began, Clark continued, the fugitive claimed that he was in fact a free black from Somerset County, Pennsylvania. (Another version says Carlisle, Pennsylvania.) He demonstrated a familiarity with that area by "rattl[ing] off names and places in Somerset County as glibly as though he was telling the truth." The runaway requested a delay in the hearing so that he could procure witnesses to support him. McKeever granted a delay of ten days and bond of one thousand dollars to guarantee the fugitive's appearance in court after this delay, much to the delight of the party from Virginia. But to their chagrin, McKeever then demanded a bond from the Virginians to vouchsafe their appearance.

Colonel W.W. McNulty signed for the fugitive slave, and the owner of the slave put down the bond to guarantee his appearance. McKeever, however, refused to accept the slave owner's money, declaring it "forfeit, not bail," much to the delight of the crowd that had gathered. He ordered the fugitive's handcuffs removed and pronounced him a free man. A free black named William Asbury then escorted the fugitive toward safety.

Sources:

"McKeever was a Righteous Judge and a Warm Abolitionist," Murdock Papers,
    McKeever Study Library

Forrest, 422–25

Washington (PA) Observer, November 20, 1884

The Plaque Book: West Middletown Houses and Their History (West Middletown,
    PA: McKeever Study Library, 1995), 6

"A Savior of Slaves," *Pittsburg Dispatch*, May 2, 1890

William McKeever
Two stars

Location: McKeever in the1830s lived in a stone house on College Street in the
village of West Middletown. His house stood adjacent to the building that
occupied the corner of College and Main streets. The 1856 Barker Map shows
this building as McNulty's Hotel. McKeever's house is no longer standing.

Site analysis: William McKeever (1758–1838), the father of Thomas and
Matthew McKeever, was one of the earliest abolitionists in Washington
County and reputedly the first in the western part of the county. According
to one story, he was outraged when a slave driver known as General Biggs
cursed and flogged several weary slaves who were part of a coffle of slaves
being dragged through West Middletown in 1830. (One version has it that
these were actually runaway slaves who had been recaptured.) McKeever became so enraged by this treatment that he began denouncing the driver and
followed the train of slaves out of the village, all the while screaming abuse at
him. Once outside the village, the driver advised McKeever to keep his
mouth shut and return home. But McKeever tore open his shirt and dared
Biggs to shoot him through the heart, as this was the only way they could
stop his bitter denunciations. As Rebecca Jones recounted in her "Reminiscences," "The neighbors were alarmed for the outcome. The general, in spite
of his temper, realized that discretion was the better part of valor. McKeever,
having at last exhausted his vocabulary, came home without accident, quite
the hero of the occasion."

McKeever reputedly harbored slaves in his attic and in a cellar hidden
by a secret trap door that was concealed by a rag carpet. According to Osborne Mitchell, as many as a dozen slaves could be concealed in this hiding

place. But as with all stories of secret rooms mentioned in connection with the Underground Railroad, this one should be taken with a grain of salt. It is McKeever's sons who were clearly involved in the Underground Railroad.

Sources:
Forrest, 424–25
1830 U.S. Census
Barker Map
Osborne Mitchell, "Abolitionists and Anti-Slavery Days," *Washington (PA) Reporter,* August 15, 1908
Rebecca C. Jones, "Reminiscences," in *Reminiscences of West Middletown, Pennsylvania,* ed. William T. Lindsey (West Middletown, PA: McKeever Study Library Association, 2002 [1910]), 5

John Stockton
Two stars

Location: Cross Creek Village

Site analysis: John Stockton was pastor of the Cross Creek Presbyterian Church for fifty years, from 1827 to 1877, and espoused his abolitionist views from the pulpit through the antebellum years. An 1820 graduate of Washington College, Stockton opened his church to other antislavery preachers and to black members. William Asbury, the noted black Underground Railroad agent, is buried in the church graveyard. Not all of Stockton's congregation agreed with his views on slavery and race. In 1849, part of the congregation left to form its own church, the Pine Grove Presbyterian Church, in protest against his views.

Stockton's connection to the Underground Railroad is unknown. Although a historian of the Cross Creek Presbyterian Church claims that the church aided many fugitives, there is no documentation to support this claim.

Sources:
Jason Haley, "Presbyterians Divided" (Unpublished paper, Washington & Jefferson College, 2001), 41–43
Alvin D. White, *History of Cross Creek Presbyterian Church* (Parsons, WV: McLain, 1969) 39, 52

Samuel Taggart
Grove United Presbyterian Church, West Middletown
Three stars

Location: 125 E. Main St., West Middletown. The original Grove Presbyterian Church stood just to the east of this site from 1818 to 1859. The current church was built in 1859.

Site analysis: Samuel Taggart (1803–1885) was minister of the Presbyterian Church in West Middletown for much of the period when the local Underground Railroad was in operation. He became known as a fiery abolitionist. Antislavery advocates published one of his sermons as a pamphlet and distributed it widely in the county.

Although West Middletown has the reputation of being wholeheartedly sympathetic to the antislavery cause, the actual situation in the village was clearly more complex. Taggart's staunchly abolitionist views caused a rift in his own congregation. Those who disagreed with Taggart's stance refused to contribute financially to the church and threatened to starve the pastor. When asked if he would "preach against slavery if he had to live on bread and water," Taggart, who had been born in Ireland, retorted that he had never said that. According to Albert McClure's recollection, however, Taggart said that he would "preach on if I had to live on buttermilk and potatoes—not a bad diet for a good old Irishman." In 1844, some thirty members of his church left to form the Patterson's Mill Associated Presbyterian Church and hired a pastor from the South.

Bitterness between this staunchly abolitionist church and some of its neighbors continued through the Civil War. According to Dr. Albert McClure, Union soldiers on furlough placed a U.S. flag on the church and provoked much resentment from local Copperheads, who threatened to tear down the flag. A group from Eldersville rode through town, shooting their guns and proclaiming for Jeff Davis. Confronted by Union soldiers defending the church, the Copperheads attempted to bribe Thomas Webster, the janitor, to take the flag down. Webster declined according to McClure's account, saying, "No, what good would $20.00 [be] to a dead man?"

This altercation resulted in one casualty. A "rebel" living on a nearby farm threatened to shoot Thomas McKeever, one of the furloughed Union soldiers. Thomas was the son of Matthew McKeever and namesake of the noted Underground Railroad agent. McClure's uncle, James, however, intervened, and struck the rebel's gun just as he was about to fire. The ball struck McClure in the thigh and remained there for the rest of his life.

Several sources link this church to the Underground Railroad. According to Forrest, "slaves were frequently concealed in the old church." Presumably Taggart would have been the agent responsible for hiding these slaves. Osborne Mitchell likewise says that the church was a station.

Sources:

Beers, 1328

Forrest, 731

Dr. Albert McClure to Roy Thompson, October 25, 1925, McKeever Study Library, West Middletown, PA

Samuel Taggart, "A Sermon by Samuel Taggart," Historical Collection, XV-f-38, Washington & Jefferson College, Washington, PA

White, *First Families and Forgotten Churches*

Osborne Mitchell, "Abolitionists and Anti-Slavery Days," *Washington (PA) Reporter*, August 15, 1908

The Plaque Book: West Middletown Houses and Their History (West Middletown, PA: McKeever Study Library, 1995), 5

WASHINGTON AREA

Tar (Tower) Adams
Five stars

Location: Tar Adams lived on Chestnut Street, west of what is now Franklin Street, according to an 1859 city directory. The exact location of Adams's residence is unknown.

Site analysis: Tar or Tower Adams (his name also appears in the census as "Tour" Adams) played an important role in the Underground Railroad in Washington, Pennsylvania. Born free in Maryland in 1788, Adams moved to Washington as a young man and began plying his trade as a gunsmith. Forrest credits him with being the first Underground Railroad agent in the county. This would suggest that he began helping fugitive slaves shortly after the War of 1812.

Adams's name appears prominently in the annals of the local Underground Railroad. Forrest relates one story testifying to Adams's prowess as a runner and indicating his Underground Railroad connections in West Middletown. According to Forrest, mounted slave catchers appeared one day in Washington. Feigning lameness, Adams overheard the slave catchers' inquiries about a fugitive. After learning about their mission, Adams took off like a bolt for West Middletown. After catching sight of Adams running at full speed, the sheriff, who had accompanied the would-be captors into Washington, informed them that their mission was now a hopeless one. When asked why, the sheriff responded that the seemingly lame man who had disappeared was in fact the fleet-footed Adams, who could outrun men on horseback to West Middletown.

Adams also appears in accounts of one of the most famous murders that occurred in antebellum Washington. In 1828, local authorities arrested Christian "Kit" Sharp and accused him of murdering his owner, Robert Carlyle, just outside of Washington. Sharp was a runaway slave who had been recaptured by Carlyle. After spending the night in Washington with his recaptured slave, Carlyle set out along the National Road. He was found murdered several miles along the road. Sharp claimed that three men had attacked his master, and that he was totally innocent of the charges against him. Many in Washington believed Sharp's story and that Tar Adams had been one of the three men. The jury believed otherwise, however, and sentenced Sharp to hang.

Adams's Underground Railroad activities continued into his old age. In 1856, Adams and Samuel McFarland guided a group of nine fugitive slaves who had escaped from Clarksburg, Virginia, to safe houses in Washington. Later Adams also helped to deliver these same fugitives into the hands of agents in Pittsburgh. Adams thus may have been involved in helping slaves gain their freedom from the beginning to the end of the Underground Railroad in Washington County.

Sources:

Forrest, 376–78, 425

Washington (PA) Observer, October 16, 1884

George H. Thurston, *Directory of the Monongahela and Youghiogheny Valleys* (Pittsburgh: A. A. Anderson, 1859), 138

Washington Borough Tax Records, 1838–1841 (microfilm), Law Library, Washington County Courthouse, Washington, PA

Henry Bolden
Two stars

Location: North Lincoln Street; exact location unknown

Site analysis: An African American, Henry Bolden (ca. 1830–1903) spent his entire life in Washington. After working as a laborer, Bolden took up the barbering trade at the age of twenty-five and practiced it until illness forced him to retire in 1900. Bolden was a well-known figure in Washington: his death in 1903 warranted a front-page obituary. Bolden was supposedly the first black in Pennsylvania to serve as a United States juror in 1870. His obituary notes that he was "in close touch with 'Underground Railroad' affairs and aided many refugees to pass safely northward." No further details are known about his Underground Railroad activities.

Source:
Washington (PA) Observer, April 18, 1903

Hugh Dorsey
Three stars

Note: It is not totally clear if the Samuel Dorsey and Hugh Dorsey who appear in the Underground Railroad literature on Washington, Pennsylvania, are one and the same person or different people. Both are described as black barbers who involved in helping fugitive slaves. It is likely that they were two individuals. McFarland specifically refers to Hugh Dorsey in his account, whereas Forrest and Crumrine mention Samuel Dorsey. Furthermore, both a Hugh Dorsey (aged thirty-three) and a Samuel Dorsey (aged thirty-eight) appear in the 1860 census.

Location: Hugh Dorsey's barber shop was located on Main Street near Maiden Street according to the 1859 Washington Directory. His residence was at Cherry Alley near Main Street. Neither of these sites has survived.

Site analysis: Comparatively little is known about Hugh Dorsey's Underground Railroad activities. He is mentioned specifically only in one instance. According to Agnes Rankin's daughter, when she was fifteen a slave owner and his four slaves stopped to spend the night at the tavern operated by her mother in what was then Rankin Town (located at the top of West Chestnut Hill in what is now part of Washington). The daughter became so incensed at the master's abuse of his slaves that she set out for help. She apparently turned to Hugh Dorsey, who spirited the three youngest slaves away to safety. The oldest of the slaves said that he was too old to flee and did not want to jeopardize the others' chances.

Sources:
McFarland, 129
Thurston, *Directory of the Monongahela and Youghiogheny Valleys*, 143
1860 U.S. Census

Samuel W. Dorsey
Three stars

Note: It is not totally clear if the Samuel Dorsey and Hugh Dorsey who appear in the Underground Railroad literature on Washington, Pennsylvania, are one and the same person or different people. Both are described as black barbers who were involved in helping fugitive slaves. It is likely that they were two individuals. McFarland specifically refers to Hugh Dorsey in his account, whereas Forrest and Crumrine mention Samuel Dorsey. Furthermore, both a Hugh Dorsey (aged thirty-three) and a Samuel Dorsey (aged thirty-eight) appear in the 1860 census.

Location: Unknown

Site analysis: Little is known about Samuel Dorsey's Underground Railroad activities. Forrest mentions only that he "devoted his life before the war to the cause of members of his race." Crumrine mentions one incident in which Dorsey was involved, that of the escape of nine slaves from Clarksburg, Virginia, in 1856. Matthew McKeever of West Middletown forwarded the group of fugitives to Washington, where Dorsey helped send them along to Canada.

Sources:
Forrest, 426
Crumrine, *History*, 262

Sarah Foster Hanna
Three stars

Location: Sarah Foster Hanna's involvement in the Underground Railroad occurred while she was principal of the Washington Female Seminary. The seminary was located at the corner of Maiden and what is now Lincoln Street. Acquired by Washington & Jefferson College in 1940, the seminary classroom became known as McIlvaine Hall, which was torn down to make way for a new science building. The original seminary building that faced Maiden Street and served as a dormitory has also been torn down.

Site analysis: George Walls is the sole source of information about Hanna's participation in the Underground Railroad. In an 1884 newspaper interview, Walls related that Mrs. Hanna had forwarded two slaves who had escaped from near Morgantown to him. "They had walked their shoes off—were in a terrible fix," Walls said of their condition when they arrived in Washington. Walls subsequently helped the two slaves escape to Pittsburgh. Walls does not specify how Mrs. Hanna came to know of the plight of the two slaves, but it is evident that they had not received any organized help until she got word to Walls. This is the only known incident of her involvement in the Underground Railroad.

Hanna was principal of the seminary from 1840 until 1874.

Sources:
Washington (PA) Observer, November 6, 1884
Crumrine, *History*, 558–60

William Hart
Two stars

Location: Unknown

Site analysis: Very little is known about William Hart's involvement in the Underground Railroad in Washington, Pennsylvania. The only known reference to Hart's activities states that even his brother, George S. Hart, knew nothing about the method he "employed to befriend fugitive slaves."

William Hart is listed as a thirty-year-old potter in the 1850 U.S. Census.

Source:
Washington (PA) Observer, November 20, 1884

Mrs. Mary (Miller) Houston (Huston)
Three stars

Location: Near Washington on the National Road. Exact location is unknown.

Site analysis: Mrs. Houston harbored a group of sixteen fugitive slaves in her barn after they had fled from Wheeling. Members of the group had been learning how to read and write when their owners, named Mitchell and Wilson, discovered this and threatened to sell them farther south. Arrangements were made to bring these slaves by night to Mrs. Houston's.

F. Julius LeMoyne spent several nights in Mrs. Houston's barn to safeguard the fugitives. It took him several days to procure carriages to take these fugitives across the Ohio River to safety.

It is unclear whether Mrs. Houston ever hid fugitive slaves on other occasions. This incident is the only one that has been recorded about her involvement in the Underground Railroad. Her name sometimes appears in historical records as "Huston." Her youngest daughter, Mary, was married to Samuel McFarland.

Source:
Crumrine, Notes
Crumrine, *History*, 564

F. Julius LeMoyne House
Five stars

Location: 49 E. Maiden Street, Washington, PA. Built in 1812, this Greek Revival stone house was the home of Dr. F. Julius LeMoyne (1798–1879).

Site analysis: The LeMoyne House is one of only several dozen Underground Railroad sites nationally that has been recognized by the National Park Service. It is by far the best-documented Underground Railroad site in Washington County. Washington County Historical Society's library, located in the house, contains some half a dozen primary sources that document LeMoyne's activities as an Underground Railroad agent.

After becoming an ardent exponent of abolitionism in the 1830s, LeMoyne apparently became involved in the Underground Railroad around

1840. Most of his efforts as an Underground Railroad agent occurred during the 1840s, before ill health increasingly confined him to his house. His activities ranged from the legal to the clearly illegal. LeMoyne on occasion met stages bearing newly manumitted slaves and helped these slaves who had been freed by their owners catch the next stage to their destination. But he also helped hide fugitive slaves and hired stages to take these runaways north to Canada.

There is no specific, concrete evidence that LeMoyne ever hid slaves in his home. However, LeMoyne's involvement in abolitionism and the Underground Railroad make it very probable that he hid runaway slaves in the house on occasion.

Sources:
Crumrine, Notes
U.S. Department of the Interior, "F. Julius LeMoyne Home," National Historical
    Landmark Nomination
LeMoyne Papers
McCulloch, *Fearless Advocate*

Samuel McFarland
Five stars

Location: Samuel McFarland owned a large farm just inside the Washington borough limits on the road to West Middletown. His house, which is no longer standing, occupied the site of present-day Washington High School on Jefferson Avenue.

Site analysis: McFarland (1795–1868) was probably the best-known white Underground Railroad agent in the borough of Washington after F. Julius LeMoyne. Born in Washington County, he graduated from Washington College and was admitted to the bar in 1827.

McFarland showed his abolitionist leanings quite early. In 1828, he defended a runaway slave, Christian "Kit" Sharp, who had been accused of murdering his owner, one Robert Carlisle, of Kentucky. However, McFarland was unable to gain an acquittal for his client, who was hanged for the murder. McFarland became one of the founding members of the Washington Anti-Slavery Society in 1835. When local abolitionists moved into politics in the 1840s, McFarland offered his name as a candidate.

After LeMoyne's health began to decline in the late 1840s, McFarland assumed the white leadership of the Washington Underground Railroad. On one occasion he harbored eighteen slaves at his residence. He was also instrumental in guiding nine fugitive slaves from Clarksburg, Virginia, to safety in Washington. This group was later conducted to Canada without incident. Osborne Mitchell observed that "It was by no means unusual for this gentleman to give shelter to six or eight runaways at the same."

McFarland had close ties with the African American Underground Railroad community in Washington. Firsthand accounts of escapes link him to George Walls, who lived in Chartiers Township, and to Tar Adams, who lived close to McFarland on West Chestnut Street.

The religious affiliations of McFarland and his wife, Mary, reflected their abolitionist convictions. In 1855 they joined the Free Presbyterian Church in West Alexander, the only antislavery church in Washington County.

Sources:
Crumrine, *History*, 547, 564
McFarland, 130
Washington (PA) Observer, October 16, 1884
Osborne Mitchell, "About the Stormy Days Before the War," *Washington (PA) Reporter*, August 15, 1908

Colin M. Reed House/Davis Memorial Hall
One star

Location: 123 E. Maiden St., Washington, PA

Site analysis: Davis Hall, on the campus of Washington & Jefferson College, is sometimes mentioned as an Underground Railroad site, but there is little foundation for this claim. Colin M. Reed Sr. (1804–1888), a banker, owned the house during the years before the Civil War and has never been linked to the cause of abolition. His name does not appear at any of the abolitionist meetings held in the county and is not mentioned in any of the county histories in connection with the Underground Railroad. His sole connection to abolitionism is his signature on a petition to Congress in 1838 denouncing the gag rule against resolutions having to do with slavery.

His name may have been linked to the Underground Railroad because of his association with the LeMoyne name. Reed was interested in the cause of female education and assisted Dr. Julius LeMoyne in establishing the Washington Female Seminary, which was initially built next door to Reed's house. A far more likely reason for the mistaken claim that the Reed house was an Underground Railroad site is that Reed's nephew, George W. Reed, married LeMoyne's daughter Madeleine. This marriage, however, did not take place until 1907—long after both Dr. LeMoyne and Colin M. Reed had died. There is fragmentary evidence that George W. Reed participated in the local Underground Railroad.

Sources:
Beers, 7, 190–91
Washington (PA) Observer, November 27, 1884
U.S. House. 25th Congress, 1st Session. "Petition from Washington Co Pa to rescind Mr. Patton's Resolution," February 14, 1838, and May 21, 1838

Tom Robinson
Four stars

Location: According to the 1855 Doran Map of Washington, Robinson's house stood on the alley east of what is now Lincoln Street between Chestnut Street and Walnut Street. The house is no longer standing.

Site analysis: Tom Robinson was a black man whom George Walls identifies as an Underground Railroad agent. In an 1884 newspaper interview, Walls said that four slaves escaping from Clarksburg, Virginia, were lodged at Robinson's house. Walls then took these four slaves to William H. McNary's farm near Canonsburg. It is likely that Robinson was a subscriber to Martin R. Delany's newspaper, the *Mystery*, as a Thomas Robinson in Washington is listed as an agent for the paper. No other historical documents can be located about Robinson. He does not even show up in the census.

Sources:
Washington (PA) Observer, October 16, 1884
Doran, T. "Map of Washington, Washington County, Pennsylvania"
Mystery (Pittsburgh, PA), December 16, 1846

Samuel Skinner
Four stars

Location: Skinner's house in Washington stood at 136 East Walnut Street between College and Lincoln Streets. Although a house still occupies this site today, it appears to be of much more recent construction.

Site analysis: George Walls identifies Samuel Skinner (1818–1859), who was black, as an Underground Railroad agent. In an 1884 newspaper interview, Walls said that five slaves from a larger group of nine fugitives escaping from Clarksburg, Virginia, were taken to Skinner's house for safekeeping. Walls later took these five fugitives to James McNary's farm, located about four miles northeast of Washington in South Strabane Township.

Samuel Skinner first appears in historical records in 1847, when he shows up in the Washington Borough Tax Records. He was assessed $125 for a house and lot on Maiden Street that year. He is listed as a thirty-two-year-old laborer in the 1850 U.S. Census.

Sources:
Washington (PA) Observer, October 16, 1884
Doran, T. "Map of Washington, Washington County, Pennsylvania"
Michael S. Batalo, "Samuel Skinner" (unpublished paper, Washington & Jefferson College, January 28, 2005)
Washington Borough Tax Records
Marshall E. Lignian, ed., *Thomas McKean's Death Register, 1820–1896, Washington, PA* (Monessen, PA: Privately printed, 1975), 32
1850 U.S. Census

George Walls
Five stars

Location: An African American born in Pennsylvania, Walls (c. 1812–1885) was a tenant farmer during most of the 1840s and 1850s in South Strabane Township. Based upon his neighbors in the 1850 census, he, his wife, and eight children lived near James McNary, not far from Chartiers Creek, in the northern part of the township. This is where he was living in 1856 during the Clarksburg escape. By 1860 he had moved across Chartiers Creek and was living in Chartiers Township as a farmer in 1860. According to Walls, he lived at the time about four miles north of Washington near Major J. H. Ewing's farm at the Meadowlands.

Based upon Walls's neighbors in the 1860 census, it is highly likely that he was living along Hickory Ridge Road near its intersection with Allison Hollow Road. (Walls did not own property in Chartiers Township, so it is impossible to locate him precisely.) The census taker began at the southern end of Hickory Ridge Road and listed the names of families such as the Robert Millers and John Boons that can readily be found on contemporary nineteenth-century maps. Walls and his five children appear after these names but before that of James C. Heron, the pastor of the United Presbyterian Church, located just beyond Allison Hollow Road.

Walls in 1884 owned a house in Washington at the corner of Chestnut and Lincoln Streets.

Site analysis: John C. McNary of Canonsburg, whose father William H. McNary was involved in the Underground Railroad, described Walls in 1884 as "the general agent of the line in this county." John distinctly remembered an incident in 1856 when Walls had brought four runaway slaves to hide in an old sheep shed full of hay on his father's farm west of Canonsburg.

Walls was one of three black Underground Railroad agents in Washington County interviewed for a series of newspaper articles that appeared in the *Washington Observer* in the fall of 1884. Walls related two episodes in which he had been involved: the escape of nine slaves belonging to Cyrus Ross of Clarksburg, Virginia, and the escape of a slave named Randolph who slipped away from his owner in Washington County.

The escape of the Clarksburg slaves is fairly well known, but Walls adds details that appear nowhere else. County historian Boyd Crumrine tells the general route they followed and lists some of the stations at which they were helped before escaping to Canada. Walls, however, specifies the people who were involved in this escape and what they did to aid the fugitives. For example, he mentions that Samuel McFarland and "a man named Adams" (probably Tar or Tower Adams, a black gunsmith) brought the slaves into Washington from West Alexander. Once in Washington, the slaves were hidden at Skinner's on Walnut Street and Tom Robinson's on Chestnut. Both Skinner and Robinson were black, and their residences can be located on the 1855 Doran Map of Washington.

Walls's own involvement with the runaways began once they had reached Washington. In the middle of the night, he took four of the slaves to William H. McNary's farm in Chartiers Township. The following night, he took the remaining fugitives to James McNary's farm in South Strabane Township.

Walls also arranged for the transportation of the fugitives to Pittsburgh. Enlisting the help of a white abolitionist named John Berry, who was a neighbor of James McNary, Walls delivered the slaves to Jarrett's Tavern, which was probably located in South Fayette Township, just across the Allegheny County line. From there a black wagoner named Joe Brooks hauled the party to Pittsburgh. Walls adds that two blacks prominent in Pittsburgh Underground Railroad circles, John Peck and Samuel Bruce, met Brooks's wagon and saw the fugitives safely on to Canada.

Walls also related the story of the deliverance of the slave named Randolph. Randolph belonged to a Carolinian by the name of James Gillespie who had been educated in Canonsburg. When Gillespie returned to visit friends, probably in the mid- or late-1840s (Walls recalled in 1884 that it was "nigh forty years ago"), he brought Randolph with him.

When Walls approached Randolph about the possibility of being a free man, Randolph indicated that he was willing to take a chance. Walls then enlisted the help of William Wassler, a black man who had often helped Walls previously. Wassler lived on Major J. H. Ewing's farm at the Meadowlands, several miles from Canonsburg. Walls hid Randolph for a night at Wassler's, then moved him to a nearby barn for two weeks.

Randolph's disappearance stirred up a hornet's nest. As Walls recounted, "We colored folks was most always called on when a black man was missing. The owner and about twenty others, with a constable, hunted, all armed, for Randolph."

When the furor had finally subsided, Joseph Lee, a white abolitionist who was a neighbor of Walls, helped to get Randolph to another safe house some thirty miles to the southwest. Randolph stayed at Michael Hackaress's in West Finley Township for a month before coming back to the Canonsburg area. Margaret McLane, Lee's sister-in-law, cut off Randolph's hair and painted him yellow in an effort to disguise him. The disguise worked. When Lee drove his barouche through Canonsburg and unexpectedly passed by Gillespie, Gillespie failed to recognize his former slave. Randolph ultimately made it to Canada.

Walls died at his residence on East Chestnut Street in Washington, PA, on August 26, 1885, at age seventy-three, of typhoid fever.

Sources:

Washington (PA) Observer, September 3, 1885, October 16, 1884; November 6, 1884

Doran, T. "Map of Washington, Washington County, Pennsylvania"

Caldwell

Barker Map

South Strabane Tax Record, 1856–1857, Washington County, Pennsylvania.

1840, 1850, 1860, 1870, 1880 U.S. Census

CANONSBURG/MEADOWLANDS AREA

John Berry
Four stars

Location: North Strabane Township, on Christy Road, about half a mile east of the intersection with Linwood Road

Site analysis: John Berry (1805–1881) was the son of William Gilmore Berry, who was noted for his abolitionist and Underground Railroad activities. John Berry's major role appears to have been that of a financier of Underground Railroad escapes. For example, Berry in 1856 provided thirty dollars to aid in the escape of nine slaves from Clarksburg, Virginia, to Pittsburgh. Berry paid for the wagon team that hauled these fugitives from Canonsburg to Pittsburgh and for other expenses. On another occasion, Berry met a carriage that was taking a fugitive to Pittsburgh and gave him all of the money he had on hand ($7.50) to help him in escaping to Canada. Berry invited the fugitive and his guides to dinner at his house, but the press of time precluded that.

Berry was a close associate of a major figure in the local Underground Railroad, George Walls. It was Walls who provided virtually all of the known information about Berry's involvement in the Underground Railroad. Walls refers to him as Squire Berry.

Sources:

Washington (PA) Observer, October 16, 1884; November 6, 1884

Beers, 124, 165, 336

Michael S. Batalo, "John Berry" (Unpublished paper, Washington & Jefferson College, 2005)

9. Home of John Berry, North Strabane Township

William Gilmore Berry
Two stars

Location: Berry's farm, Peach Garden Farm, was located about a mile south of Canonsburg. Route 519 divides what was once his three-hundred-acre farm, purchased in 1835. The brick house that he built on the northern half of this property has apparently been torn down. His son Matthew's house, located south of Route 519 on part of the original Berry farm, is still standing, although in dilapidated condition. In about 1850, Berry built a house in Canonsburg at 404 W. Pike Street and began living there. A Sunoco station now occupies this site.

Site analysis: This site is not very well documented. A reference in Beers is the only source of information about Berry's Underground Railroad activities. According to Beers, Berry (1781–1866) was a prominent name in the local Underground Railroad network, associated with "Dr. F. Julius Le-Moyne, Maj. Samuel McFarland, W. H. McNary, Joseph Lee and others."

Berry "gave liberally of his means to establish and maintain the Underground Railroad," Beers adds. George Walls, one of the major Underground Railroad agents in the vicinity of Canonsburg, adds that John Berry, William's son, was a frequent financial contributor to the cause. John Berry lived on a farm some five miles southeast of Canonsburg in North Strabane Township.

Sources:
Beers, 124, 336, 165
Wallace, 6–7
Washington (PA) Observer, October 16, 1884
Crumrine, *History*, 377

Daniel Houston
One star

Location: Chartiers Township. The exact location is unknown. Houston lived in what was then called Houstonville.

Site analysis: Daniel Houston's connection to the Underground Railroad is tenuous. Beers is the only source that mentions his name: "Daniel Houston was opposed to slavery and was, no doubt, connected with the underground railway, but he had his own views. Dr. Brownson asked him if he was going to the Abolitionist meeting at Pittsburgh; he said: No! he was in favor of colonization." Houston's support of colonization makes it highly unlikely that he was involved in the Underground Railroad.

Source:
Beers, 165

Joseph Lee
Four stars

Location: Joseph Lee's residence was in South Strabane Township. In 1843 he bought land from his father, Samuel Lee, that was located on Chartiers Creek in the northwest corner of the township. The original land warrant was taken out by Thomas Rankin. The description of the property in the deed listing

Lee's neighbors as Daniel Moore and James (?) Quail makes it clear which property was his. The development of the I-79 corridor along Chartiers Creek and of the Meadowlands Race Track has greatly changed the landscape of this site.

Site analysis: Joseph Lee apparently played an important role in the local Underground Railroad, although he does not appear in any of the recent literature on the topic. Furthermore, virtually all historical trace of him has disappeared. He does not show up in any antebellum census. The only clear mark he has left is his purchase of a farm in 1843 from his father.

Some measure of Lee's stature among his contemporaries, however, can be gained from Beers's assessment of William Gilmore Berry's role in the Underground Railway. Beers states that Berry was associated in this activity with "Dr. F. Julius LeMoyne, Maj. Samuel McFarland, W. H. McNary, Joseph Lee and others." In providing this list of names, Beers was clearly pointing to what he considered the white leadership of the local Underground Railroad.

George Walls provides specific details about Lee's involvement. Around 1845, Walls approached Lee about helping to move a slave named Randolph who had escaped from his owner at Walls's instigation. The slave owner was a former student in Canonsburg who had come back to visit friends in Canonsburg, accompanied by his slave. Walls had hidden Randolph in local barns for several weeks, but the irate owner continued to search for his lost slave. Before attempting to send Randolph to Canada, Walls decided to move him to an unsuspected location: Michael Hackaress's in West Finley Township. Lee drove his wagon to the barn where Randolph had been hidden and took Randolph to Hackaress's.

Lee and his relations also played a role in Randolph's ultimate escape to Canada. Lee's sister-in-law, Margaret McLane, helped to disguise Randolph by cutting his hair, fashioning some whiskers for him, and painting his skin yellow. The disguise was so effective, according to Walls, that the slave owner did not even recognize Randolph when he was driven past him in a carriage through Canonsburg. Lee evidently accompanied Randolph to Pittsburgh.

On another occasion, Lee rode into Pittsburgh on horseback to warn John Peck, a prominent African American stationmaster, that several fugitive slaves from Morgantown would be forwarded to Peck the following day. Walls gives the impression that he turned to Lee whenever he had need of assistance.

Sources:
Washington (PA) Observer, November 6, 1884
Beers, 124, 165, 336
W. F. Horn, *The Horn Papers: Early Westward Movement on the Monongahela and Upper Ohio, 1765–1795*, 3 vols. (New York: Hagstrom, 1945), 3:80

James S. McNary
Four stars

Location: The farm that James McNary bought in 1857 was located about four miles northeast of Washington in North Strabane Township. It was located on Munce Road near its intersection with Christy Road. The house is still standing. McNary at the time of the Clarksburg Nine's escape was living nearby in South Strabane Township.

Site analysis: James S. McNary (1810–1902) and his brother William, who owned a farm in nearby Chartiers Township, were both abolitionists. While William was clearly involved in the local Underground Railroad, James might be characterized as a reluctant participant.

George Walls, a black Underground Railroad agent who probably lived in South Strabane Township, told a newspaper reporter in 1884 that he brought five fugitive slaves from Washington to James McNary's farm in 1859 (the actual date of the escape is 1856) and hid them in McNary's sheep shed for a week. (Walls evidently lived very close to McNary.) McNary was apparently not informed that Walls had hidden the slaves there. As Walls recounted, "I don't think Jim knew they were there, till the boys began to feel lively, and he saw them dance 'Juba' on top of the shed." (The Juba was a dance named after Master Juba, the stage name of William Henry Lane, a free black from Rhode Island who was acclaimed as the best dancer of his age and is widely acknowledged as the inventor of tap dance.) McNary subsequently asked Walls to move the fugitives along. Walls promised to relocate them in several days.

Walls subsequently delivered this party to Jarrett's Tavern, a stop in South Fayette Township in Allegheny County. From there the group of fugitives was taken to Pittsburgh and finally to Canada. Although McNary clearly was not happy to be hosting a group of fugitive slaves, it is important that Walls counted on his sympathies.

Sources:

Washington (PA) Observer, October 16, 1884

Beers, 330

Crumrine, *History*, 880–81

Lisa Traiger, "'Juba!' Celebrates Tap's Old Master," *Washington Post*, December 6, 2012

William H. McNary
Five stars

Location: McNary's farm, Fine View Farm, 395 Plum Run Road, is located about two and one-half miles northwest of Canonsburg in Chartiers Township. Plum Run Road is the extension of North Main Street in Houston, PA.

Site analysis: William H. McNary (1805–1877) and his brother James S. McNary were both involved in the local Underground Railroad. According to Beers, William was one of the original abolitionists in Washington County. McNary broke with the pastor of his own church and many of his relatives over the question of slavery. The Canonsburg area was not receptive to anti-slavery views, at least initially. When McNary brought Dr. F. Julius LeMoyne from nearby Washington to deliver an abolitionist speech, he was unable to get permission from any church, school, or public hall in the borough. LeMoyne was eventually forced to give his speech in a public street.

McNary was one of the local organizers of the Republican Party. In 1855 he attended a convention in Pittsburgh to organize a party dedicated to stopping the expansion of slavery. McNary a year later sponsored the first Republican speeches in Washington County.

McNary reportedly "helped many a fugitive in his flight for liberty," according to Crumrine. We know of one specific incident in which he was involved. George Walls, a black Underground Railroad agent who lived in South Strabane Township, told a newspaper reporter in 1884 of an episode in which he brought four fugitives from Washington to McNary's farm in the middle of the night in 1856. John C. McNary, William's son, likewise remembered these runaway slaves' arrival at his father's farm. Walls's interview suggests that Fine View Farm was a frequent stop on the Underground Railroad.

The black community of Canonsburg held McNary in high esteem. When he died in 1877, many of the men of that community requested the honor of walking bareheaded beside his funeral bier.

Sources:
Washington (PA) Observer, October 16, 1884
Beers, 12, 165, 336
Crumrine, *History*, 718

William Wassler
Four stars

Location: The 1860 census shows Wassler (his name appears as Wasler on the census) living in Chartiers Township with his wife and five children. According to George Walls, Wassler lived on the farm of Major John H. Ewing and was apparently his hired man.

Site analysis: George Walls's account in the *Washington Observer* is the only source of information about Wassler's Underground Railroad activities. According to Walls, who lived near Ewing's farm, Wassler frequently helped Walls with escapes.

One notable instance of Wassler's help involved Randolph, the slave of a Carolinian who had been educated in Canonsburg. Randolph decided to seek freedom when he accompanied his owner on a visit to Canonsburg. After Walls had enticed Randolph to run away, Wassler hid the slave on the Ewing farm.

In another incident related by Walls, Wassler was harboring a fugitive slave from the Morgantown area when a man purporting to be a missionary stopped at Wassler's. Wassler declined to fall for this ruse and learned from the escaped slave that the missionary was none other than his owner. Wassler got word to Walls of the imminent danger faced by the fugitive, and the two engineered the escape of this slave to Pittsburgh and beyond.

Sources:
Washington (PA) Observer, November 6, 1884
1860 U.S. Census

MONONGAHELA AREA
(For the Bowman family, see George Norris below.)

Beckett Mansion
One star

Location: Exact site is unknown, but it stood near Daggs Ferry on the Monongahela River, between Monongahela and Webster.

Site analysis: This is a poorly documented site that appears in only one source. The *Monongahela Area 200th Anniversary* booklet declares, "It is known that Ginger Hill was a station as was 'the great and pillared Beckett mansion in 1845.'"

"Beckett mansion" probably refers to a substantial log house that Joseph Beckett erected in 1785 along the Monongahela River, near a ferry that came to be known as Daggs Ferry. The Beckett mansion was actually the ferry house. It became known as Daggs Ferry when John Daggs married the widow of Joseph's son, John, in 1818. The ferry was abandoned shortly after Daggs and his wife moved to Washington, Pennsylvania, in 1822. The house is sometimes referred to as the Beckett-Daggs Mansion. It was torn down in 1888.

Sources:

Monongahela Area 200th Anniversary, 1769–1969 (Monongahela, PA: Monongahela Publishing, 1969), 52

Marta Burns, "Joseph Beckett of Rostraver and Forward Townships," in Mon Valley Biographies, *Mid Monongahela Valley History and Geography* (Michael A. Donaldson, 1999), http://freepages.genealogy.rootsweb.ancestry.com/~pamonval/bios/biobeckettjoseph.html

Bethel AME Church, Monongahela
Five stars

Location: Corner of Main and Seventh Street, Monongahela. The present church was completed in 1871.

Site analysis: The Bethel AME Church has long been linked to the Underground Railroad, in large measure because of William Ralph's membership in the church. Ralph was the major figure in the Underground Railroad in the Monongahela area. (See the entry on Ralph for more details.)

The Bethel AME Church's beginnings date to 1833, when Paul Quinn helped to organize it. It is one of the oldest African American churches in southwestern Pennsylvania. The first AME church was built about 1845 at the corner of Geary Street and Fair Street (now Sixth Street).

The first pastor of the church was Samuel Clingman. Among the founding members of the congregation were Rachel Bowman, Elijah Bowman, John Bowman, Ruth Ann Bowman, and Thomas Bowman. It is likely that the Bowmans mentioned by Howard Wallace as being Underground Railroad agents in the nearby Maple Creek area were related to these Bowmans.

The Bethel AME Church was placed on the National Register of Historic Places in 2002.

Sources:

Gary Thomas, "Bethel AME Church to Mark 171st Anniversary," *Pittsburgh Tribune-Review*, August 29, 2004

Washington County History & Landmarks Foundation, "Bethel African Methodist Episcopal Church," Landmark Registry (2017), http://www.washcolandmarks .com/index.php?component=landmark_registry&task=viewFull&id=9

U.S. Department of the Interior, National Park Service, "Bethel African American Episcopal Church of Monongahela City," NP Gallery, National Register of Historic Places (11/7/2002), https://npgallery.nps.gov/AssetDetail?assetID= 8192fe7b-2c6e-474e-ac93-efe3927bb866

David Longwell House
Zero stars

Location: 711 West Main Street, Monongahela

Site analysis: Although there are rumors that the Longwell House was an Underground Railroad stop, they do not appear to have any basis. David Longwell, who was a riverboat captain, did not leave his father's farm until about 1860. Only then did he buy the lot on which the current house (built in 1872) now stands. If Longwell did indeed work as an Underground Railroad operative, he did so for a very short time.

The main reason for not considering the Longwell House as an authentic Underground Railroad site is that it was not built until 1872.

Sources:

Washington County History & Landmarks Foundation, "Longwell House," Landmark Registry (2017), http://www.washcolandmarks.com/index.php?component=landmark_registry&task=viewFull&id=45

Robert Van Atta, "Virginians Came to Area, Brought Slavery with Them," *Pittsburgh Tribune-Review*, January 12, 1997

Milton Maxwell
Three stars

Location: According to the 1860 census, Milton Maxwell owned a farm valued at $1,500 near Ginger Hill in Carroll Township. The exact location of this site is unknown, but it seems reasonable to infer that Maxwell's farm was located near Benjamin Williams's farm, since the Williams and Maxwell families appear very close together in the census.

Site analysis: Howard Wallace mentions Ginger Hill as being one of the alternative routes from his father's house in Centerville. Maxwell forwarded passengers from Ginger Hill to Pittsburgh.

The 1850 census identifies Milton Maxwell as a thirty-year-old mixed-race farmer living in Carroll Township with his wife Mary, two children, and a woman who may have been his mother. According to the census, Wallace possessed no property then. By 1860 Maxwell had acquired a farm of his own. By 1870, he and his wife had moved to Iowa.

Sources:
Wallace, 5
1850, 1860, 1870 U.S. Census
Barker Map

George Norris and Bowman Family Sites
Three stars

Location: Fox Stop Road, Fallowfield Township, in the Maple Creek area

Site analysis: The 1876 Caldwell atlas of Washington County shows the George Norris family and Bowman families living on a tributary of the north branch of Maple Creek near Fox Trot Road in eastern Fallowfield Township. No evidence of the small black community that once lived in this hollow apparently exists today. The construction of a railroad line in the early twentieth century through the Maple Creek valley has resulted in considerable change to the local topography. The railroad used a huge amount of fill to carry it over the tributary where the Bowmans and Norrises once lived.

The Norris and Bowman families were part of the black Underground Railroad network that ran through eastern Washington County. According to Howard Wallace, fugitive slaves were guided from Centerville to the Maple Creek area and then directed by the Bowmans and Norrises to a river crossing near modern-day Donora. Once they had crossed the Monongahela, fugitives found shelter in a black community near Belle Vernon and then were guided north to Pittsburgh.

The 1850 census lists George Norris as a thirty-eight-year-old farmer who owned property valued at $735. He was married and had four children.

The same census records two black families named Bowman living in Fallowfield Township at this time. Lydia Bowman, age forty-six, had four children living with her and owned property worth $300. Samuel Bowman was a propertyless, thirty-one-year-old laborer. Living with him were a wife, four children, and another adult male named Bowman who may have been his brother. Both of these families in 1860 apparently were neighbors of George Norris, since they appear on either side of Norris on the enumeration list.

Sources:
Wallace, 4–5
Caldwell
1850, 1860 U.S. Census

William Ralph
Five stars

Location: William Ralph's home after the Civil War stood on West Main Street between Tenth and Eleventh Streets (formerly Elm and Walnut) in Monongahela. A book published in 1908 states that Ralph's home stood across the street from the "present" residence of T. S. McCurdy.

Before the Civil War, Ralph lived in a house that was built on a lot that he purchased in 1839. This house at the corner of Main Street and West Alley (between modern-day Sixth and Seventh Streets) was a block from the J. B. Taylor residence.

Site analysis: William Ralph (ca. 1813–1897) was a major figure in Monon-gahela's Underground Railroad. Initially a stage boy, Ralph later entered business as a barber and coal dealer. (He appears in the 1860 census as a teamster.) Ralph also became an itinerant AME minister. He served briefly as pastor of the Little Zion AME Church near Centerville.

It is through Joseph Armstrong that we know about Ralph's involve-ment in the Underground Railroad. Armstrong as a young boy frequently stayed with his aunt, Mrs. J. B. Taylor, whose house stood a block away from Ralph's on West Main Street. His aunt was a "violent abolitionist of the outspoken kind" who became acquainted with Ralph because he supplied her with coal. On several occasions, Mrs. Taylor harbored fugitive slaves in the barn behind her house at Ralph's request. Armstrong vividly remem-bered the time he was asked to row fugitive slaves across the Monongahela after Ralph had delivered them to his aunt's barn. Armstrong believed that Ralph's own stable was "too public for business of this kind." Joseph Arm-strong in 1908 remembered Ralph as "the representative colored man of the town for fifty years, a man of gigantic frame and great strength with a char-acter above reproach."

Sources:
Armstrong, "Boyhood Days," 148–49
Monongahela Daily Record, February 16, 1897
Pittsburgh Tribune-Review, August 29, 2004
Caldwell, map of Monongahela
Andrew Chess Plan Book, Monongahela, Recorder of Deeds Office, Washington
    County, PA
J. W. Lockhart Plan Book, Recorder of Deeds Office, Washington County, PA

J. B. Taylor (Joseph Armstrong)
Four stars

Location: 715 Main Street, Monongahela. The house is still standing. The barn in which runaway slaves were hidden was razed in the late nineteenth or early twentieth centuries.

Site analysis: Although the owner of this house was Joseph B. Taylor, it is Taylor's wife Mary and his nephew who are connected to the Underground

Railroad. The nephew, Joseph Armstrong, recalled when he was approximately seventy that as a young boy of ten or eleven he had rowed fugitive slaves across the Monongahela River. Armstrong became involved in the Underground Railroad through his aunt, Mrs. Joseph B. Taylor, whom he characterized as a "violent abolitionist." Her acquaintance with the Reverend William Ralph, who was her coal dealer, resulted in her barn becoming a stop on the Underground Railroad. She assisted Ralph by allowing fugitives to stay in the hayloft of her barn. (Ralph's own stable was too public for the business of hiding slaves.) Armstrong remembered that his aunt had asked him several times to row fugitives across the river, where he was met by a man who spirited the runaways away toward Pittsburgh.

Armstrong is buried in Monongahela Cemetery.

Source:
Armstrong, "Boyhood Days," 148–49

CENTERVILLE AND WEST BROWNSVILLE AREA

Nathan Cleaver
Three stars

Location: 533 Deems Park Road, West Pike Run Township

Site analysis: According to local historian W. Floyd Gillis, this farm belonged to Nathan Cleaver (1801–1887) and may have been an Underground Railroad stop. A Quaker, Cleaver in 1851 employed a fugitive slave named Renols Parker. Howard Wallace's account states that slave catcher Bob Stump and "eight rough men from Virginia" who were heavily armed found Parker at work in Cleaver's field. Parker made a dash for the house, where he hastily made his way up the narrow stairs. When Stump and his men arrived at the house, Parker threatened that he would bash in the brains of anyone who attempted to climb the stairs and capture him. This threat had its desired effect on his pursuers.

A standoff soon developed. Stump vowed that "he would have his man," but a crowd of neighbors sympathetic to Parker soon surrounded the house. Eventually, as darkness loomed, two of these neighbors, a black man named Henry Smith and a white man named Isaac Vaile, promised Stump that they would deliver Parker to Stump in Brownsville the next morning. Their promise, however, was nothing but a ruse. Parker went to Canonsburg with his family and eventually, following the advice of Howard Wallace, to Canada.

Family tradition also supports the contention that the Cleavers were involved in the Underground Railroad. According to Helen R. Harris, the story goes that a grandchild once found a black man hiding in the barn back before the Civil War. When she asked her grandfather about the presence of this man, he indicated that the man was a fugitive slave attempting to get to Canada. The child then asked if hiding the slave were against the law. The grandfather replied, "There are times when God's law is more important than man's law."

Sources:

Wallace, 6–7

California Area Historical Society, *California, Pennsylvania: Images of America* (Charleston, SC: Arcadia, 2003), 52

Beers, 878

Helen L. Harris to Joan Ruzika, August 1, 1991, in Washington County Historical Society archives, Washington, PA

Amos Griffith
No Rating

Location: 98 Spring Road, West Pike Run Township. Griffith's house may still be standing. An older cut-stone foundation is still partially visible underneath renovations made in the last half century to the current house. Griffith's original house may be part of the current structure. Griffith sold his farm to Joseph Garwood in 1857. Garwood's name appears on an 1856 map of Washington County. It is likely that Garwood leased the Griffith farm before he purchased the property.

Site analysis: Amos Griffith (ca. 1798–1871) has no known Underground Railroad credentials, but he was clearly an important figure in Washington County abolitionism. One of the last Quakers in the county, Griffith was among half a dozen people in the county in 1847 who subscribed to an abolitionist periodical. He also probably had some connection to John B. Vashon, the noted African American Pittsburgh abolitionist. Vashon's half-sister Virginia lived with Griffith's family, according to the 1850 census.

Griffith and his wife Edith ultimately moved to Mount Pleasant, Ohio, where he died in 1871.

Sources:

Barker Map

Deed Book 1R, book 3, S, 451, Washington County Courthouse, Washington, PA

M. H. Urquhart to S. P. Noble, Box A24, Folder 1, LeMoyne Papers

Paul N. D. Thornell, "The Absent Ones and the Providers: A Biography of the Vashons," *Journal of Negro History* 83, no. 4 (Autumn 1998): 286–87

Job Johnson Hotel
Four stars

Location: Corner of First and Wood Streets, California, PA. The hotel is no longer standing.

Site analysis: Job Johnson was one of the founders of California, Pennsylvania. Johnson was an antislavery advocate who, along with several of his friends, left the Greenfield Methodist Church over that church's stance on slavery. His hotel reportedly contained two hiding places for fugitive slaves, one in the basement and another on the second floor. Nan Hornbake, the author of a book on California's history, claimed to have seen the second-floor hideaway, which consisted of little more than a closet. According to that same author's account, fugitive slaves were taken from boats that anchored at the Monongahela wharf to the safety of Johnson's Hotel and then forwarded to Washington, Pennsylvania. Crumrine states that Johnson was one of a relatively few whites in eastern Washington County who was willing to lend a hand to fugitive slaves.

Samuel S. Rothwell, another member of California's Underground Railroad network, reminisced many years later about an incident involving Johnson to the *Monongahela (PA) Daily Republican.* Johnson had been hiding two men and a woman in a garret when a slave catcher appeared at Johnson's. Looking at the closed door leading to the garret, the slave catcher demanded, "Where does that stairway lead to?" Pointing to a nearby shotgun, Johnson replied, "It is the shortest way to hell, for you, my man, if you dare to go one single step that way." By the time the slave catcher reappeared with help, Johnson had whisked the fugitive slaves along the way.

Sources:
Hornbake, 19–20
Serinko, *California University of Pennsylvania*, 37
Beers, 799
Crumrine, *History*, 629
"Slavery Days," *Monongahela (PA) Daily Republican*, September 22, 1893

Latta Stone House
One star

Location: Mount Tabor Road, Roscoe, Allen Township

Site analysis: The Latta Stone House is a poorly documented Underground Railroad site. The only reference to its being a stop is an article by Mary Herron in the *Washington Observer*, October 29, 1937.

According to Herron, the back bedroom of the house contains a well-concealed trapdoor that leads to the attic, where fugitive slaves supposedly found refuge. However, Herron provides no details on specific escapes or on the owner's activities as an Underground Railroad agent.

The house was built between 1803 and 1805 by Allen Stockdale. It became known as the Latta House when it was acquired by William Latta (1777–1862).

Sources:
Washington (PA) Observer, October 29, 1937
Beryl Redfield, "The Latta Stone House," *Latta Genealogy Newsletter* 18, http://www
    .latta.org/Articles/Stone%20House.htm

Little Zion AME Church and Cemetery
Two stars

Location: Woods Run Road, near Centerville, PA

Site analysis: This church is no longer standing, although the footprint of the small building can still be seen. The nearby cemetery for members of the church is overgrown. Few of the grave markers are still standing.

Augustus R. Green organized the Little Zion African Methodist Episcopal Church in 1844. Meetings were held at the home of Abraham Lowdrake until 1850, when the congregation erected a log building. The congregation built a frame church at the present site several miles northeast of Centerville in 1880.

Although the church is not mentioned in any of the existing accounts of the local Underground Railroad, it is still an important site. Several of its members played important roles in assisting fugitive slaves in the Centerville area. Among them were William Wallace, father of Howard Wallace, Samuel Wheeler, and William Ralph, a Monongahela Underground Railroad agent who served briefly as pastor of this church.

Sources:
Forrest, 635
Crumrine, *History*, 992
Wallace, 3–7

James Moffitt
Three stars

Location: James Moffitt lived in a house on Bridge Street in West Brownsville at the corner of Bridge and Main Streets. The house is no longer standing; it apparently was taken down to improve a highway intersection. Although Moffitt had died by the time the 1870 census was taken, his widow E. (Elizabeth) J. Moffitt appears as the owner of this house in the 1876 Caldwell atlas of West Brownsville.

Site analysis: Several sources mention Moffitt's participation in the Underground Railroad but offer no specific details on the nature of his participation. Howard Wallace mentions Moffitt as one of the friends of the African American conductors in eastern Washington County. George Walls, in the November 6, 1884, edition of the *Washington Observer* singles out "Squire Moffatt" as the person who gave refuge to fugitive slaves who were crossing the Monongahela River near Brownsville and sent them on to Pittsburgh.

Note: *Moffitt* appears to be the correct spelling of his name. The major evidence here is that the 1850 census shows a James Moffitt living in West Brownsville with the designation of "Esq" after his name. His occupation is listed as "gentleman." Wallace also identifies him as "James Moffitt, Esq."

Sources:
Wallace, 7
Washington (PA) Observer, November 6, 1884
1850, 1860, 1870 U.S. Census
Caldwell

Lewis Shutterly House
Two stars

Location: 800 Park Street, California, PA. The stone house is still standing.

Site analysis: There is little documentation for this site. The Shutterly house is mentioned as being a place of refuge when it was too dangerous for fugitives to be taken to Job Johnson's Hotel in California. The caption to the photograph of the Shutterly house that appears in *California, Pennsylvania* states that the house is "believed" to have been an Underground Railroad station.

Lewis Shutterly (1821–1869) appears in the 1860 census as a thirty-nine-year-old coal merchant. He was married and had three children.

Sources:
Hornbake, 20
1860 U.S. Census
California Area Historical Society, *California, Pennsylvania,* 16

Samuel Taylor Farm
No Rating

Location: 153 Linton Road, near Centerville

Site analysis: Samuel Taylor was one of the Quaker neighbors to whom William Wallace turned when he needed help in transporting fugitive slaves. Taylor was willing to let Wallace borrow his horses, Old Suse and Bill, even after they had put in a hard day in the fields when the need arose.

Source:
Wallace, 4

William and Howard Wallace
Four stars

Location: Route 481, about half a mile northeast from that road's intersection with the Old National Pike in Centerville

Site analysis: The Wallaces' house is no longer standing. According to local historian Floyd Gillis, it stood in a small depression close to the road, on the northern side of Route 481. When Howard Wallace, William's son, wrote his account of the Underground Railroad in the early twentieth century, Lewis Deems was living in the house.

Howard Wallace (1831–1921) recalled that his father's house was one of the main stops on the Underground Railroad in eastern Washington County. Underground Railroad agents in Brownsville would forward their cargo to the Wallace homestead in West Pike Run Township. The house had a large cellar in which fugitives hid during the daylight hours.

Wallace records the names of a number of blacks who assisted with the transportation of fugitive slaves toward their next destination. These included Benjamin Wheeler, Sam Wheeler, Joseph Steward, and Henry Smith. In addition, Wallace singles out several white Quakers who assisted his father's Underground Railroad operations. Nathan Pusey and Samuel Taylor often loaned their horses to help escaping slaves.

Three routes led from the Wallace station to Pittsburgh. The main one was to the Maple Creek area, where the Bowman and Norris families rendered aid. From there, fugitives made their way to a station near Belle Vernon and then on to Pittsburgh. Howard Wallace also took fugitives on occasion to Milton Maxwell, who lived in Ginger Hill. Fugitives were occasionally sent to Canonsburg as well.

Source:
Wallace, 3–7

William Ward
One star

Location: 141 Chestnut Road, Twilight Borough

Site analysis: Local folklore and family stories suggest that the Ward House may have been an Underground Railroad stop, but there is no hard evidence to support this conclusion. The house was constructed before the Civil War:

the date inscribed in the kitchen is 1842. There are rumors that tunnels once led from the basement, although these have never been found.

According to Frank Watkins, who was born and lived in this locality for a long time, local tradition holds that the Reverend William Ward, a Methodist minister, was converted into an abolitionist by the writings of Harriet Beecher Stowe and housed fugitive slaves in his substantial brick house. "Some of the aged residents, who lived through that time, would tell us youngsters tales of seeing black people scurrying into and out of the Ward House," he observes in a letter to Joan Ruzika. "Perhaps these tales were meant to entertain?"

The Ward House does not appear in any written records of the Underground Railroad. One circumstantial reason for thinking that Ward may have been involved in the Underground Railroad is that his son Wilson named his second son LeMoyne, presumably after the famed Underground Railroad agent and doctor from Washington, Pennsylvania. Whether or not this name was intended to celebrate LeMoyne's activities as a conductor or as a doctor is impossible to know, but it does suggest a connection between the two families.

Sources:

Beers, 1457

Frank Watkins to Joan Ruzika, undated letter (ca. 1991), Washington County Historical Society archives

NOTES

INTRODUCTION

1. Larry Gara was the first to point out that the existing histories of the Underground Railroad were largely the histories of white abolitionists as the heroes of the institution and neglected the role of African Americans; see *The Liberty Line: The Legend of the Underground Railroad* (Lexington: University of Kentucky Press, 1961), 190–94. Charles L. Blockson pioneered the study of African American involvement in the Underground Railroad in the 1980s; see *The Underground Railroad: First-Person Narratives of Escapes to Freedom in the North* (New York: Prentice Hall, 1987) and *The Hippocrene Guide to the Underground Railroad* (New York: Hippocrene Books, 1994).

2. Colson Whitehead, *The Underground Railroad* (New York: Doubleday, 2016).

3. The Fiji house is now located on East Chestnut Street.

4. I should point out that docents in my recent visits to the LeMoyne House have emphasized that the incident described above is a "story" and may not be "history." A version of this story appears in the Washington County Historical Society's "Docent Guide: The LeMoyne House," typescript, n.d. (ca. 1993), 1.

5. Margaret C. McCulloch, *Fearless Advocate of the Right: The Life of Francis Julius LeMoyne, M.D., 1798–1879* (Boston: Christopher Publishing House, 1941), 159; Earle R. Forrest, *The House of Romance* (Washington, PA: Washington County Historical Society, 1964), 18–19.

6. Eric Foner, *Gateway to Freedom: The Hidden History of the Underground Railroad* (New York: W. W. Norton, 2015), 124–25, 148–49.

7. Fergus M. Bordewich, "History's Tangled Threads," *New York Times*, February 2, 2007.

8. See Gara, *Liberty Line*, 1–21.

9. Gara, *Liberty Line*, 2.

10. Gara, *Liberty Line*, 2–4, 143–48.

11. Wilbur H. Siebert, *The Underground Railroad from Slavery to Freedom* (New York: Macmillan, 1898; repr. New York: Russell & Russell, 1967).

12. David W. Blight, "Why the Underground Railroad, and Why Now?: A Long View," in *Passages to Freedom: The Underground Railroad in History and Memory,* ed. David W. Blight (Washington, DC: Smithsonian Books, 2004), 240.

13. Gara, *Liberty Line,* 194.

14. Gara, *Liberty Line,* 1–2, 192–94.

15. Gara, *Liberty Line,* xi–xiii, 2; Siebert, *Underground Railroad,* appendix E.

16. Blight, "Introduction: The Underground Railroad in History and Memory," in Blight, *Passages to Freedom,* 3.

17. Matthew Pinsker, "Vigilance in Pennsylvania: Underground Railroad Activities in the Keystone State, 1837–1861" (draft context study; Harrisburg: Pennsylvania Historical and Museum Commission, 2000), 4–5; David G. Smith, *On the Edge of Freedom: The Fugitive Slave Issue in South Central Pennsylvania* (New York: Fordham University Press, 2013), 5–7.

18. See Charles L. Blockson, "Escape from Slavery: The Underground Railroad," *National Geographic,* July 1984, 3–39; *The Underground Railroad in Pennsylvania* (Jacksonville, NC: Flame International, 1981); and *Hippocrene Guide to the Underground Railroad.*

19. Foner, *Gateway to Freedom,* 1–27.

20. John Hope Franklin and Loren Schweninger, *Runaway Slaves: Rebels on the Plantation* (New York: Oxford University Press, 1999), 98–101, 116–19, 367; Foner, *Gateway to Freedom,* 13–14; Smith, *On the Edge of Freedom,* 6–7.

21. Gary W. Gallagher, *Causes Won, Lost, and Forgotten: How Hollywood and Popular Art Shape What We Know about the Civil War* (Chapel Hill: University of North Carolina Press, 2008), 9–10.

22. Gara, *Liberty Line,* xiii, 2.

23. Blight, *Passages to Freedom,* 2–3.

24. Blight, *Passages to Freedom,* 239.

25. Fergus M. Bordewich, *Bound for Canaan: The Underground Railroad and the War for the Soul of America* (New York: Amistad Press, 2005), 370–72.

26. Blight, *Passages to Freedom,* 241.

27. Blight, *Passages to Freedom,* 3–6.

28. Richard Fausset and Alan Blinder, "Era Ends as South Carolina Lowers Confederate Flag," *New York Times,* July 11, 2015.

29. Jacqueline L. Tobin and Raymond G. Dobard, *Hidden in Plain View: A Secret Story of Quilts and the Underground Railroad* (New York: Doubleday, 1999).

30. Unsigned review of *Hidden in Plain View: A Secret Story of Quilts and the Underground Railroad,* by Jacqueline L. Tobin and Raymond G. Dobard, accessed September 7, 2017, http://www.amazon.com/Hidden-Plain-View-Underground-Railroad/dp/0385497679/ref=s.

31. Unsigned review of *Hidden in Plain View*, by Tobin and Dobard, accessed October 26, 2017, https://www.thriftbooks.com/w/hidden-in-plain-view-a-secret -story-of-quilts-and-the-underground-railroad_jacqueline-l-tobin_raymond -g-dobard/252658/#isbn=0385497679.

32. Leigh Fellner, "Betsy Ross Redux: The Underground Railroad 'Quilt Code'" (Pensacola, FL: Hart Cottage Quilts, 2006), i–iii, https://web.archive.org /web/20130120160626/http://ugrrquilt.hartcottagequilts.com/betsy%20ross%20 redux.pdf.

33. One notable exception is Peter P. Hinks, who developed a set of criteria for evaluating the authenticity of Underground Railroad sites in Connecticut. Hinks proposed accrediting sites in only seven of the twenty-seven towns that he examined. See David W. Blight, "Why the Underground Railroad, and Why Now?: A Long View," in *Passages to Freedom*, ed. Blight, 235.

34. Pinsker, "Vigilance in Pennsylvania," 10.

35. Blight, *Passages to Freedom*, 2.

36. Foner, *Gateway to Freedom*, 14.

37. Pinsker, "Vigilance in Pennsylvania," 4; Smith, *On the Edge of Freedom*, 6–7; Keith P. Griffler, *Front Line of Freedom: African Americans and the Forging of the Underground Railroad in the Ohio Valley* (Lexington: University Press of Kentucky, 2004), xi–xiv; J. Blaine Hudson, *Fugitive Slaves and the Underground Railroad in the Kentucky Borderland* (Jefferson, NC: McFarland, 2002), 3–10; Cheryl Janifer LaRoche, *Free Black Communities and the Underground Railroad: The Geography of Resistance* (Urbana: University of Illinois Press, 2014); Stanley Harrold, *Subversives: Antislavery Community in Washington, DC, 1828–1865* (Baton Rouge: Louisiana State University Press, 2003).

38. Griffler, *Front Line of Freedom*, xiii.

39. Daniel Carpenter and Colin D. Moore, "When Canvassers Became Activists: Antislavery Petitioning and the Political Mobilization of American Women," *American Political Science Review* 108, no. 3 (August 2014): 486; Smith, *On the Edge of Freedom*, 9.

40. Smith, *On the Edge of Freedom*, 14–18

41. Smith, *On the Edge of Freedom*, 1–8, 14–15; Laurence A. Glasco, ed., *The WPA History of the Negro in Pittsburgh* (Pittsburgh: University of Pittsburgh Press, 2004), 104.

42. On the lack of scholarly studies of the Underground Railroad in western Pennsylvania, see Pinsker, "Vigilance in Pennsylvania," 77. On Pittsburgh, see R. J. M. Blackett, "'Freedom, or the Martyr's Grave': Black Pittsburgh's Aid to the Fugitive Slave," in *African Americans in Pennsylvania: Shifting Historical Perspectives*, ed. Joe William Trotter and Eric Ledell Smith (University Park: Pennsylvania State University Press, 1997), and *Making Freedom: The Underground Railroad and the Politics of Slavery* (Chapel Hill: University of North Carolina Press, 2013).

CHAPTER ONE. The Twilight of Slavery

1. For the broader picture of the contest between slavery and abolitionism in Pennsylvania, see Gary B. Nash and Jean R. Soderlund, *Freedom by Degrees: Emancipation in Pennsylvania and its Aftermath* (New York: Oxford University Press, 1991).

2. Glasco, *WPA History*, 35–40.

3. Earle R. Forrest, *History of Washington County, Pennsylvania,* 3 vols. (Chicago: S. J. Clarke, 1926), 1:314–18.

4. Washington County was initially part of three Virginia counties (Ohio, Monongalia, and Yohogania), but the early settlements were established in Yohogania County. Forrest, *History of Washington County*, 1:406–7.

5. R. Eugene Harper, *The Transformation of Western Pennsylvania, 1770–1800* (Pittsburgh: University of Pittsburgh Press, 1991), 12–13.

6. Nash and Soderlund, *Freedom by Degrees*, 4–7.

7. Boyd Crumrine, *History of Washington County, Pennsylvania* (Philadelphia: L. H. Everts, 1882), 222. The original "Washington County Negro Register from 1782 to 1851" is located in Washington & Jefferson College's Historical Collection, folder XV-j-238. Subsequent references to this register come from Charles Morton Ewing, ed., "Washington County Slave Record," (Washington, PA, 1951), a paginated typescript of the register, Washington & Jefferson College, Historical Collection, XV-j-238.5. For statistics on slave owners and population, see Raymond M. Bell, "Black Persons in Early Washington County, Pennsylvania," typescript, 1978, Historical Collection, Miller Library, Washington & Jefferson College, 1, 4, 8.

8. Harper, *Transformation of Western Pennsylvania*, 55.

9. For township statistics, see Ewing, "Washington County Slave Record," 1–4; R. Bell, "Black Persons," 2–3, and Raymond M. Bell, "List of Slave Owners in Washington County, Pennsylvania, 1782," *National Geographical Society Quarterly* 59, no. 1 (1971): 22–23; Forrest, *History of Washington County,* 1:407; Shelby Weaver-Splain and Craig Stutman, *African American Multiple Properties Documentation Form (MPDF)* (Harrisburg: Pennsylvania Historical and Museum Commission, 2010), 8.

10. Nash and Soderlund, *Freedom by Degrees*, 89.

11. Harper, *Transformation of Western Pennsylvania*, 55.

12. Robert Wallace Brewster, "The Rise of the Antislavery Movement in Southwestern Pennsylvania," *Western Pennsylvania Historical Magazine* 22 (1939): 3; Thomas Slaughter, *The Whiskey Rebellion: Frontier Epilogue to the American Revolution* (New York: Oxford, 1986), 67; Forrest, *History of Washington County*, 1:407, 410, 454; *Washington (PA) Reporter*, March 21, 1814.

13. Harper, *Transformation of Western Pennsylvania*, ix–xi, 53–55.

14. Edward M. Burns, "Slavery in Western Pennsylvania," *Western Pennsylvania Historical Magazine* 8, no. 4 (1925): 207; *Rural Reflections of Amwell Township,*

Washington County, Pennsylvania, 4 vols. (Amwell Township, PA: Bicentennial Committee of Amwell Township, 1977–1981), 4:174.

15. Forrest, *History of Washington County*, 1:412.

16. Crumrine, *History of Washington County*, 223.

17. Forrest, *History of Washington County*, 1:408; Glasco, *WPA History*, 42.

18. Nash and Soderlund, *Freedom by Degrees*, 4–5, 112, 121.

19. Nash and Soderlund, *Freedom by Degrees*, 141.

20. Nash and Soderlund, *Freedom by Degrees*, 4–5, 111; Brewster, "Rise of the Antislavery Movement," 3.

21. R. Bell, "Black Persons," 1, 4, 8; Ewing, "Washington County Slave Record," 38; Harper, *Transformation of Western Pennsylvania*, 8; Richard L. Forstall, ed., *Population of States and Counties of the United States: 1790–1990* (Washington, DC: United States Census Bureau, 1996), 139, https://www.census.gov/population/www/censusdata/pop1790-1990.html.

22. Ewing, "Washington County Slave Record," 37–38; Nash and Soderlund, *Freedom by Degrees*, 111.

23. George Swetnam, *Pittsylvania Country* (New York: Duell, Sloan & Pearce, 1951), 179; Nash and Soderlund, *Freedom by Degrees*, 110; Glasco, *WPA History*, 43.

24. R. Bell, "Black Persons," 2.

25. Forrest, *History of Washington County*, 1:412–13.

26. Ewing, "Washington County Slave Record," 4; Crumrine, *History of Washington County*, 986–87; U.S. Bureau of the Census, Decennial Census of Population and Housing, 1800, 1810, https://www.census.gov/prod/www/decennial.html (hereafter "U.S. Census"); R. Bell, "Black Persons," 8.

27. Will Book 2, Washington County Wills, Washington County Courthouse, Washington, PA; Crumrine, *Washington County*, 986–87; U.S. Census, 1810, 1820; R. Bell, "Black Persons," 8.

28. Glasco, *WPA History*, 49.

29. *Western Telegraph and Washington Advertizer*, February 9, 1796, quoted in William J. Switala, *Underground Railroad in Pennsylvania* (Mechanicsburg, PA: Stackpole Books, 2001), 70.

30. Glasco, *WPA History*, 52.

31. *Washington (PA) Reporter*, January 17, 1814; July 25, 1814; November 6, 1815.

32. Paul Finkelman, "The Kidnapping of John Davis and the Adoption of the Fugitive Slave Law of 1793," *Journal of Southern History* 56, no. 3 (August 1990): 400–3; Whitfield J. Bell Jr., "Washington County, Pennsylvania, in the Eighteenth Century Antislavery Movement," *Western Pennsylvania Historical Magazine* 25 (1942): 136–39; Richard S. Newman, *The Transformation of American Abolitionism: Fighting Slavery in the Early Republic* (Chapel Hill: University of North Carolina Press, 2002), 4–6.

33. Finkelman, "Kidnapping of John Davis," 401–2.

34. Finkelman, "Kidnapping of John Davis," 403–8; Memorial to Thomas Mifflin, May 31, 1791, in *Calendar of Virginia State Papers and Other Manuscripts*, ed. William P. Palmer (Richmond: Commonwealth of Virginia, 1885) 5: 320–21, https://dcms.lds.org/delivery/DeliveryManagerServlet?dps_pid=IE113634.

35. Finkelman, "Kidnapping of John Davis," 421–22; Nash and Soderlund, *Freedom by Degrees*, 114–15; W. Bell, "Washington County," 136–39.

36. Henrietta Buckmaster, *Let My People Go: The Story of the Underground Railroad and the Growth of the Abolition Movement* (Boston: Beacon Press, 1941), 20; Benjamin Quarles, *Black Abolitionists* (New York: Oxford University Press, 1969), 144; Nash and Soderlund, *Freedom by Degrees*, 194–97; Griffler, *Front Line of Freedom*, 19–22.

37. W. Bell, "Washington County," 137–41.

38. Swetnam, *Pittsylvania Country*, 179–80; W. Bell, "Washington County," 137–41.

39. Common Pleas Court Records, Washington County, PA, #94, Feb Term, 1799; R. Bell, "Black Persons," 1.

40. Newman, *Transformation of American Abolitionism*, 76–77, 207; Ewing, "Washington County Slave Record," 6. Reddick's membership certificate in the PAS can be found in Washington & Jefferson College's Historical Collection, xvj 446.

41. Ewing, Washington County Slave Record, 32.

42. Miller v. Dwilling, in Thomas Sergeant and William Rowle Jr., *Reports of Cases Adjudicated in the Supreme Court of Pennsylvania* (Philadelphia, 1818–1829), 14:442–46; Nash and Soderlund, *Freedom by Degrees*, 185, 195; Brewster, "Rise of the Antislavery Movement," 4.

43. *Rural Reflections of Amwell Township*, 4:175; Deed Book 1R, 258, Washington County.

44. Nash and Soderlund, *Freedom by Degrees*, 179–86; David W. Galenson, "The Rise and Fall of Indentured Servitude in the Americas: An Economic Analysis," in Robert Whaples and Dianne C. Betts, eds., *Historical Perspectives on the American Economy* (New York: Cambridge University Press, 1995), 123.

45. R. Bell, "Black Persons," 5.

46. R. Bell, "Black Persons," 4–5; *Washington (PA) Reporter*, August 11, 1823, quoted in Earle R. Forrest, ed., "Historical Items, Washington County, Pa," (1963) 6:13, Washington County Historical Society.

47. Nash and Soderlund, *Freedom by Degrees*, 201.

48. Smith, *On the Edge of Freedom*, 23.

49. Forrest, *History of Washington County*, 1:414.

50. "Dido Munts the Slave," Historical Collection, Washington & Jefferson College.

51. Griffler, *Front Line of Freedom*, 22.

52. R. Bell, "Black Persons," 2–3; U.S. Bureau of the Census, *Eighth Census* (Washington, DC: Bureau of the Census, 1864).

53. U.S. Bureau of the Census, *Seventh Census* (Washington, DC: Bureau of the Census, 1851).

54. Ellen Eslinger, "Freedom without Independence: The Story of a Former Slave and Her Family," *Virginia Magazine of History and Biography* 114 (2006): 266–67.

55. Eslinger, "Freedom without Independence," 267–68.

56. Eslinger, "Freedom without Independence," 269, 272–86.

57. *Washington (PA) Reporter*, April 16, 1897, 4.

58. R. Bell, "Black Persons," 6–7; Carter Woodson, *Free Negro Heads of Families in the United States in 1830* (Washington, DC: Association for the Study of Negro Life and History, 1925), 151–52; John Hope Franklin and Albert A. Moss Jr., *From Slavery to Freedom: A History of African Americans*, 7th ed. (New York: Mc-Graw-Hill, 1994), 151.

59. Gary B. Nash, *Forging Freedom: The Formation of Philadelphia's Black Community, 1720–1840* (Cambridge, MA: Harvard University Press, 1988), 79.

60. U.S. Bureau of the Census, *Seventh Census*; Nash, *Forging Freedom*, 248.

61. Nash, *Forging Freedom*, 127–31; 193.

62. As quoted in Nash, *Forging Freedom*, 114.

63. R. Bell, "Black Persons," 6; Elbert Matthews, "Church History: St. Paul AME Church, 1818–1987" (Washington, PA: St. Paul AME Church, 1987); Forrest, *History of Washington County*, 1:848; Crumrine, *History of Washington County*, 524; Leon F. Litwack, *North of Slavery: The Negro in the Free States, 1790–1860* (Chicago: University of Chicago Press, 1961), 191–94.

64. Bordewich, *Bound for Canaan*, 226.

65. Gary Thomas, "Bethel AME Church to Mark 171st Anniversary," *Pittsburgh Tribune-Review*, August 29, 2004.

66. Forrest, *History of Washington County*, 1:635; Crumrine, *History of Washington County*, 992; Howard Wallace, "A Historical Sketch of the Underground Railroad from Uniontown to Pittsburgh" (Uniontown, PA: Privately printed, 1903) 3–7.

67. Daniel Arnet, James Brown, and F. L. Chambers to F. Julius LeMoyne, October 23, 1843, LeMoyne Papers, Box A24, Washington County Historical Society, Washington, PA; Forrest, *History of Washington County*, 1:712.

68. Smith, *On the Edge of Freedom*, 18.

CHAPTER TWO. Radical Abolitionism and
the Arrival of the Underground Railroad

1. Griffler, *Front Line of Freedom*, 42, 48, 72–73; Forrest, *History of Washington County*, 1:378, 425.

2. Siebert, *Underground Railroad*, 33–34; Bordewich, *Bound for Canaan*, 133–46.

3. Siebert, *Underground Railroad*, 27–28, 301; Franklin and Moss, *From Slavery to Freedom*, 108–9; Benjamin Drew, *A North-Side View of Slavery: The Refugee* (Boston: John P. Jewett, 1856; repr. 1968), 19–28.

4. *Washington (PA) Reporter*, June 25, 1810, May 2, 1814, in *Abstracts of the Washington, Pa., Reporter, 1808–1814*, ed. Bonnie Malmat (Apollo, PA: Closson Press, 1990), 36–37, 174.

5. *Washington (PA) Reporter*, January 27, 1814.

6. Siebert, *Underground Railroad in Pennsylvania*, 37, 43–46; Gara, *Liberty Line*, 173–74.

7. Switala, *Underground Railroad in Pennsylvania*, 43–44, 59; Peter Kolchin, *American Slavery,. 1619–1877* (New York: Hill and Wang, 2003), 94–99.

8. Thomas B. Searight, *The Old Pike: A History of the National Road* (Uniontown, PA: printed by author, 1894), 109–10.

9. Bordewich, *Bound for Canaan*, 90–91; Searight, *Old Pike*, 121.

10. McCulloch, *Fearless Advocate*, 158.

11. Bordewich, *Bound for Canaan*, 90–91, 99–102; Josiah Henson, *The Life of Josiah Henson, Formerly a Slave, Now an Inhabitant of Canada, as Narrated by Himself* (Boston: Arthur D. Phelps, 1849), 21–25, http://docsouth.unc.edu/neh/henson49/menu.html.

12. *Washington (PA) Reporter*, June 10, 1822, June 2, 1823, in Forrest, "Historical Items," 6:3, 6:12.

13. Searight, *Old Pike*, 109.

14. Searight, *Old Pike*, 223–24, 337.

15. Forrest, *History of Washington County*, 1:376–78.

16. Forrest, *History of Washington County*, 1:378, 425; Jean Fritz, *Brady* (New York: Puffin Books, 1987).

17. Forrest, *History of Washington County*, 1:425.

18. John Asbury, "Asbury-Adams Roots" (Washington, PA: self-published, ca. 1992), Washington County Historical Society, 1–2, 6, 8; James Simpson, *History of the Cross Creek Graveyard and the Cross Creek Cemetery* (1894; repr., Parsons, WV: McClain Printing, 1969), 14; *Washington (PA) Reporter*, November 20, 1884; Carter Woodson, *Free Negro Heads of Families in the United States in 1830* (Washington, DC: Association for the Study of Negro Life and History, 1925), 152; 1830 U.S. Census.

19. Gara, *Liberty Line*, 3–7; Griffler, *Front Line of Freedom*, 79–80.

20. William W. Freehling, *The Road to Disunion: Secessionists at Bay, 1776–1854* (New York: Oxford University Press, 1990), 155.

21. *Washington (PA) Reporter*, July 31, 1820, July 21, 1820; Randall M. Miller and William Pencak, eds., *Pennsylvania: A History of the Commonwealth* (University Park: Pennsylvania State University Press, 2002), 597.

22. Bordewich, *Bound for Canaan*, 136.

23. Forrest, *History of Washington County*, 1:416; Brewster, "Rise of the Antislavery Movement," 7; *Claysville (PA) Recorder*, August 13, 1915; *The LeMoyne*

Home: 1812–1935 (Hollywood, CA: Hollycrafters, 1935), 7, in Washington & Jefferson College Historical Collection, W&J, xv j 189; *Washington (PA) Examiner,* May 1, 1830, June 1, 1830.

24. Forrest, *History of Washington County,* 1:416–18; Helen Turnbull Waite Coleman, *Banners in the Wilderness: Early Years of Washington and Jefferson College* (Pittsburgh: University of Pittsburgh Press, 1956), 134–41; Memorial, Committee on the District of Columbia, Petitions and Memorials (HR20A-G5.1), January 19–26, 1829, Folder 4, 20th Congress, Records of the U.S. House of Representatives, Record Group 233, National Archives, Washington, DC.

25. Newman, *Transformation of American Abolitionism,* 96–98, 117; Walter M. Merrill, *Against the Wind: A Biography of William Lloyd Garrison* (Cambridge, MA: Harvard University Press, 1963), 4; Eric Burin, "Rethinking Northern White Support for the African Colonization Movement: The Pennsylvania Colonization Society as an Agent of Emancipation," *Pennsylvania Magazine of History and Biography* 127, no. 2 (2003): 203.

26. Brewster, "Rise of the Antislavery Movement," 7–8.

27. Newman, *Transformation of American Abolitionism,* 99–100; Eric Burin, "Rethinking Northern White Support," 206.

28. James Brewer Stewart, *Holy Warriors: The Abolitionists and American Slavery* (New York: Hill and Wang, 1996), 44–45; Quarles, *Black Abolitionists,* 16–18.

29. Newman, *Transformation of American Abolitionism,* 103; Quarles, *Black Abolitionists,* 23–29; Stewart, *Holy Warriors,* 58–59.

30. *Liberator* (Boston, MA), December 15, 1843.

31. Daniel Arnet et al. to F. J. LeMoyne, LeMoyne Papers, Box A24, Washington County Historical Society, Washington, PA; Miller and Pencak, *Pennsylvania,* 168.

32. Tunde Adeleke, *Without Regard to Race: The Other Martin Robinson Delany* (Jackson: University Press of Mississippi, 2003), 40–52; Glasco, *WPA History,* 85–87.

33. Burleigh to LeMoyne, June 29, 1841, Box A24, LeMoyne Papers; Glasco, *WPA History,* 85.

34. *Mystery* (Pittsburgh, PA), December 16, 1846; Siebert, *Underground Railroad,* appendix E, 431–34; *Washington (PA) Observer,* October 16, 1884.

35. Stewart, *Holy Warriors,* 44–45.

36. Newman, *Transformation of American Abolitionism,* 114–15; Stewart, *Holy Warriors,* 58–59.

37. The Presbyterian minister George Bourne was the first American to call for the "immediate and total abolition" of slavery in 1816. The British abolitionist Elizabeth Heyrick popularized the idea of "immediate not gradual emancipation" in her 1824 pamphlet bearing the same title, but it was Garrison who popularized the doctrine of immediatism in an American context. Merton L. Dillon, *Benjamin Lundy and the Struggle for Negro Freedom* (Urbana: University of Illinois Press,

1966), 15; Adam Hochshild, *Bury the Chains: Prophets and Rebels in the Fight to Free an Empire's Slaves* (New York: Mariner Books, 2006), 324.

38. James Brewer Stewart, "From Moral Suasion to Political Confrontation: American Abolitionists and the Problem of Resistance, 1831–1861," in *Passages to Freedom*, ed. Blight, 69–70.

39. Newman, *Transformation of American Abolitionism*, 115.

40. Merrill, *Against the Wind*, 41–44; Ronald G. Walters, *American Reformers, 1815–1860*, rev. ed. (New York: Hill & Wang, 1997), 77–80.

41. David Brion Davis, *Inhuman Bondage: The Rise and Fall of Slavery in the New World* (New York: Oxford University Press, 2006), 258–60.

42. Stewart, *Holy Warriors*, 37–43; Walters, *American Reformers*, 82–85.

43. Edward Magdol, *The Antislavery Rank and File: A Social Profile of the Abolitionists' Constituency* (Westport, CT: Greenwood Press, 1986), xi, 15–22, 47.

44. Stewart, *Holy Warriors*, 37–43.

45. Walters, *American Reformers*, 80–81; Merrill, *Against the Wind*, 77–81; Bordewich, *Bound for Canaan*, 153.

46. Brewster, "Rise of the Antislavery Movement," 8; John L. Myers, "The Early Anti-Slavery Agency System in Pennsylvania, 1833–1837," *Pennsylvania History* 21 (1964): 66–68; Joe Smydo, "Freedom for the Slaves, Progress for the Town: Pragmatic Abolitionism in Washington County, Pennsylvania, during the 1830s and 1840s" (unpublished seminar paper, Duquesne University, 2012), 13–14.

47. Glasco, *WPA History*, 104; Smith, *On the Edge of Freedom*, 61–70, 214.

48. William Lee Miller, *Arguing about Slavery: The Great Battle in the United States Congress* (New York: Alfred A. Knopf, 1996), 82.

49. Owen W. Muelder, *Theodore Dwight Weld and the American Anti-Slavery Society* (Jefferson, NC: McFarland, 2011), 36–41.

50. Glasco, *WPA History*, 130.

51. Myers, "Early Anti-Slavery Agency System," 66–69; Bordewich, *Bound for Canaan*, 158–59; *Washington Examiner*, June 20, 1835; *Our Country* (Washington, PA), June 12, 1835, June 19, 1835.

52. Theodore D. Weld to Mrs. C. LeMoyne Wills, December 22, 1872, Le-Moyne Papers.

53. Rebecca Harding Davis, *Bits of Gossip* (Boston: Houghton Mifflin, 1904), 168.

54. Osborne Mitchell, "About the Stormy Days before the War," *Washington (PA) Reporter*, August 15, 1908; McCulloch, *Fearless Advocate*, 31–32, 108–28, 134–36; R. Davis, *Bits of Gossip*, 168.

55. Extra to *Washington (PA) Examiner*, August 15, 1835, Washington & Jefferson College Historical Collection, xv-j-399.

56. Joseph McFarland, *Twentieth Century History of Washington County* (Chicago: Richmond-Arnold, 1910), 130; David Grimsted, *American Mobbing, 1828–1861: Toward Civil War* (New York: Oxford University Press, 1998), 66.

57. Brewster, "Rise of the Antislavery Movement," 11–12; Myers, "Early Anti-Slavery Agency," 71–75.

58. Forrest, *History of Washington County*, 1:419–20; McFarland, *Twentieth Century History*, 130; McCullough, *Fearless Advocate*, 117; Joe Smydo, "Freedom for the Slaves," 10–11; Myers, "Early Anti-Slavery Agency," 71–75; "The Washington Rioters," *Liberator* (Boston, MA), November 26, 1836.

59. Grimsted, *American Mobbing*, 19–22, 35–37; Glasco, *WPA History*, 131.

60. Forrest, *History of Washington County*, 1:420–21; Grimsted, *American Mobbing*, 58–61.

61. *Our Country* (Washington, PA), July 11, 1836.

62. McCulloch, *Fearless Advocate*, 118–19. As Grimsted notes, mobbing in other Northern cities brought converts to the abolitionist cause: *American Mobbing*, 58.

63. Joe Smydo, "Unlikely Partners: Collaboration between Colonizationists and Radical Abolitionists in Washington County, Pennsylvania, during the 1830s" (MA thesis, Duquesne University, 2016), 1–3, 92–105.

64. LeMoyne to Joseph Templeton, April 6, 1837, Box A24, LeMoyne Papers; Stewart, *Holy Warriors*, 45.

65. Miller, *Arguing about Slavery*, 73.

66. McCulloch, *Fearless Advocate*, 125–26; Forrest, *History of Washington County*, 1:421–22.

67. American Colonization Society, *African Repository and Journal*, vol. 10 (Washington, DC: James C. Dunn, 1834), 118, https://books.google.com/books?id=wMcNAAAAQAAJ.

68. *Washington (PA) Examiner*, June 27, 1835.

69. R. J. M. Blackett, "Fugitive Slaves and the Struggle against Slavery in Western Pennsylvania" (lecture, Center for Africanamerican Urban Studies & the Economy [CAUSE] Conference, Carnegie Mellon University, Pittsburgh, PA, February 6, 2016).

70. Forrest, *History of Washington County*, 1:426; *Washington (PA) Reporter and Tribune*, August 30, 1860. I am indebted to R. J. M. Blackett for pointing out the latter source.

71. Smydo, "Unlikely Partners," 2–3, 16–27.

72. Miller, *Arguing about Slavery*, 107–11.

73. U.S. Congress, House, Journal, 24th Congress, Records of the House of Representatives, Record Group 233, 1st session, February 29, 1836, 413, National Archives, Washington, DC. http://memory.loc.gov/cgi-bin/ampage?collId=llhj&file Name=029/llhj029.db&recNum=412&itemLink=r?ammem/hlaw:@field(DOCID +@lit(hj02962))%230290413&linkText=1.

74. Susan Zaeske, *Signatures of Citizenship: Petitioning, Antislavery, and Women's Political Identity* (Chapel Hill: University of North Carolina Press, 2003), 69–72; Miller, *Arguing about Slavery*, 103.

75. Sweney's name appears as "Sweeney" in some accounts. Smydo, "Unlikely Partners," 105.

76. U.S. Congress, House, "Petition from Washington County, PA, to rescind Mr. Patton's Resolution," February 14, 1838, and "Petition from Washington County, PA, to rescind Mr. Patton's Resolution," May 21, 1838, both in Library of Congress Collection HR 25A, 25th Congress, Records of the House of Representatives, Record Group 233, National Archives, Washington, DC; Siebert, *Underground Railroad*, 434; Smydo, "Unlikely Partners," 105.

77. Miller, *Arguing about Slavery*, 316; Zaeske, *Signatures of Citizenship*, 2–7.

78. I am grateful to Natalie Rocchio, archives specialist, National Archives and Records Administration, for discovering this petition. U.S. House, Journal, 25th Congress, "Petition of 118 Ladies of Washington Co Pa for the Abolition of Slavery . . . ," February 14, 1838, Library of Congress Collection HR25A, Records of the Congress of the U.S., Record Group 233, National Archives, Washington, DC; Beth A. Salerno, *Sister Societies: Women's Antislavery Societies in Antebellum America* (DeKalb: Northern Illinois University Press, 2005), 183–84.

79. Personal communication from Natalie Rocchio, February 6, 2016.

80. See "Geographic Distribution of Antislavery Signatures to U.S. House, 25th Congress," in Carpenter and Moore, "When Canvassers Became Activists," 486.

81. Dwight L. Dumond, *Antislavery: The Crusade for Freedom* (Ann Arbor: University of Michigan Press, 1961), 172–73, 179; Brewster, "Rise of the Antislavery Movement," 9; McCulloch, *Fearless Advocate*, 125–26, 134; Weld to Mrs. C. LeMoyne Wills, December 22, 1872.

82. John Stauffer, *The Black Hearts of Men: Radical Abolitionists and the Transformation of Race* (Cambridge, MA: Harvard University Press, 2002), 20; Forrest, *History of Washington County*, 1:419–21; *Washington (PA) Patriot*, June 10, 1848, in Washington & Jefferson College Historical Collection.

83. "Helltown," in West Middletown Scrapbook, McKeever Study, West Middletown, 264.

84. Forrest, *History of Washington County*, 1:421–22, 424; *Washington (PA) Reporter*, August 15, 1908.

85. Alvin D. White, *First Families and Forgotten Churches* (Washington, PA: Quality Quick, 1992), 91–93; Jason Haley, "Presbyterians Divided: Antislavery and Washington County Abolitionists" (unpublished seminar paper, Washington & Jefferson College, 2001), 32, 37–40.

86. Matthew McKeever, "Recollections of John Brown," letter dated September 11, 1880, in *Washington Observer*, June 7, 1890; Stephen B. Oates, *To Purge This Land with Blood: A Biography of John Brown* (New York: Harper & Row, 1970), 49.

87. James McElroy, "Recollections," in *Reminiscences of West Middletown, Pennsylvania*, ed. William T. Lindsey (West Middletown, PA: McKeever Study Library Association, 2002 [1910]), 2, 10–12, 14.

88. Letter of Mrs. R. C. Jones, April 1, 1910, in West Middletown Recollections, McKeever Study Library, West Middletown, PA; Dorothy Sterling, *Ahead of Her Time: Abby Kelley and the Politics of Antislavery* (New York: W. W. Norton, 1991), 104–5, 211–15.

89. *Claysville (PA) Recorder*, May 28, 1915; *Washington (PA) Observer*, January 4, 1904; U.S. Congress, 25th Congress, Third Session, Journal of the House of Representatives, December 20, 1838, 114.

90. 1840 U.S. Census; *Claysville (PA) Recorder*, May 28, 1915.

91. *Claysville (PA) Recorder*, May 28, 1915.

92. Crumrine, *History of Washington County*, 981; *Claysville (PA) Recorder*, March 12, 1915, August 20, 1915.

93. "Session Book of the Free Presbyterian Church of West Alexander," West Alexander Presbyterian Church archives, West Alexander, PA. See also Jason A. Haley, "Washington County Presbyterians: Abolitionism in a Divided Denomination" (honors thesis, Washington & Jefferson College, 2002), 32–36; *Washington (PA) Observer*, January 5, 1904.

94. Job Johnson et al. to LeMoyne, July 24, 1843, Box A24, LeMoyne Papers.

95. James Miller to LeMoyne, September 21, 1837, and Joseph Miller to LeMoyne, August 2, 1837, both in Box A24, LeMoyne Papers.

96. Pennsylvania Anti-Slavery Society Western District Minutes, 1837–1838, Heinz History Center, Pittsburgh, PA.

97. Andrew E. Murray, *Presbyterians and the Negro* (Philadelphia: Presbyterian Historical Society, 1966), 88–89.

98. Haley, "Washington County Presbyterians," 12–14.

99. Murray, *Presbyterians and the Negro*, 65, 103–6; Robert T. Handy, *A History of the Churches in the United States and Canada* (New York: Oxford University Press, 1977), 185–86; Brewster, "Rise of the Antislavery Movement," 16.

100. Murray, *Presbyterians and the Negro*, 90–91, 118–26; Haley, "Washington County Presbyterians," 32–36; "Session Book of the Free Presbyterian Church of West Alexander."

101. Sydney E. Ahlstrom, *A Religious History of the American People* (Garden City, NY: Image Books, 1975), 1:343; Haley, "Washington County Presbyterians," 14.

102. Murray, *Presbyterians and the Negro*, 127–30; Haley, "Washington County Presbyterians," 9–11; Frederick J. Blue, *No Taint of Compromise: Crusaders in Antislavery Politics* (Baton Rouge: Louisiana State University Press, 2005), 140–43.

103. Haley, "Washington County Presbyterians," 14, 32.

104. Handy, *History of the Churches*, 168–69; Ahlstrom, *Religious History of the American People*, 1:541–44, 2:112.

105. Regis J. Serinko, *California University of Pennsylvania: The People's College in the Monongahela Valley*, 2nd ed., (Roscoe, PA: Roscoe Ledger, 1992), 37; William H. Burleigh to LeMoyne, July 20, 1841, Box A24, LeMoyne Papers.

106. Forrest, *History of Washington County*, 1:592–94; Howard Wallace, "Historical Sketch," 5. Joseph Miller, who invited LeMoyne to address citizens in eastern Washington County, clearly was a Quaker, as is evidenced by his use of "thee" and "eighth month." Miller to LeMoyne, August 2, 1837, Box A24, LeMoyne Papers.

107. Paul N. D. Thornell, "The Absent Ones and the Providers: A Biography of the Vashons," *Journal of Negro History* 83, no. 4 (Autumn 1998): 286–87. I am indebted to Pat Trimble for pointing out the relationship between Vashon and Griffith.

108. Smith, *On the Edge of Freedom*, 61, 70–72, 214.

109. Magdol, *Antislavery Rank and File*, 21–25.

110. *Washington (PA) Patriot*, June 10, 1848, in Washington & Jefferson College Historical Collection; McCullough, *Fearless Advocate*, 145–46.

111. *Washington (PA) Patriot*, June 10, 1848, in Washington & Jefferson College Historical Collection; U.S. Congress, Senate, *Biographical Dictionary of the United States Congress, 1774–1989*, Senate Document 100–34, 1989, 970.

112. M. H. Urquhart to S. P. Noble, February 11, 1847, Box A24, Folder 1, LeMoyne Papers.

113. Brewster, "Rise of the Antislavery Movement," 15.

114. Stewart, *Holy Warriors*, 66–74.

115. Magdol, *Antislavery Rank and File*, xi–xiv, 21–25, 37–47; Glasco, *WPA History*, 103.

116. Eric D. Dutchess, "Between Frontier and Factory: Washington, Pennsylvania, 1810–1870" (Ph.D. dissertation, West Virginia University, 2012), 1–7, 28, 89, 102–6; Magdol, *Antislavery Rank and File*, xi–xiv, 138; Smith, *On the Edge of Freedom*, 9–10.

117. Smith, *On the Edge of Freedom*, 15, 71–72.

118. Haley, "Washington County Presbyterians," 12–14.

119. Bordewich, *Bound for Canaan*, 126–46; *Washington (PA) Observer*, June 7, 1890.

120. Siebert, *Underground Railroad*, 35–38; Griffler, *Front Line of Freedom*, 73; Bordewich, *Bound for Canaan*, 161–62. On the connection between organized abolitionism and the Underground Railroad, see also Muelder, *Theodore Dwight Weld*, 25.

121. Bordewich, *Bound for Canaan*, 153–54.

122. Stewart, "From Moral Suasion to Political Confrontation," in Blight, *Passages to Freedom*, 77–79; Grimsted, *American Mobbing*, 66.

123. Richard O. Boyer, *The Legend of John Brown: A Biography and a History* (New York: Knopf, 1973), 312–15.

124. Newman, *Transformation of American Abolitionism*, 145.

125. Stewart, "From Moral Suasion to Political Confrontation," in Blight, *Passages to Freedom*, 79; Stewart, *Holy Warriors*, 88–93.

126. McCullough, *Fearless Advocate*, 139–41; Ira V. Brown, "An Antislavery Agent: C. C. Burleigh in Pennsylvania, 1836–1837," *Pennsylvania Magazine of History and Biography* 105, no. 1 (1981): 78.

127. Stewart, *Holy Warriors*, 93–94.

128. McCulloch, *Fearless Advocate*, 134.

129. Stewart, *Holy Warriors*, 88–93; Walters, *American Reformers*, 86–92; McCulloch, *Fearless Advocate*, 130–33; Forrest, *History of Washington County*, 1:427.

130. McCulloch, *Fearless Advocate*, 130–33; Stewart, "From Moral Suasion to Political Confrontation," in Blight, *Passages to Freedom*, 86; Grimsted, *American Mobbing*, 73.

131. Lewis Woodson to LeMoyne, June 21, 1842, Box A24, LeMoyne Papers; McCulloch, *Fearless Advocate*, 139–40; Walters, *American Reformers*, 85–86; Glasco, *WPA History*, 85.

132. James M. McPherson, *Ordeal by Fire: The Civil War and Reconstruction*, 2nd ed. (New York: McGraw-Hill, 1992), 65–67. On the Douglass visit, see "Slavery Days," *Monongahela (PA) Daily Republican*, September 22, 1893.

133. *Our Country* (Washington, PA), July 21, 1836; McCulloch, *Fearless Advocate*, 140, 261.

134. Pennsylvania Anti-Slavery Society Western District Minutes, 1837–1838, Heinz History Center, Pittsburgh, PA.

135. See also the analysis of LeMoyne's movement into the Underground Railroad in U.S. Department of the Interior, National Park Service, "F. Julius Le-Moyne Home," National Historical Landmark Nomination (1997), 10–14.

CHAPTER THREE. The Legendary Underground Railroad in Washington County

1. Gara, *Liberty Line*, 1–2.

2. Fergus M. Bordewich, "History's Tangled Threads," *New York Times*, February 2, 2007, A19.

3. Gara, *Liberty Line*, 17.

4. Gara, *Liberty Line*, 7, 172, 191; Siebert, *Underground Railroad*, 346; E. W. R. Ewing, *Northern Rebellion and Southern Secession* (Richmond, VA: J. L. Hill, 1904), 254.

5. Pinsker, "Vigilance in Pennsylvania," 21; Stanley Harrold, *Border War: Fighting over Slavery before the Civil War* (Chapel Hill: University of North Carolina Press, 2010), 39–40.

6. Gara, *Liberty Line*, 40.

7. Pinsker, "Vigilance in Pennsylvania," 20–21.

8. Bordewich offers an estimate of between 70,000 and 150,000, but argues that 100,000 might be the best estimate; *Bound for Canaan*, 436–37. Franklin and

Schweninger believe that between 1,000 and 2,000 slaves escaped per year between 1830 and 1860—thus between 30,000 and 60,000; *Runaway Slaves*, 367; Eric Foner, *Gateway to Freedom*, 152.

9. Gara, *Liberty Line*, 38–40; Bordewich, *Bound for Canaan*, 436–37.

10. Franklin and Schweninger, *Runaway Slaves,* xiv, 17–48; Peter Kolchin, *American Slavery*, 158–60.

11. Hudson, *Fugitive Slaves*, 162; Bordewich, *Bound for Canaan*, 436–37; Harrold, *Border War*, 39–40.

12. Siebert, *Underground Railroad*, 378; Gara, *Liberty Line*, 38–40; Kolchin, *American Slavery*, 158; Smith, *On the Edge of Freedom*, 6; Ewing, *Northern Rebellion and Southern Secession*, 254.

13. Drew, *North-Side View*, v.

14. Robin Winks, *The Blacks in Canada: A History* (New Haven: Yale University Press, 1971), 233–40.

15. Michael Wayne, "The Black Population of Canada West on the Eve of the American Civil War: A Reassessment Based on the Manuscript Census of 1861," *Histoire Social/Social History* 28 (1995): 466–70.

16. Griffler, *Front Line of Freedom*, 25.

17. Drew, *North-Side View*, 149–50, 239–47. Black men and women who emigrated to Canada from free states arrived in virtually equal numbers, whereas black men constituted 62 percent of those migrating or fleeing from slave states. Wayne, "Black Population of Canada West," 471–74.

18. The estimate is Bordewich's, *Bound for Canaan*, 436.

19. Pinsker, "Vigilance in Pennsylvania," 14.

20. Gara, *Liberty Line*, 40; Davis, *Inhuman Bondage*, 264–65.

21. Gara, *Liberty Line*, 143–48.

22. Davis, *Inhuman Bondage*, 265; Stanley W. Campbell, *The Slave Catchers: Enforcement of the Fugitive Slave Law, 1850-1860* (Chapel Hill: University of North Carolina Press; New York: W. W. Norton, 1972), 10–12; Stewart, *Holy Warriors*, 107.

23. Davis, *Inhuman Bondage*, 265; Campbell, *Slave Catchers*, 23–25.

24. Harriett Beecher Stowe, *Uncle Tom's Cabin* (New York: Penguin, 1998), 99.

25. Gara, *Liberty Line*, 127–28.

26. Campbell, *Slave Catchers*, vi–vii, 147–49, 207.

27. Siebert, *Underground Railroad*, 342–43, 378.

28. Siebert, *Underground Railroad*, 379; William Freehling, *Road to Secession*, 165; 1850 U.S. Census.

29. Ancestry.com, U.S. Federal Census—Slave Schedules, 1850 and 1860 (Provo, UT: Ancestry.com Operations Inc, 2010), http://search.ancestry.com/search/group /usfedcen; Siebert, *Underground Railroad*, 378–79.

30. Campbell, *Slave Catchers*, 199–207.

31. Ancestry.com, U.S. Federal Census—Slave Schedules, 1850 and 1860.

32. Freehling, *Road to Secession*, 165; Siebert, *Underground Railroad*, 378; Gara, *Liberty Line*, 38–40.

33. Bordewich, *Bound for Canaan*, 196; Smith, *On the Edge of Freedom*, 27–31.

34. Drew, *North-Side View*, 46–53.

35. Griffler, *Front Line of Liberty*, 90–91.

36. Forrest, *History of Washington County*, 1:426; *Washington (PA) Observer*, June 7, 1890; Paul Weyand, "The Anti-Slavery Movement in Beaver County," in Joseph H. Bausman, *History of Beaver County, Pennsylvania* (New York: Knickerbocker Press, 1904), 2:1140.

37. *Washington (PA) Observer*, November 20, 1884. On the making of the Underground Railroad legend, see Gara, *Liberty Line*, 143–91.

38. Burns, "Slavery in Western Pennsylvania," 211. I made my estimate before encountering Burns's article.

39. Gara, *Liberty Line*, 91; Switala, *Underground Railroad in Pennsylvania*, 144; Bordewich, *Bound for Canaan*, 356.

40. Gara, *Liberty Line*, 69–70.

41. *Washington (PA) Observer*, January 5, 1904.

42. Smith, *On the Edge of Freedom*, 35–38; Harrold, *Subversives*.

43. Gara, *Liberty Line*, 42–45; Smith, *On the Edge of Freedom*, 29–30.

44. *Washington (PA) Observer*, January 5, 1904.

45. Howard Wallace's "A Historical Sketch of the Underground Railroad from Uniontown to Pittsburgh" appeared originally as a pamphlet. Because it was privately printed, there is no publication date. Internal evidence indicates that he wrote his account after 1891. His account can also be found in Nan Hornbake, *History and Development of California, Pa.: One Hundred Years of Progress* (California, PA: California Centennial Committee, 1949), 20–24.

46. Gara, *Liberty Line*, 58–62; Griffler, *Front Line of Freedom*, 100.

47. Eber Pettit, *Sketches in the History of the Underground Railroad* (Fredonia, NY: W. McKinistry & Son, 1879; repr., Freeport, NY: Books for Libraries Press, 1971), 27–28.

48. Pettit, *Sketches in the History*, 28–29.

49. Pettit, *Sketches in the History*, 30–31.

50. Frederick Douglass, *Narrative of the Life of Frederick Douglass*, ed. David W. Blight, 2nd ed. (Boston: Bedford/St. Martin's, 2003), 112.

51. For Greene County stations, see Switala, *Underground Railroad in Pennsylvania*, 74–75.

52. Robert S. Starobin, ed., *Blacks in Bondage: Letters of American Slaves*, 2nd ed. (New York: New Viewpoints, 1974; repr., Princeton, NJ: Markus Wiener Publishers, 1994), 150–53; Smith, *On the Edge of Freedom*, 31–32.

53. See "David Thompson's Story" in *Slave Testimony: Two Centuries of Letters, Speeches, Interviews, and Autobiographies*, ed. John W. Blassingame (Baton

Rouge: Louisiana State University Press, 1977), 532–33. Recollections from the 1880s differ slightly about the timing of this escape. Crumrine places the escape in 1856, whereas African American conductors who were interviewed about the escape for an 1884 newspaper article on the Underground Railroad date it to 1859. See Crumrine's handwritten notes in "Underground Railway," xv-j-380, Historical Collection, Miller Library, Washington & Jefferson College, and *Washington (PA) Observer*, October 16, 1884. However, the *Pittsburg Dispatch* of August 6, 1856, which discusses a slave hunt in Greene County for nine fugitives from the Clarksburg area, establishes with near certainty that the escape occurred in 1856.

54. David Thompson, interview in "The McCurdy Station," *The Underground Railroad in Pennsylvania*, vol. 1, Siebert Papers, Ohio Historical Society, Columbus, Ohio.

55. David Thompson, interview in "The McCurdy Station," *Underground Railroad in Pennsylvania*.

56. "David Thompson's Story," in Blassingame, *Slave Testimony*, 532–33.

57. *Washington (PA) Observer*, October 16, 1884.

58. See, for example, William J. Switala, *Underground Railroad in Delaware, Maryland, and West Virginia* (Mechanicsburg, PA: Stackpole Books, 2004), 118–22; Connie Park Rice, *Our Monongalia: A History of African Americans in Monongalia County, West Virginia* (Terra Alta, WV: Headline Books, 1999), 23; Slave schedules for 1850 and 1860, Ancestry.com.

59. I am indebted to Patrick Trimble for pointing out this incident to me. For accounts of the Pruntytown escape, see *Wheeling Intelligencer*, November 6, 1858; *Pittsburgh Gazette*, November 9, 1858; and *Virginia Free Press*, November 18, 1858. Several of these items were reprinted from the *Morgantown Star*. See also the Slave Schedule for Taylor County, Virginia, 1860 U.S. Census, where the ten fugitive slaves are reported missing; Ancestry.com, U.S. Federal Census—Slave Schedules, 1860.

60. Forrest, *History of Washington County*, 1:425–26.

61. "Letters of Dr. F. J. LeMoyne, an Abolitionist of Western Pennsylvania," *Journal of Negro History*, 18, no. 4 (1933): 465–66.

62. Boyd Crumrine Papers, Historical Collection, Miller Library, Washington and Jefferson College, Washington, PA.

63. Pettit, *Sketches in the History*, 17–23.

64. Philip J. Schwartz, *Migrants against Slavery: Virginians and the Nation* (Charlottesville: University Press of Virginia, 2001), 35; Forrest, *History of Washington County*, 1:426–27.

65. Wallace, "Historical Sketch." For McKeever's account, see Forrest, *History of Washington County*, 1:426–27; Smith, *On the Edge of Freedom*, 27–29.

66. *Washington (PA) Observer*, October 16, 1884.

67. Gara, *Liberty Line*, 99–100; Pinsker, "Vigilance in Pennsylvania," 16; Smith, *On the Edge of Freedom*, 27.

68. Forrest, *History of Washington County*, 1:426–27.

69. Anonymous to F. Julius LeMoyne, September (?) 1851, LeMoyne Papers, Washington County Historical Society. On the Christiana Riot, see Switala, *Underground Railroad in Pennsylvania*, 25–26.

70. Forrest, *History of Washington County*, 1:426; Gara, *Liberty Line*, 97–98.

71. Joseph Taylor Armstrong, "My Boyhood Days in Monongahela City," *Historical Magazine of Monongahela's Old Home Week Celebration* (1908): 148–49; *Washington (PA) Observer*, October 16, 1884, November 20, 1884; Forrest, *History of Washington County*, 1:425; Bordewich, *Bound for Canaan*, 232.

72. I was asked once after a presentation on the local Underground Railroad if it was true that a tunnel ran from LeMoyne's house to the crematorium. See also McCulloch, *Fearless Advocate*, 159; U.S. Department of the Interior, "F. Julius LeMoyne Home," 1997, 7, 15–16.

73. Gara, *Liberty Line*, xiv.

74. Dave Molter, "Area Man Recalls Woman Who Taught Him about Life," *Washington (PA) Observer-Reporter*, July 25, 1990.

75. *Washington (PA) Observer*, October 16, 1884; Forrest, *History of Washington County*, 1:425; Ibid.; Asbury, "Asbury-Adams Roots," 2.

76. Crumrine, "Underground Railway"; *Washington (PA) Observer*, November 6, 1884.

77. Forrest, *History of Washington County*, 1:425.

78. Wallace, "Historical Sketch," 6–7; "McKeever Was a Righteous Judge and a Warm Abolitionist," Murdock Papers, McKeever Study Library, West Middletown, PA.

79. *Washington (PA) Observer*, October 16, 1884; Crumrine, *History of Washington County*, 881.

80. Stowe, *Uncle Tom's Cabin*, 212.

81. "McKeever Was a Righteous Judge," Murdock Papers.

82. See *Washington (PA) Observer*, November 20, 1884, for a slightly different account of this same incident.

83. "McKeever Was a Righteous Judge," Murdock Papers. See also Asbury, "Asbury-Adams Roots," 1–2, 6, 8; Simpson, *History of the Cross Creek Graveyard*, 14; *Washington (PA) Reporter*, November 20, 1884; Woodson, *Free Negro Heads of Families*, 152.

84. See McCulloch, *Fearless Advocate*, 263n175.

85. Gant to LeMoyne, June 7, 1847, in LeMoyne Papers, Box A24, Folder 1; *National Era* (Washington, DC), January 7, 1847; "Underground Railroad Site to be Preserved," *Cincinnati Enquirer*, November 18, 2002, http://enquirer.com/editions/2002/11/18/loc_amrep18.html.

86. Thomas Lee to LeMoyne, May 8, 1847, LeMoyne Papers, Box A24, Folder 1.

87. McCulloch, *Fearless Advocate*, 159.

88. W. H. Brisbane to LeMoyne, 1844, LeMoyne Papers, Box A24; *Washington (PA) Reporter*, March 16, 1844; John Niven, *Samuel P. Chase: A Biography* (New York: Oxford University Press, 1995), 213–14; William H. Brisbane, "Speech

of Rev. Wm H. Brisbane lately a slaveholder in South Carolina; containing an account of the change in his views on the subject of slavery" (speech to the Female Anti-Slavery Society of Cincinnati, 1840), Wisconsin Historical Society Archives (Wis Mss VD, box 1); online facsimile at http://www.wisconsinhistory.org/turning points/search.asp?id=23.

89. J. H. Beers, *Commemorative Biographical Record of Washington County, Pennsylvania* (Chicago: J. H. Beers, 1893), 7, 190–91; U.S. House, "Petition from Washington County, Pa., to Rescind Mr. Patton's Resolution."

90. Boyd Crumrine Papers.

91. U.S. Department of the Interior, "F. Julius LeMoyne House," 17.

92. Gara, *Liberty Line*, xii–xiv, 3–18.

93. For local examples, see Molter, "Area Man Recalls Woman Who Taught Him About Life," *Washington (PA) Observer-Reporter*, July 25, 1990, and Colleen Bente, "Underground Railroad Sneaked through Washington County," *Washington (PA) Observer-Reporter*, March 3, 1991; Scott Beveridge, "The Fugitives: Runaway Slaves Find Route to Freedom," *Washington (PA) Observer-Reporter*, February 23, 1997.

94. Forrest, *History of Washington County*, 1:261.

95. *Washington (PA) Reporter*, August 15, 1908.

96. *Washington (PA) Observer*, October 16, 1884.

CHAPTER FOUR. The Underground Railroad Network in Washington County

1. Smith, *On the Edge of Freedom*, 30.

2. Diane Miller, "The Places and Communities of the Underground Railroad: The National Park Service Network to Freedom," in *Passages to Freedom*, ed. Blight, 279–81.

3. Smith, *On the Edge of Freedom*, 30–31.

4. Forrest, *History of Washington County*, 1:424; McCulloch, *Fearless Advocate*, 157; Switala, *Underground Railroad in Pennsylvania*, 74.

5. Cheryl Janifer LaRoche, *Free Black Communities and the Underground Railroad*, xii.

6. U.S. Bureau of the Census, *Fifth Census* (Washington, DC: National Archives and Records Administration, 1831); Siebert, *Underground Railroad*, 379.

7. For population figures, see 1850 and 1860 U.S. Census; Crumrine, *History of Washington County*, 261; Connie Park Rice, *Our Monongalia*, 23.

8. Rice, *Our Monongalia*, 23.

9. William J. Switala, *Underground Railroad in Delaware, Maryland, and West Virginia*, 102.

10. Wallace, "Historical Sketch," 3; Michael Sajna, "Underground Railroad Leaves Tracks in Southwestern Pennsylvania," *Pittsburgh Tribune-Review*, February 25, 1990.

11. Lorraine Walls-Perry, *Reaping the Harvest: A History of the Crockett Family* (Bloomington, IN: AuthorHouse, 2004), 1–12.

12. U.S. Bureau of the Census, *Seventh Census* (Washington, DC: National Archives and Records Administration, 1851); Wallace, "Historical Sketch," 6.

13. Siebert, *Underground Railroad,* 123; Pettit, *Sketches in the History*, 32.

14. Boyd Crumrine Papers.

15. Ibid.; McElroy, "Recollections," 10; Paul Weyand, "Anti-Slavery Movement in Beaver County," 2:1141.

16. Forrest, *History of Washington County*, 1:424. For Gray's obituary and reminiscences, see *Washington Reporter*, January 9, 1906.

17. Switala, *Underground Railroad in Pennsylvania*, 74; Marlene Bransom and William Allen Davison, *Early African American Life in Waynesburg, Greene County, Pennsylvania* (Indiana, PA: A. G. Halldin, 2002), 13–16.

18. Crumrine, "Underground Railway"; Crumrine, *History of Washington County*, 261; *Washington (PA) Observer*, October 16, 1884; David Thompson, interview in "The McCurdy Station," *Underground Railroad in Pennsylvania*. Thompson, in his interview with Siebert, said that the McCurdy station was ten miles north of Pittsburgh, but his geography was off here. The only Joseph McCurdy living in the region was located in Greene County. U.S. Bureau of the Census, *Seventh Census* (Washington, DC: National Archives and Records Administration, 1851).

19. Forrest, *History of Washington County*, 1: 425–26.

20. *Washington (PA) Observer*, January 5, 1904; 1830, 1840, 1850, 1860 U.S. Census.

21. *Washington (PA) Observer*, January 5, 1904; Harold Hutchison, letter to author, October, 24, 2006; Helen Barnhart Morris, Obituary of John McCoy, in "Old Scrap Book," (1983), 102, Genealogical Collection, Citizens Library, Washington, PA.

22. Forrest, *History of Washington County*, 1:424; *Washington (PA) Observer*, January 5, 1904; *Claysville Recorder*, August 20, 1915, November 30, 1928; *Washington (PA) Daily Reporter*, March 7, 1903; *Washington (PA) Observer*, November 6, 1884; 1840, 1850, and 1860 U.S. Census.

23. *Washington (PA) Observer*, January 5, 1904; *Washington (PA) Reporter*, October 17, 1866; *Wheeling (WV) Intelligencer*, August 1, 1910.

24. *Washington (PA) Observer*, January 5, 1904.

25. Ibid.; Forrest, *History of Washington County*, 1:424; *Claysville Recorder*, May 28, 1915, July 24, 1926.

26. *Claysville Recorder*, July 24, 1926.

27. White, *First Families and Forgotten Churches*, 91–93; Haley, "Presbyterians Divided," 32.

28. Forrest, *History of Washington County*, 1:424; Brewster, "Rise of the Antislavery Movement," 5.

29. Forrest, *History of Washington County*, 1:424.

30. McElroy, "Recollections," 10.

31. Ibid.

32. Ibid.

33. Forrest, *History of Washington County*, 1:427.

34. *Washington (PA) Observer*, November 20, 1884.

35. McKeever, "Recollections of John Brown," letter dated September 17, 1880, reprinted in *Washington (PA) Observer*, June 7, 1890; Oates, *To Purge this Land with Blood*, 49.

36. Boyer, *Legend of John Brown*, 347–53; Forrest, *History of Washington County*, 1:424.

37. "Conversations with James W. Murdock," recorded by Jack and Jane Fulcher, ca. 1952, typescript, 10–11, Murdock Papers.

38. Switala, *Underground Railroad in Pennsylvania*, 79.

39. Switala, *Underground Railroad in Pennsylvania*, 75.

40. *Washington (PA) Observer*, October 16, 1884.

41. *National Era* (Washington, DC), June 5, 1851; Haley, "Presbyterians Divided," 36; Forrest, *History of Washington County*, 1:410.

42. McCulloch, *Fearless Advocate*, 156, 166–67, 174. A notice of this meeting and mention of LeMoyne appeared in *Frederick Douglass's Paper*, July 23, 1852.

43. McFarland, *Twentieth Century History of Washington County*, 130; McCulloch, *Fearless Advocate*, 122, 173–76; *Washington (PA) Reporter*, August 15, 1908.

44. *Washington (PA) Observer*, October 16, 1884. Crumrine in his unpublished notes says that Thomas Marquis and J. P. Miller helped move the Clarksburg fugitives to Clouse's shop. See his "Underground Railway."

45. *Washington (PA) Observer*, October 16, 1884.

46. *Washington (PA) Observer*, November 6, 1884, September 3, 1885. For Hackaress, see U.S. Bureau of the Census, *Sixth Census* (Washington, DC: National Archives and Records Administration, 1841) and "A Very Aged Negro Dead," *Pittsburgh Press*, September 7, 1895; *Claysville (PA) Recorder*, July 17, 1936.

47. Weaver-Splain and Stutman, *African American MDPF*, 8.

48. "Map of Washington, Washington County, Pennsylvania" (Philadelphia: T. Doran, 1855); 1860 U.S. Census. See Bolden's obituary in the *Washington (PA) Observer*, April 18, 1903.

49. *Liberator* (Boston, MA), August 29, 1856.

50. Hudson, *Fugitive Slaves*, 93. The *Chronicle*'s report was reprinted in "Tarred and Feathered," *Baltimore Sun*, August 16, 1856. It mentions that slave owners had pursued "a number of slaves" from Virginia to Washington, PA.

51. McFarland, *Twentieth Century History of Washington County*, 129.

52. Ibid., 130; Crumrine, *History of Washington County*, 261.

53. *Washington (PA) Observer*, November 20, 1884; Deed Book 57, 464, and Deed Book 59, 88, Washington County Courthouse, Washington, PA; Library and Archives Canada, *Census of 1851*, https://www.bac-lac.gc.ca/eng/census/1851/Pages/1851.aspx.

54. *Washington (PA) Observer*, November 6, 1884.

55. *Washington (PA) Observer*, October 16, 1884, November 6, 1884; David Thompson, interview in "The McCurdy Station," *Underground Railroad in Pennsylvania*; George H. Thurston, *Directory for 1856–57 of Pittsburgh and Allegheny Cities* (Pittsburgh: George H. Thurston, 1856), 183. Thompson, in his interview with Siebert, offers a different route, but it is difficult to make sense of his itinerary. He says that he took "the cars" from Allegheny City to a village, where he and six other fugitives took a carriage and at some point traveled through Bridgeport, Ohio—an unlikely destination, given that it is opposite Wheeling on the Ohio River. The *Observer's* account and Thompson's do agree that the Clarksburg fugitives boarded a boat on Lake Erie and eventually went to Windsor.

56. Boyd Crumrine Papers. For a description of routes out of Washington, see also Switala, *Underground Railroad in Pennsylvania*, 78–79.

57. Wallace, "Historical Sketch," 4–7.

58. Campbell, *Slave Catchers*, 199–207.

59. Wallace, "Historical Sketch," 4–7. George Walls also identified James Moffitt as an agent who helped assist fugitives in getting to Pittsburgh. *Washington (PA) Observer*, October 16, 1884. "West Brownsville," in Caldwell Atlas.

60. Wallace, "Historical Sketch," 4–5; 1850, 1860 U.S. Census; "Fallowfield Township," in J. A. Caldwell, *Caldwell's Illustrated Historical Centennial Atlas of Washington County* (Condil, Ohio: J. A. Caldwell, 1876). Peter Cleaver and John Frye appear as agents in Orlando S. Love, "The Underground Railroad of California, PA, and Vicinity," *Theses, Senior Class, 1900*, 2 vols. (Southwestern State Normal School, California, PA, 1900), 2:34.

61. Wallace, "Historical Sketch," 5; Gara, *Liberty Line*, 103.

62. Wallace, "Historical Sketch," 6–7; 1850, 1860, and 1870 U.S. Census.

63. Wallace, "Historical Sketch," 5.

64. In addition to the presence of Parker on the Cleaver farm, family tradition indicates that the Cleavers harbored fugitive slaves; Helen L. Harris, letter to Joan Ruzika, August 1, 1991, in Washington County Historical Society archives.

65. Wallace, "Historical Sketch," 6–7. Also see Campbell, *Slave Catchers*.

66. Wallace, "Historical Sketch," 7.

67. Crumrine, *History of Washington County*, 261; Hornbake, *History and Development of California, Pennsylvania*, 19–20; Serinko, *California University of Pennsylvania*, 37; Love, "Underground Railroad of California," 2:33; "Slavery Days," *Monongahela (PA) Daily Republican*, September 22, 1893; Mary Herron, "Latta Stone House is Most Perfect Virginia Mansion in This Area," *Washington (PA) Observer*, October 29, 1937.

68. Armstrong, "My Boyhood Days in Monongahela City," 148–49; *Washington (PA) Observer-Reporter*, October 1, 1989.

69. Ancestry.com, 1850 and 1860 U.S. Federal Census—Slave Schedules.

70. Pinsker, "Vigilance in Pennsylvania," 6; Smith, *On the Edge of Freedom*, 2–3, 16–18, 30–32; Hudson, *Fugitive Slaves*, 2–4, 34–53.

71. Some historians, including J. Blaine Hudson, have argued that mass escapes such as that executed by the Clarksburg Nine imply the existence of an Underground Railroad presence. Two other mass escapes from this region in the late 1850s and early 1860s lend some credence to Hudson's point. However, no other evidence substantiates this claim in western Virginia. Hudson, *Fugitive Slaves*, 80.

72. Blackett, *Making Freedom*, 1–2.

73. Thomas Lee to Doctors Lemoin (*sic*) and Templeton, May 8, 1847, Letters, File A23, LeMoyne Papers.

74. Blackett, "Freedom, or the Martyr's Grave," 149–50, 159–63; Blackett, "Fugitive Slaves and the Struggle Against Slavery in Western Pennsylvania"; Switala, *Underground Railroad in Pennsylvania*, 88–89.

75. Weyand, "Anti-Slavery Movement in Beaver County," 2:1142–46.

76. Switala, *Underground Railroad in Pennsylvania*, 79.

77. Smith, *On the Edge of Freedom*, 22–23.

78. Campbell, *Slave Catchers*, 201.

79. Anonymous to Dr. F. J. LeMoyne, September 1851, File A-23, LeMoyne Papers.

80. Blackett, "Freedom, or the Martyr's Grave," 163.

81. Blackett, "Freedom, or the Martyr's Grave," 157.

82. *Washington (PA) Examiner*, October 26, 1850.

83. Adeleke, *Without Regard to Race*, 66–69; Laurence A. Glasco, "Double Burden: The Black Experience in Pittsburgh," in *City at the Point: Essays on the Social History of Pittsburgh*, ed. Samuel P. Hays (Pittsburgh: University of Pittsburgh Press, 1989), 72–73; Blackett, "Fugitive Slaves."

CONCLUSION. The End of the Line

1. See Griffler, *Front Line of Freedom*, 4.

2. Alicyn Wiedrich, "Segregation and Civil Rights in Washington, Pennsylvania, 1945–1975" (Honors thesis, Washington & Jefferson College, 2011). On the North in general, see Thomas J. Sugrue, *Sweet Land of Liberty: The Forgotten Struggle for Civil Rights in the North* (New York: Random House, 2009).

3. *Claysville (PA) Recorder*, February 25, 1916.

4. David W. Blight, "Why the Underground Railroad, and Why Now?: A Long View," in *Passages to Freedom*, ed. Blight, 241.

5. See, for example, Griffler's *Front Line of Freedom* and LaRoche's *Free Black Communities and the Underground Railroad*.

6. Foner, *Gateway to Freedom*.

7. Harrold, *Border War*, 13–14; Gara, *Liberty Line*, 7.

BIBLIOGRAPHY

PRIMARY SOURCES

American Colonization Society. *African Repository and Journal.* Vol. 10. Washington, DC: James C. Dunn, 1834. https://books.google.com/books?id=wMcN AAAAQAAJ.

Andrew Chess Plan Book. Monongahela, Recorder of Deeds Office, Washington County, PA.

Barker, J. "Barker's Map of Washington County, Pennsylvania." North Hector, NY: William J. Barker, 1856.

Boyd Crumrine Papers, Historical Collection, Miller Library, Washington & Jefferson College, Washington, PA.

Brisbane, William H. "Speech of Rev. Wm H. Brisbane lately a slaveholder in South Carolina; containing an account of the change in his views on the subject of slavery." Speech to the Female Anti-Slavery Society of Cincinnati, 1840. Wisconsin Historical Society Archives (Wis Mss VD, box 1); online facsimile at http://www.wisconsinhistory.org/turningpoints/search.asp?id=23.

Claysville (PA) Recorder, 1904–1928.

Common Pleas Court Records, Washington County, PA, #94.

Crumrine, Boyd. "Underground Railway." Historical Collection, Miller Library, Washington & Jefferson College, Washington, PA.

Deed Books 1R, 57, and 59. Washington County, Washington County Courthouse.

"Dido Munts the Slave." Historical Collection, Miller Library, Washington & Jefferson College, Washington, PA.

Doran, T. "Map of Washington, Washington County, Pennsylvania." Philadelphia: T. Doran, 1855.

Ewing, Charles Morton, ed. "Washington County Slave Record," Typescript. 1951. Historical Collection, Miller Library, Washington & Jefferson College.

Genealogical Collection, Citizens Library, Washington, PA.

Henson, Josiah. *The Life of Josiah Henson, Formerly a Slave, Now an Inhabitant of Canada, as Narrated by Himself.* Boston: Arthur D. Phelps, 1849. http://docsouth .unc.edu/neh/henson49/menu.html.

Hutchison, Harold. Letter to author, October 24, 2006.

J. W. Lockhart Plan Book. Recorder of Deeds Office, Washington County, PA.

LeMoyne Papers, Washington County Historical Society, Washington, PA.

"Letters of Dr. F. J. LeMoyne, an Abolitionist of Western Pennsylvania," *Journal of Negro History,* 18, no. 4 (1933): 451–74.

Library and Archives Canada. *Census of 1851.* https://www.bac-lac.gc.ca/eng/census /1851/Pages/1851.aspx.

Map of Ohio County, West Virginia. Wheeling, WV: Koller and Conrad, 1918.

McElroy, James. "Recollections," in *Reminiscences of West Middletown, Pennsylvania,* edited by William T. Lindsey. West Middletown, PA: McKeever Study Library Association, 2002 [1910].

McKeever, Matthew. "Recollections of John Brown." Letter dated September 11, 1880. Reprinted in *Washington (PA) Observer,* June 7, 1890.

Murdock Papers, McKeever Study Library, West Middletown, PA.

Mystery (Pittsburgh, PA), 1846.

Our Country (Washington, PA), 1835.

Pennsylvania Anti-Slavery Society Western District Minutes, 1837–1838, Heinz History Center, Pittsburgh, PA.

Pittsburgh Gazette, 1858.

"Session Book of the Free Presbyterian Church of West Alexander." West Alexander Presbyterian Church archives, West Alexander, PA.

Thurston, George H. *Directory for 1856–57 of Pittsburgh and Allegheny Cities.* Pittsburgh: George H. Thurston, 1856.

———. *Directory of the Monongahela and Youghiogheny Valleys.* Pittsburgh: A. A. Anderson, 1859.

The Underground Railroad in Pennsylvania. Vol. 1. Siebert Papers, Ohio Historical Society, Columbus, OH.

U.S. Bureau of the Census. Decennial Census of Population and Housing, 1790–1860. https://www.census.gov/programs-surveys/decennial-census/decade.html.

———. *Fifth Census.* Washington, DC: National Archives and Records Administration, 1831.

———. *Sixth Census.* Washington, DC: National Archives and Records Administration, 1841.

———. *Seventh Census.* Washington, DC: National Archives and Records Administration, 1851.

U.S. House. 20th Congress. Memorial, Committee on the District of Columbia, Petitions and Memorials (HR20A-G5.1), January 19–26, 1829, Folder 4, Records of the U.S. House of Representatives, Record Group 233, National Archives, Washington, DC.

———. 24th Congress, First Session. Records of the House of Representatives, Record Group 233, February 29, 1836, 413, National Archives, Washington, DC. http://memory.loc.gov/cgi-bin/ampage?collId=llhj&fileName=029/llhj029 .db&recNum=412&itemLink=r?ammem/hlaw:@field(DOCID+@lit(hj02962)) %230290413&linkText=1.

———. 25th Congress, First Session. "Petition from Washington Co Pa to rescind Mr. Patton's Resolution," February 14, 1838 and May 21, 1838, Library of Congress Collection HR25A, Records of the House of Representatives, Record Group 33, National Archives, Washington, DC.

———. 25th Congress, First Session. "Petition of 118 Ladies of Washington Co Pa for the Abolition of Slavery . . ." February 14, 1838, Library of Congress Collection HR25A, Records of the Congress of the US, Record Group 233, National Archives, Washington, DC.

Virginia Free Press, 1858.

Washington Borough Tax Records. Microfilm. Law Library, Washington County Courthouse, Washington, PA.

Washington County Negro Register from 1782 to 1851. Historical Collection, Miller Library, Washington & Jefferson College.

Washington (PA) Examiner.

Washington (PA) Observer.

Washington (PA) Patriot, 1845–1849.

Washington (PA) Reporter, 1808–1908.

West Middletown Recollections, McKeever Study Library, West Middletown, PA.

West Middletown Scrapbook, McKeever Study Library, West Middletown, PA.

Wheeling (Virginia) Intelligencer, 1856–1858.

Wheeling (WV) Intelligencer, 1910.

Will Books, Washington County Wills, Washington County Courthouse, Washington, PA.

SECONDARY SOURCES

Adeleke, Tunde. *Without Regard to Race: The Other Martin Robinson Delany*. Jackson: University Press of Mississippi, 2003.

Ahlstrom, Sydney E. *A Religious History of the American People*. 2 vols. Garden City, NY: Image Books, 1975.

Ancestry.com. U.S. Federal Census—Slave Schedules. Provo, UT: Ancestry.com Operations Inc, 2010. http://search.ancestry.com/search/group/usfedcen.

Armstrong, Joseph Taylor. "My Boyhood Days in Monongahela City." *Historical Magazine of Monongahela's Old Home Week Celebration* (1908): 148–49.

Asbury, John. "Asbury-Adams Roots." Washington, PA: self-published, ca. 1992. Washington County History Society, Washington, PA.

Batalo, Michael S. "John Berry." Unpublished paper, Washington & Jefferson College, 2005.

———. "Samuel Skinner." Unpublished paper, Washington & Jefferson College, January 28, 2005.

Beers, J. H. *Commemorative Biographical Record of Washington County, Pennsylvania.* Chicago: J. H. Beers, 1893.

Bell, Raymond M. "Black Persons in Early Washington County, Pennsylvania." Typescript. 1978. Historical Collection, Miller Library, Washington & Jefferson College.

———. "List of Slave Owners in Washington County, Pennsylvania, 1782." *National Geographical Society Quarterly* 59, no. 1 (1971); 22–23.

Bell, Whitfield J., Jr. "Washington County, Pennsylvania, in the Eighteenth Century Antislavery Movement." *Western Pennsylvania Historical Magazine* 25 (1942): 136–39.

Blackett, R. J. M. "'Freedom, or the Martyr's Grave': Black Pittsburgh's Aid to the Fugitive Slave." In *African Americans in Pennsylvania: Shifting Historical Perspectives*, edited by Joe William Trotter and Eric Ledell Smith. University Park: Pennsylvania State University Press, 1997.

———. "Fugitive Slaves and the Struggle against Slavery in Western Pennsylvania." Lecture presented at the Center for Africanamerican Urban Studies & the Economy (CAUSE) Conference, Carnegie Mellon University, February 6, 2016.

———. *Making Freedom: The Underground Railroad and the Politics of Slavery.* Chapel Hill: University of North Carolina Press, 2013.

Blassingame, John W., ed. *Slave Testimony: Two Centuries of Letters, Speeches, Interviews, and Autobiographies.* Baton Rouge: Louisiana State University Press, 1977.

Blight, David W., ed. *Passages to Freedom: The Underground Railroad in History and Memory.* Washington: Smithsonian Books, 2004.

Blockson, Charles L. "Escape from Slavery: The Underground Railroad." *National Geographic*, July 1984, 3–39.

———. *The Hippocrene Guide to the Underground Railroad.* New York: Hippocrene Books, 1994.

———. *The Underground Railroad: First-Person Narratives of Escapes to Freedom in the North.* New York: Prentice Hall, 1987.

———. *The Underground Railroad in Pennsylvania.* Jacksonville, NC: Flame International, 1981.

Blue, Frederick J. *No Taint of Compromise: Crusaders in Antislavery Politics.* Baton Rouge: Louisiana State University Press, 2005.

Bordewich, Fergus M. *Bound for Canaan: The Underground Railroad and the War for the Soul of America.* New York: Amistad Press, 2005.

Boyer, Richard O. *The Legend of John Brown: A Biography and a History.* New York: Knopf, 1973.

Bransom, Marlene, and William Allen Davison. *Early African American Life in Waynesburg, Greene County, Pennsylvania.* Indiana, PA: A. G. Halldin, 2002.

Brewster, Robert Wallace. "The Rise of the Antislavery Movement in Southwestern Pennsylvania." *Western Pennsylvania Historical Magazine* 22 (1939): 1–18.

Brown, Ira V. "An Antislavery Agent: C. C. Burleigh in Pennsylvania, 1836–1837." *Pennsylvania Magazine of History and Biography* 105, no. 1 (1981): 66–84.

Buckmaster, Henrietta. *Let My People Go: The Story of the Underground Railroad and the Growth of the Abolition Movement.* Boston: Beacon Press, 1941.

Burin, Eric. "Rethinking Northern White Support for the African Colonization Movement: The Pennsylvania Colonization Society as an Agent of Emancipation." *Pennsylvania Magazine of History and Biography* 127, no. 2 (2003): 197–229.

Burns, Edward M. "Slavery in Western Pennsylvania." *Western Pennsylvania Historical Magazine* 8, no. 4 (1925): 204–14.

Caldwell, J. A. *Caldwell's Illustrated Historical Centennial Atlas of Washington County.* Condil, Ohio: J. A. Caldwell, 1876.

California Area Historical Society. *California, Pennsylvania: Images of America.* Charleston, SC: Arcadia, 2003.

Campbell, Stanley W. *The Slave Catchers: Enforcement of the Fugitive Slave Law, 1850–1860.* Chapel Hill: University of North Carolina Press, 1970; New York: W. W. Norton, 1972.

Carpenter, Daniel, and Colin D. Moore. "When Canvassers Became Activists: Antislavery Petitioning and the Political Mobilization of American Women." *American Political Science Review* 108, no. 3 (August 2014): 479–98.

Coleman, Helen Turnbull Waite. *Banners in the Wilderness: Early Years of Washington and Jefferson College.* Pittsburgh: University of Pittsburgh Press, 1956.

Crumrine, Boyd. *History of Washington County, Pennsylvania with Biographical Sketches. . . .* Philadelphia: L. H. Everts, 1882.

Davis, David Brion. *Inhuman Bondage: The Rise and Fall of Slavery in the New World.* New York: Oxford University Press, 2006.

Davis, Rebecca Harding. *Bits of Gossip.* Boston: Houghton Mifflin, 1904.

Dillon, Merton L. *Benjamin Lundy and the Struggle for Negro Freedom.* Urbana: University of Illinois Press, 1966.

Douglass, Frederick. *Narrative of the Life of Frederick Douglass.* Edited by David W. Blight. 2nd ed. Boston: Bedford/St. Martin's, 2003.

Drew, Benjamin. *A North-Side View of Slavery: The Refugee.* Boston: John P. Jewett, 1856; reprint, New York: Johnson, 1968.

Dumond, Dwight L. *Antislavery: The Crusade for Freedom.* Ann Arbor: University of Michigan Press, 1961.

Dutchess, Eric D. "Between Frontier and Factory: Washington, Pennsylvania, 1810–1870." Ph.D. diss., West Virginia University, 2012.

Eslinger, Ellen. "Freedom without Independence: The Story of a Former Slave and Her Family." *Virginia Magazine of History and Biography* 114 (2006): 262–91.

Ewing, E. W. R. *Northern Rebellion and Southern Secession.* Richmond, VA: J. L. Hill, 1904.

Finkelman, Paul. "The Kidnapping of John Davis and the Adoption of the Fugitive Slave Law of 1793." *Journal of Southern History* 56, no. 3 (August 1990): 397–422.

Foner, Eric. *Gateway to Freedom: The Hidden History of the Underground Railroad*. New York: W. W. Norton, 2015.

Forrest, Earle R., ed. "Historical Items, Washington County, Pa." 6 vols. Washington County Historical Society, 1963.

———. *History of Washington County, Pennsylvania*. 3 vols. Chicago: S. J. Clarke, 1926.

———. *The House of Romance*. Washington, PA: Washington County Historical Society, 1964.

Forstall, Richard L., ed. *Population of States and Counties of the United States: 1790–1990*. Washington, DC: United States Census Bureau, 1996. https://www.census.gov/population/www/censusdata/pop1790-1990.html.

Franklin, John Hope, and Albert A. Moss Jr. *From Slavery to Freedom: A History of African Americans*. 7th ed. New York: McGraw Hill, 1994.

Franklin, John Hope, and Loren Schweninger. *Runaway Slaves: Rebels on the Plantation*. New York: Oxford University Press, 1999.

Freehling, William W. *The Road to Disunion: Secessionists at Bay, 1776–1854*. New York: Oxford University Press, 1990.

Fritz, Jean. *Brady*. New York: Puffin Books, 1987.

Galenson, David W. "The Rise and Fall of Indentured Servitude in the Americas: An Economic Analysis." In *Historical Perspectives on the American Economy*, edited by Robert Whaples and Dianne C. Betts, 110–40. New York: Cambridge University Press, 1995.

Gallagher, Gary W. *Causes Won, Lost, and Forgotten: How Hollywood and Popular Art Shape What We Know about the Civil War*. Chapel Hill: University of North Carolina Press, 2008.

Gara, Larry. *The Liberty Line: The Legend of the Underground Railroad*. Lexington: University of Kentucky Press, 1961; repr. 1996.

Glasco, Laurence A. "Double Burden: The Black Experience in Pittsburgh." In *City at the Point: Essays on the Social History of Pittsburgh*, edited by Samuel P. Hays, 69–110. Pittsburgh: University of Pittsburgh Press, 1989.

———, ed. *The WPA History of the Negro in Pittsburgh*. Pittsburgh: University of Pittsburgh Press, 2004.

Griffler, Keith P. *Front Line of Freedom: African Americans and the Forging of the Underground Railroad in the Ohio Valley*. Lexington: University Press of Kentucky, 2004.

Grimsted, David. *American Mobbing, 1828–1861: Toward Civil War*. New York: Oxford University Press, 1998.

Haley, Jason. "Presbyterians Divided: Antislavery and Washington County Abolitionists." Unpublished paper, Washington & Jefferson College, 2001.

———. "Washington County Presbyterians: Abolitionism in a Divided Denomination." Honors thesis, Washington & Jefferson College, 2002.

Handy, Robert T. *A History of the Churches in the United States and Canada*. New York: Oxford University Press, 1977.

Harper, R. Eugene. *The Transformation of Western Pennsylvania, 1770–1800*. Pittsburgh: University of Pittsburgh Press, 1991.

Harrold, Stanley. *Border War: Fighting over Slavery before the Civil War*. Chapel Hill: University of North Carolina Press, 2010.

———. *Subversives: Antislavery Community in Washington, DC, 1828–1865*. Baton Rouge: Louisiana State University Press, 2003.

Hochschild, Adam. *Bury the Chains: Prophets and Rebels in the Fight to Free an Empire's Slaves*. New York: Mariner Books, 2006.

Horn, W. F. *The Horn Papers: Early Westward Movement on the Monongahela and Upper Ohio, 1765–1795*. 3 vols. New York: Hagstrom, 1945.

Hornbake, Nan. *History and Development of California, Pa.: One Hundred Years of Progress*. California, PA: California Centennial Committee, 1949.

Hudson, J. Blaine. *Fugitive Slaves and the Underground Railroad in the Kentucky Borderland*. Jefferson, NC: McFarland, 2002.

Kolchin, Peter. *American Slavery, 1619–1877*. New York: Hill and Wang, 1993.

LaRoche, Cheryl Janifer. *Free Black Communities and the Underground Railroad: The Geography of Resistance*. Urbana: University of Illinois Press, 2014.

The LeMoyne Home: 1812–1935. Hollywood, CA: Hollycrafters, 1935. Washington & Jefferson College Historical Collection, xv j 189, Washington, PA.

Lignian, Marshall E. ed., *Thomas McKean's Death Register, 1820–1896, Washington, PA*. Monessen, PA: Privately printed, 1975.

Lindsey, William T., ed. *Reminiscences of West Middletown, Pennsylvania*. West Middletown, PA: McKeever Study Library Association, 2002 [1910].

Litwack, Leon F. *North of Slavery: The Negro in the Free States, 1790–1860*. Chicago: University of Chicago Press, 1961.

Love, Orlando S. "The Underground Railroad of California, PA, and Vicinity." *Theses, Senior Class, 1900*. 2 vols. Southwestern State Normal School, California, PA, 1900. 2:29–35.

Magdol, Edward. *The Antislavery Rank and File: A Social Profile of the Abolitionists' Constituency*. Westport, CT: Greenwood Press, 1986.

Malmet, Bonnie, ed. *Abstracts of the Washington, Pa., Reporter, 1808–1814*. Apollo, PA: Closson Press, 1990.

Matthews, Elbert. "Church History: St. Paul AME Church, 1818–1987." Washington, PA: St. Paul AME Church, 1987.

McCulloch, Margaret C. *Fearless Advocate of the Right: The Life of Francis Julius LeMoyne, M.D., 1798–1879*. Boston: Christopher Publishing House, 1941.

McFarland, Joseph. *Twentieth Century History of Washington County*. Chicago: Richmond-Arnold, 1910.

McPherson, James M. *Ordeal by Fire: The Civil War and Reconstruction*, 2d ed. New York: McGraw-Hill, 1992.

Merrill, Walter M. *Against the Wind: A Biography of William Lloyd Garrison*. Cambridge, MA: Harvard University Press, 1963.

Miller, Randall M., and William Pencak, eds. *Pennsylvania: A History of the Commonwealth*. University Park: Pennsylvania State University Press, 2002.

Miller, William Lee. *Arguing about Slavery: The Great Battle in the United States Congress*. New York: Alfred A. Knopf, 1996.

Monongahela Area 200th Anniversary, 1769–1969. Monongahela, PA: Monongahela Publishing, 1969.

Muelder, Owen W. *Theodore Dwight Weld and the American Anti-Slavery Society*. Jefferson, NC: McFarland, 2011.

Murray, Andrew E. *Presbyterians and the Negro*. Philadelphia: Presbyterian Historical Society, 1966.

Myers, John L. "The Early Anti-Slavery Agency System in Pennsylvania, 1833–1837." *Pennsylvania History* 21 (1964): 62–86.

Nash, Gary B. *Forging Freedom: The Formation of Philadelphia's Black Community, 1720–1840*. Cambridge, MA: Harvard University Press, 1988.

Nash, Gary B., and Jean R. Soderlund. *Freedom by Degrees: Emancipation in Pennsylvania and Its Aftermath*. New York: Oxford University Press, 1991.

Newman, Richard S. *The Transformation of American Abolitionism: Fighting Slavery in the Early Republic*. Chapel Hill: University of North Carolina Press, 2002.

Niven, John. *Samuel P. Chase: A Biography*. New York: Oxford University Press, 1995.

Oates, Stephen B. *To Purge This Land with Blood: A Biography of John Brown*. New York: Harper & Row, 1970.

One Hundred Seventy-Fifth Anniversary of Presbyterianism at West Alexander, PA. West Alexander, PA: United Presbyterian Church, 1965.

Pettit, Eber. *Sketches in the History of the Underground Railroad*. Fredonia, NY: W. McKinistry & Son, 1879. Reprint, Freeport, NY: Books for Libraries Press, 1971.

Pinsker, Matthew. "Vigilance in Pennsylvania: Underground Railroad Activities in the Keystone State, 1837–1861." Harrisburg: Pennsylvania Historical and Museum Commission, 2000. Draft context study presented at Black History Conference, Harrisburg, PA, April 27, 2000.

The Plaque Book: West Middletown Houses and Their History. West Middletown, PA: McKeever Study Library, 1995.

Quarles, Benjamin. *Black Abolitionists*. New York: Oxford University Press, 1969.

Rice, Connie Park. *Our Monongalia: A History of African Americans in Monongalia County, West Virginia*. Terra Alta, WV: Headline Books, 1999.

Rural Reflections of Amwell Township, Washington County, Pennsylvania. 4 vols. Amwell Township, PA: Bicentennial Committee of Amwell Township, 1977–1981.

Salerno, Beth A. *Sister Societies: Women's Antislavery Societies in Antebellum America*. DeKalb: Northern Illinois University Press, 2005.

Schwartz, Philip J. *Migrants against Slavery: Virginians and the Nation*. Charlottesville: University of Virginia Press, 2001.

Searight, Thomas B. *The Old Pike: A History of the National Road*. Uniontown, PA: printed by author, 1894.

Sergeant, Thomas, and William Rowle Jr. *Reports of Cases Adjudicated in the Supreme Court of Pennsylvania*. 17 volumes. Philadelphia, 1818–1829.

Serinko, Regis J. *California University of Pennsylvania: The People's College in the Monongahela Valley*. Roscoe, PA: Roscoe Ledger, 1992.

Siebert, Wilbur H. *The Underground Railroad from Slavery to Freedom*. New York: Macmillan, 1898. Reprint, New York: Russell & Russell, 1967.

Simpson, James. *History of the Cross Creek Graveyard and the Cross Creek Cemetery*. 1894. Reprint, Parsons, WV: McClain Printing, 1969.

Slaughter, Thomas P. *The Whiskey Rebellion: Frontier Epilogue to the American Revolution*. New York: Oxford, 1986.

Smith, David G. *On the Edge of Freedom: The Fugitive Slave Issue in South Central Pennsylvania*. New York: Fordham University Press, 2013.

Smydo, Joe. "Freedom for the Slaves, Progress for the Town: Pragmatic Abolitionism in Washington County, Pennsylvania, during the 1830s and 1840s." Unpublished seminar paper, Duquesne University, 2012.

———. "Unlikely Partners: Collaboration between Colonizationists and Radical Abolitionists in Washington County, Pennsylvania, during the 1830s." MA thesis, Duquesne University, 2016.

Starobin, Robert S., ed. *Blacks in Bondage: Letters of American Slaves*. 2nd ed. New York: New Viewpoints, 1974. Reprint, Princeton, NJ: Markus Wiener, 1994.

Stauffer, John. *The Black Hearts of Men: Radical Abolitionists and the Transformation of Race*. Cambridge, MA: Harvard University Press, 2002.

Sterling, Dorothy. *Ahead of Her Time: Abby Kelley and the Politics of Antislavery*. New York: W. W. Norton, 1991.

Stewart, James Brewer. *Holy Warriors: The Abolitionists and American Slavery*. New York: Hill and Wang, 1996.

Still, William. *The Underground Rail Road*. 1871. Reprint, Chicago: Johnson Publishing, 1970.

Stowe, Harriet Beecher. *Uncle Tom's Cabin*. New York: Penguin, 1998.

Sugrue, Thomas J. *Sweet Land of Liberty: The Forgotten Struggle for Civil Rights in the North*. New York: Random House, 2009.

Swetnam, George. *Pittsylvania Country*. New York: Duell, Sloane, & Pearce, 1951.

Switala, William J. *Underground Railroad in Delaware, Maryland, and West Virginia*. Mechanicsburg, PA: Stackpole Books, 2004.

———. *Underground Railroad in Pennsylvania*. Mechanicsburg, PA: Stackpole Books, 2001.

Thornell, Paul N. D. "The Absent Ones and the Providers: A Biography of the Vashons." *Journal of Negro History* 83, no. 4 (Autumn 1998): 284–301.

Tobin, Jacqueline, and Raymond G. Dobard. *Hidden in Plain View: A Secret Story of Quilts and the Underground Railroad*. New York: Doubleday, 1999.

U.S. Department of the Interior. National Park Service. "F. Julius LeMoyne Home." National Historic Landmark Nomination, 1997.

Wallace, Howard. "Historical Sketch of the Underground Railroad from Uniontown to Pittsburgh." Uniontown, PA: privately printed, 1903.

Walls-Perry, Lorraine. *Reaping the Harvest: A History of the Crocket Family*. Bloomington, IN: AuthorHouse, 2004.

Walters, Ronald G. *American Reformers, 1815–1860*. Rev. ed. New York: Hill and Wang, 1997.

Wayne, Michael. "The Black Population of Canada West on the Eve of the American Civil War: A Reassessment Based on the Manuscript Census of 1861." *Histoire Social/Social History* 28 (1995): 465–85.

Weaver-Splain, Shelby, and Craig Stutman. *African American Multiple Properties Documentation Form (MPDF)*. Harrisburg: Pennsylvania Historical and Museum Commission, 2010.

Weyand, Paul. "The Anti-Slavery Movement in Beaver County," in *History of Beaver County, Pennsylvania*, edited by Joseph H. Bausman, 1141–54. 2 vols. New York: Knickerbocker Press, 1904.

White, Alvin D. *First Families and Forgotten Churches*. Washington, PA: Quality Quick, 1992.

———. *History of Cross Creek Presbyterian Church*. Parsons, WV: McLain, 1969.

Whitehead, Colson. *The Underground Railroad*. New York: Doubleday, 2016.

Wiedrich, Alicyn. "Segregation and Civil Rights in Washington, Pennsylvania, 1945–1975." Honors thesis, Washington & Jefferson College, 2011.

Winks, Robin W. *The Blacks in Canada: A History*. New Haven: Yale University Press, 1971.

Woodson, Carter. *Free Negro Heads of Families in the United States in 1830*. Washington, DC: Association for the Study of Negro Life and History, 1925.

Zaeske, Susan. *Signatures of Citizenship: Petitioning, Antislavery, and Women's Political Identity*. Chapel Hill: University of North Carolina Press, 2003.

INDEX

———————

Page numbers in italics refer to maps or photographs; page numbers in bold refer to tables.

W. THOMAS MAINWARING

is a professor of history at Washington & Jefferson College.